FACTORIES AND FOOD STAMPS

Richard Weisskoff

FACTORIES AND FOOD STAMPS

The Puerto Rico Model of Development

THE JOHNS HOPKINS UNIVERSITY PRESS

BALTIMORE AND LONDON

Richard Weisskoff is an associate professor of economics at Bar Ilan University
in Ramat Gan, Israel. He has been a senior consultant to the Harvard Institute
for International Development, and he has taught at Yale University, Iowa State
University, and the University of Puerto Rico. He has also been called upon
to testify on Puerto Rico and the Caribbean before U.S. Congressional Subcommittees.

© 1985 The Johns Hopkins University Press
All rights reserved
Printed in the United States of America

The Johns Hopkins University Press, 701 West 40th Street, Baltimore, Maryland 21211
The Johns Hopkins Press Ltd, London

The paper in this book is acid-free and meets the guidelines for permanence
and durability of the Committee on Production Guidelines for Book Longevity
of the Council on Library Resources.

Library of Congress Cataloging in Publication Data

Weisskoff, Richard.
Factories and food stamps.

(The Johns Hopkins studies in development)
Bibliography: p.
Includes index.
1. Puerto Rico—Economic conditions—1952—.
2. Puerto Rico—Economic policy. I. Title. II. Series.

HC154.5.W45 1985   338.97295   85-5163
ISBN 0-8018-3273-X (alk. paper)

For my parents,
David and Anne

Contents

IV. THE HISTORICAL SETTING

V. THE FUTURE

List of Illustrations

Figures

Photographs

List of Tables

Preface

IN ANCIENT Thebes, King Cadmus ruled an orderly city and honored the traditional gods. His daughter Agave raised a temperamental and stubborn son, Pentheus, to whom an aging Cadmus yielded the throne.

But the world outside was changing, and a new god, Dionysus, walked the earth and commanded worship in his way, with wine. King Pentheus, spiteful of the new god, mocked him, and provoked him by outlawing his worship. So Dionysus decided to visit Pentheus . . .

Disguised as an Old Man, Dionysus entered Thebes and invited Pentheus to accompany him and secretly view the Bacchic rites of the city's maidens in their frenzied dancing. Once near the scene of the ceremonies, the Old Man suggested that Pentheus climb a tree to better view the rites without himself being seen. The King did so and the guide went off.

At once the maniacal women spotted an animal in the tree; thinking it a mountain lion, they surrounded the tree and shook it till the lion fell. Beside themselves with drink and power, they attacked it savagely and ripped the lion apart, limb by limb. Agave, queen mother of Thebes, took its head home, as a trophy to her father.

> I have let fall
> The shuttle by the loom, and raised my hand
> For higher things, to slay from out the land
> Wild beast! See, in mine arms I bear the prize,
> . . . .
> Take it, and call a feast.

THIS THEME, the archetype from Euripides' *The Bacchae,* describes the process of economic development as it has become known to us, especially, as the Puerto Rico model.

Acknowledgments

A STUDY that spans the decade and a great number of places owes thanks to many sponsors and individuals. Financial support came initially from the Yale Concilium on International Affairs, which viewed Puerto Rico in its Latin American context; from the Manpower Administration, U.S. Department of Labor, which was concerned with the migratory implications of the model; the Social Science Research Council; and the Economics Program of the National Science Foundation. The views presented in this book are solely the responsibility of the author.

Data for the early computer model were assembled and processed in New Haven, Connecticut, with the able assistance of Laurie Nisonoff, Edward Wolff, Paul Singerman, and Richard Levy, and in Cambridge, Massachusetts, with the help of Martin Leinwand and Martin Beatty. Revisions of the early model and its extension to the Caribbean were undertaken with the assistance of Faustino Ccama at Iowa State University (Ames), and a complete manuscript was typed by Diane Grimm. A two-month visit to Puerto Rico was extended by several years and was followed by further research in Washington, D.C. I am especially thankful to the students and staff of the University of Puerto Rico at Río Piedras, the Colegio-Universitario at Cayey, the Catholic University of Ponce, the Puerto Rico Planning Board, the Instituto Politécnico de México, and the American University in Washington, D.C., who labored with me in courses analyzing the Puerto Rico model of development.

I am indebted also to friends, officials, and colleagues in Puerto Rico who have been unfailingly encouraging and cooperative: *Don* Jaime Benítez, who disagrees cordially with many of my ideas; *Don* Gordon Lewis, dean of Caribbeanists, author, teacher, inspiring critic; Professor Rafael Corrada Guerrero, then Director of the Centro de Investigaciones Sociales of the University of Puerto Rico, who facilitated my visiting lectureship there in 1978–79; José Antonio Herrero, fearless analyst of the Puerto Rican economy; and Oscar Lamourt Valentín of Lares, printer. For their assistance with data and advice, I have been long indebted to Dr. Miguel Echenique of the Puerto Rico Development Bank; Suriel Sanchez, Benjamín Batista, and Augustina M. de Rubín of the Puerto Rico Planning Board; and Alejandro Guzman, who reviewed an early complete draft of the model. I owe special thanks to Ellen Hawes, Marnie Allen, Chuco Quintero Rivera, Angel Luis Ruíz, Manuel Sigüenza, Richard Funkhauser, Delsie Gandia, Orlando Espadas, Neftalí García, Juan A. Castañer, and many other colleagues for their encouragement and tutoring.

In the United States, special acknowledgment must be made to Gus Ranis, then Director of the Yale Economic Growth Center, who provided a provocative intellectual climate for this research to grow in; James Tobin, who was later to direct his own project in Puerto Rico; Hollis Chenery, who always thought of Puerto Rico as an economic unit; Wassily Leontief, who, like Professor Chenery, had participated in the early think-tank operations on that island; Anne Carter, who provided the support at the Harvard Economic Research Project for the tools of analysis; and Raymond Beneke, economics chairman at Iowa State University, who facilitated the pursuit of further fieldwork and publication.

In Washington, D.C., I am grateful to Joseph Grunwald of the Brookings Institution and to Ben Stephansky of the Carnegie Endowment for International Peace; to Isabel Letelier, Saul Landau, and Marcus Raskin of the Institute for Policy Studies; to the Congressional Office of the Commonwealth of Puerto Rico; and to Gary Bikel, Grace Horowitz, and other colleagues of the Food and Nutrition Service, U.S. Department of Agriculture. In New York City, I acknowledge the counsel of Gilberto Gerena-Valentín, councilman from the South Bronx, and Frank Bonilla, Director of the Centro de Estudios Puertorriqueños of the City University.

Thanks to Francis Nissel of Monsey, New York, and Ruth Wachsler of Tel Aviv for typing the final manuscript; to Dorit Bek and Nati Shpunt for preparing the graphics; to Diane Hammond for editing; Michael Perelman for comments; and Michael J. Weisskoff, global troubleshooter.

Statistics and graphs cannot acknowledge the consultations of many other friends and colleagues, too numerous to mention here, who have shared their impressions and advice in my wanderings. I am especially indebted to my neighbors in the countryside of Humacao, Cayey, and Lares.

Finally, I would like to recall the memories of three people who have been particularly important in this work. Stephen Hymer, former professor at Yale, spurred his younger colleagues to contemplate less orthodox models and explore the edges of political economy. He has left us to carry on in his tradition. Angel Rodríguez Cristóbal, mountain farmer from Ciales, Puerto Rico, appeared one cold winter evening at the Quaker Meeting House in Des Moines, Iowa, to explain the dilemma of his people as he saw it. His talk rekindled my interest in Puerto Rico, and on my return to the island we became better acquainted. I attended Angel's appearance in federal court in San Juan, where he was sentenced to one year in federal prison for trespassing on a navy beach on the island of Vieques. Midway through his term in Tallahassee, Florida, Angel was found hanged in his cell. *Don* Juan Corretjer, dedicated revolutionary and inspiring mentor, encouraged my field work and writing during my stay in Puerto Rico. His writing and personal example, daring and idealistic, remain challenges of scholarship and morality. Inspired by the memory of these fallen colleagues, let this book help clarify the conditions of our people.

FACTORIES AND FOOD STAMPS

CHAPTER 1

Introduction: The Puerto Rico Model
of Development

THE EXPERIENCES that led to this study began in July of 1962, when a young college sophomore labored for a household moving company in Hato Rey, Puerto Rico. At summer's end the eighteen-year-old returned to Cambridge, Massachusetts, to continue his studies of Latin American economic development. The student became a college professor, and his former employer became one of the island's most distinguished business leaders.[1] The first spiral of our story ends nearly two decades later when the student returned to the University of Puerto Rico to relay some of his findings and write the chapters of this book. But he soon left the capital to work as a farmhand and orangepicker in the mountains of Lares. There he was confronted by a situation that he had uncovered in his academic investigations ten years earlier. The past he had recorded and the future he had projected had become the present. The second spiral had begun.

THIS IS a book about a model and an economy. By model, I mean a set of ideas that are already current and are brought together in a way that helps us understand how the world works. It also helps us make informed guesses about the likely effects of different policies on future events.

By economy, I intend the Puerto Rican economy and how the system by which a people makes its livelihood has changed during recent decades. The purpose of this book is to understand the economy of Puerto Rico by means of a set of ideas, that is, the model, which is the blueprint the observer constructs *after* some study and which supposedly tells us about the inner workings of the society.

Practitioners of modern economics face an embarrassment of riches: there are many standard models to choose from. The task of this book is to present a particular model and apply it concretely and statistically to the Puerto Rican situation. The model, as we shall see, is also applicable to other countries, especially in the Caribbean, and to other small, dependent nations elsewhere in the world.

Models in themselves can be powerful tools, as they guide our understanding of how the economy operates, much like the knowledge of theoretical aerodynamics adds to our appreciation of an airplane's flight. Yet riding in an airplane, or even

1

piloting one, at no time presupposes a scientific understanding of aerodynamics or of meteorology.

Nevertheless, models serve as a guide to public policy. Economists constantly advise statesmen and politicians as to the likely consequences of budget changes, laws, and regulations, just as a pilot facing a sudden change of winds makes adjustments in the flight plan in view of his or her theoretical and practical understanding of how the airplane operates. New models are sought when the ship of state faces a crisis: inflation, unemployment, business bankruptcy, trade deficits, credit scarcity. Recommendations of the attending economist are based on the model that underlies the conventional thinking of that time and that is critical to the type of intervention that is prescribed.

Any analogies of the economic system to mechanical or physical phenomena fail, however, because the so-called science of economics deals with human beings, our collective material and social behavior. A model must summarize our most important thinking about how society meets its everyday material needs to feed, clothe, and house itself, to stay healthy, to engage in work and play—in short, to live. This is the correct preoccupation of modern economics.

The task of understanding and analyzing the economy becomes especially urgent when a people presses against the limits of life. The urgency is most noticeable when a people is deprived of food and protection from the elements. Today, one nation looks at its neighbor and asks, How is it that you are so poor and I am so wealthy? The American public is periodically gripped with such questioning, almost soul-searching. Sometimes this questioning is reflected in political devices, such as President John F. Kennedy's Alliance for Progress and the Peace Corps or President Lyndon B. Johnson's War on Poverty. It also becomes reflected in the work of scholars who follow the fashions. Third World people, however, face such questions daily, not periodically. Continually, they ask, Why are we as a society so poor, and they—America and the industrialized nations—so wealthy?

Puerto Rico, with half the per capita income of the poorest state in the United States, poses a double dilemma. Compared to the United States, Puerto Rico is indigent. But compared to Latin America and the Caribbean nations, which are themselves better off relative to the Asian or African peoples, Puerto Rico is rich.[2] Is Puerto Rico poor or wealthy? This question takes on two further dimensions. If Puerto Rico is *within* the United States, it therefore should be compared to states like Mississippi and Louisiana, or regions like Appalachia and the Ozarks. However, if Puerto Rico is *outside* the United States, it should be treated like other small developing nations. This is precisely the historical dilemma of Puerto Rico: it is internal and external to the United States *at the same time*.

Puerto Rico was ceded by Spain in 1898 to the United States, and until 1952 was directly if loosely administered by the Congress through its committees and by the president through his appointed governor. Classified as a territory, a colony, even a possession, Puerto Rico became a commonwealth in 1952, linked in some permanent way to the United States but unforeseen in the Constitution.[3] At the same time, Puerto Rico stands very much *outside* the United States, an island economy, a society with its own resources and labor force in a naturally defined physical space, a nation in its own right before the Spanish cession, a people with its own coherence.

By being both *inside* and *outside* the world's leading industrial power, the people of Puerto Rico, like many other Third World peoples, are subject to two sets of economic laws. The first set is external, made by both U.S. policy (congressional restrictions on trade and shipping, federal budgets, and administrative rules) and by the U.S. labor market, which affects wages and the general level of economic activity. The second set of economic laws is interior, reflecting Puerto Rico's own rules and own logic. This last point is often minimized or overlooked entirely. It may well be that the U.S. economy is the tail that wags the dog, but it is also true that the tail has a dog.

Parallel to these two sets of laws are at least two viewpoints. The first viewpoint is that the development problem is external and must be approached fundamentally in its international dimension. The backwardness of Puerto Rico, the argument goes, is due to the colonial status it has sustained for five hundred years, manipulating first the Spanish and now the American administrations in order to survive as a society. One side, then, concludes that Puerto Rico should enter the United States like any other state and take an equal position like any other peculiar economic region within the metropolis. The opposing side would have Puerto Rico become a politically independent country, with appropriate detailed arrangements to be negotiated with the United States regarding such issues as trade and travel, citizenship, the public debt, and foreign aid. Both positions seem to have a common theme: that the economic problem can be approached, indeed solved, only as part of the solution to the status question.

The second viewpoint is to look *within* Puerto Rico for a solution to its problems—for example, the efficient use of land, people, the island's geographical position, and natural resources. This viewpoint typically provokes a chorus of lamentation, the standard liturgy of poverty: the scarcity of resources, the density of population, the absence of capital and skilled labor, etcetera, etcetera—key phrases in the usual aid-requesting ideology that development economists have made popular and refined in the past three decades. To this has recently been added a vocabulary of dependence: Puerto Rico is not only poor but, worse, it has become completely dependent. And so the problem is thrown back again to the external conditions. In the meantime, teams of consulting economists are called in periodically to offer their authoritative and studied opinions on what can be done within the current framework.

This book takes a more positive tack with respect to the second set of economic laws. Without denying the urgency of some new political outcome, this treatise deals with the daily operation of the Puerto Rico economy as it is currently constituted and holds that the long-term political solution may eventually be reached on the basis of the present economy. The choice of political status—

commonwealth, statehood, or independence—if made through the electoral process, will to a large extent be based on the people's ability to project their livelihoods under each proposed arrangement. An island with 60 percent of its people dependent on food stamps and the rest working in foreign-owned factories or in federally supported government offices can hardly be expected to elect a status that might jeopardize that arrangement. On the other hand, the prospect of statehood for an island that has sent half its people into economic exile is like asking the United States to accept what appears to be an economic desert, America's poorhouse, as an equal partner.

The point is simple: the much-discussed political options are not options at all as long as the economic base is ignored. Hence, the purpose of this book is to clarify how the parts of Puerto Rico's economy fit together, how they function, and what their effects on the society are. But economics, as it has come to us, is a lopsided science. It looks only at the material side of life and at those aspects that can be quantified. Economists count the number of "things" and give them a number in money terms. These are the labels hung on the products of people's labor, the vocabulary of economics. My intent is to use this vocabulary and to quantify the concepts, attaching values to these notions in order to understand how the material base—the economy—functions, and then to offer solutions on the basis of this understanding.

The Puerto Rican economy faces a perpetual crisis. The management of this crisis in the day-to-day administration of the colony, much like guiding a canoe routinely through the rapids, has gone by different names. In the 1930s, it was called the Puerto Rico Reconstruction Administration (Franklin Delano Roosevelt's New Deal). In the fifties, it became Operation Bootstrap (guest industries), the escape valve (mass migration), tourism, and tax exemption. Then CETA grants and food stamps in the 1970s, free trade zones and banking centers in the 1980s. There is always room for a new gimmick, a new solution.

The approach taken in this treatise is more candid and demanding: candid in showing how the simple gimmicks applied by today's politicians, like the single bonanza crops or minerals sought by early promoters in the Caribbean, fail to resolve the needs of the people for life and livelihood; demanding in requiring that the path to the future be extricated from the lessons of the past and built on the existing economic base.

Puerto Rico today is administered from three capitals: San Juan, Washington, D.C., and New York City. All three have short memories. Expediency and protection of existing interests have substituted for judiciousness and scholarship. This study is intended as a contribution to redressing that imbalance.

WE LEARN at least three lessons from the worlds that comprehend Puerto Rico and the United States: the history of each of the peoples and the relationship between the two. The material history of Puerto Rico provides us with a record of its economic base, of how the people who inhabited that island satisfied their own needs and, through exchange, the needs of others. The history of the exchange itself is the relationship. This study deals with only one fraction of the story, the material basis of Puerto Rico. It is necessarily partial and incomplete. The tools of analysis, however, are so powerful that when we focus on this part of the story the findings, through narrow, are quite remarkable. What we lose in breadth we gain in depth.

The point of departure is the present, which was once the future. The Puerto Rican computer model made in 1970 for 1980 has come of age. In that model, I first projected backward to 1960, much like the pole vaulter paces backward to gauge the number of steps before the running leap. Then a mechanical robot— which consists of nothing more than a mass of observed suppositions written in equation form, a series of interconnected chains and spirals—was set in forward motion along different paths. Each path represented a different scenario for the economy. And on reaching its destination, I asked the robot questions about what it saw in the economy: How many people were to be employed? What was their work, their wealth, the distribution of their riches? Such was my exercise in both retrospective and prospective economics.

The results were both comforting and alarming. The comfort came from the optimism and prosperity that the majority of paths led to. Only one scenario warned of the possibility of real danger and its consequences. "Compared with the actual 1970 distribution," I wrote in 1971, "the 1980 projections of the distribution of occupational needs present an alarming picture . . . these results point to the likelihood of continued out-migration of substantial numbers of unemployable male laborers, despite the rise in overall employment."[4]

Both the worst and best have come about. The Puerto Rican economy, once connected by many real or imagined harnesses to the American economy, ground to a halt by the mid-seventies. The American government also turned around and, rather than allow Puerto Rico to rely exclusively on the private sector for its trade and investment, began to pour billions of dollars directly into its survival system. The patient was taken off the kidney machine and put into an oxygen tent, when, according to another view, neither was needed. The insurance company paid all the bills. One did not have to be clairvoyant to forecast the 1980 developments. Knowing the prior routes and the existing structure provided the raw materials for our robot. What was unexpected was the creative, and to some observers the destructive, reaction in Puerto Rico to the American "solution" to their crisis.

In the first section of this book I briefly sketch the Puerto Rican economy and present the 1980 predictions made in 1971, together with the actual developments as the data became available by 1982. Then follows a road map, if you will, of the route I took, with guidebooks to the inner workings of the economy. Vital concepts are presented with sketches and examples to avoid the confusion for lay readers usually provoked by specialized vocabulary and shorthand codes.

In the second section are more extensive descriptions of the economic situation in Puerto Rico, the economic response to the food stamp intervention, and the situation of Puerto Ricans living in the United States.

In part three the Puerto Rico model is restored to its rightful place as a prototype for small, open, developing countries. In doing this, I examine the Caribbean in more detail, specifically the labor-surplus model that guides much current thinking about such countries. Part four provides some historical background. I conclude with reflections about my model and the labor-surplus model, suggesting a specific program for Puerto Rico.

My work demands a new model for 1990, a reprogramming of our old robot friend. I abstain from that task in this volume. I have learned too much about my first Frankenstein to either junk or resuscitate him, although both must be done eventually. My task here is to present my pioneering experiences for what they may contribute toward planning the future.

As this book goes to press, historical events overtake the reader, the author, and the economy. The crisis in Puerto Rico is so persistent and the responses so forthcoming that new developments underscore the relevance of the approach and findings of this book. Data available by mid-1985 tend not only to endorse the model but also the need for immediate remedy. The migration of "substantial numbers of unemployable male laborers," predicted by the model for the 1970s, it now appears, was merely postponed a decade. According to recent statistics from the Puerto Rico Planning Board, 142,000 Puerto Ricans have migrated from the island from 1980 to 1984, more than in any other five-year period since the 1950s.

The economic program outlined in chapter 17 now takes on unprecedented urgency. The Puerto Rico model has indeed come of age.

I

The Model and the Economy:
The Future as Present

CHAPTER 2

The Economy at a Glance

How We View the Economy

HOW DOES an economy work? To most of the world, the mechanism that produces for our material needs appears almost like a magical black box. Men and women earn money in some way, and they buy things—objects or services—ranging from ashtrays to xeroxing. That Mexican sugar dissolves in Brazilian coffee poured into a Japanese cup that was baked in a French kiln forged with Chinese manganese mystifies no one. The coffee tastes good, and the system seems to work well enough.

There are times, however, when the black boxes break down. The goods don't get delivered, the factories shut down or move away, and the sugar seems too plentiful here and too scarce there. At these historical points, every coffee drinker begins to ask about the infinitely complex connections that once seemed to function so smoothly for so long. An economic model is our guide through the black boxes of one particular economy—a prototypical economy, as we shall see—from which we can learn much more than we might at first expect.

We have two immediate tasks. The first is to look at the real economy and at how it has operated. Based on that overview, we then construct our imitation, or paper-doll replica complete with moving parts, our mechanical robot, and let it do some historical chores. Then we turn our robot loose and, having pointed it in a given direction, watch it while it walks. Does it crash into hidden walls in this future time and alert us to their possible existence? Does it find for us a path that we, having watched the robot's labor, can then undertake for ourselves?

The selection of the characteristics that will form the bones and springs of our mechanical robot is itself problematic, for that very selection presupposes a model from which we seek objective information. For example, do we seek information on gross national product expressed in dollars or do we calculate the quantity of labor spent in all the factories and farms expressed in person-hours? Do we track the value of everything that is produced by a society or only that which is consumed? The value of oranges, the number of oranges, the number of orange pickers, or the number of orange eaters? The answers to these questions all presuppose a prior notion of how the economy operates. Hence, our empirical sketch and the deepening of our theoretical understanding based on that sketch must go hand in hand.[1]

For better or for worse, we are not starting from scratch: there exist traditional modes of describing and comparing economic performance, which embody much of the conventional wisdoms. These accounts are living, quantitative narratives of a society's material odyssey and at the same time are the double-entry bookkeeping records of the nation, a summary of who owes who how much. The tellers of these material tales are the national accountants.[2]

My sketch of the Puerto Rican economy begins with a description of its most superficial economic record, for our model must not only accurately imitate that record and its changes but provide as well a logical description of the mechanics that lie beneath the surface. I then must construct the robot piece by piece and make it imitate the expressions of the past, like programming it to recite the lines of a well-known play. This step is called the calibration of the model, measuring the actual paces to get the size of the historical stride at which our robot hobbles along. If our robot can do this much, I may be in a position to postulate the processes by which the parts interact, how the wires connect and how the various systems or pieces move in harmony with one another. The next step is to set the creature in motion with instructions and to dutifully record its progress at each task and along each path. The records of these ramblings are called forecasts, predictions, and are treated at times as high prophecy or at other times as the ravings of a crackpot.[3]

The final stage to my investigation, usually omitted from publication reports, is the evaluation of the forecasts after the time has elapsed. The failure of predicted events to occur might lead the observer to challenge the entire underlying scheme or simply to recalculate when the expected event is to occur.[4] In economics, we are taught, the variables are so numerous and their interactions so complicated that we cannot possibly expect accuracy in our forecasts. The computerized prophecies may be temporarily acclaimed in business and political circles and policies reformulated in the light of their forecasts. Fortunes may be made or lost on the spin of a computer disk. But once the expected events have or have not come to pass, the high priests may be well on to a new, improved version of their forecaster, more complicated and supposedly more accurate, for some other time or place.[5] Rarely are the carriers of ill omens commissioned again to carry out their task, especially if their warnings prove true.

I make several claims about my model of the Puerto Rican economy. I claim first to have correctly identified the underlying structure. Second, that relationships between pieces of the structure have been correctly identified. And third, that, using all this information, the guesses about the future have been correct. That these warnings were partly ignored in Puerto Rico, although not by economists in other island nations, is political history.

Economic Performance, 1950–80: Gross Product

Puerto Rico in 1950 was, according to most conventional criteria, a prototypical developing country just beginning to grow. Gross product per person, the traditional measure of the standard of living of people, nearly quadrupled from 1950 to 1980, rising from $400 per person to $1,281 (see table 2.1). That the population grew 45 percent while the gross product rose 364 percent is conventionally cited as evidence of its advancement toward a "higher" phase of growth.[6] Gross product per person is a shorthand concept, an abbreviation. Its increase implies simply that the value of the numerator, national production, has risen by more than the value of the denominator, the number of people living on the island. The rest is simple division. This fraction, however, is used commonly as a price-tag measurement of an economy, revealing even less than the name of the country yet identifying the country's position on some international scale of welfare and progress.

Other dimensions in Puerto Rico, also abbreviated nicknames of characteristics, report high material growth. Personal income, consumption, and investment all rose more than 400 percent in the thirty years, marking material satiety and the successful accumulation of objects and capital. They also reflect the great strides the economy made in providing for its current and future needs.

The figures also tell a contrary story. That consumption has nearly equaled or exceeded personal income implies that no net savings were formed in the society.[7] On the national level, there has been no abstention from consumption, only absention from saving. The enormous perennial imbalances in the flow of funds into and out of the country that result from an excess of imports over exports (net sales to rest of world) suggest a tremendous openness, or attachment, to outside markets—in this case, to the U.S. economy. The growth of imports or the decline of exports, which the negative balance signals, go hand in hand with the growth of consumption, investment, and production. They are one and the same.

The imbalance, however, warns us that the import bill must be paid now or later in some way, in kind or in cash. In the meantime, the imbalance sets up stresses: how is the living standard maintained? How are present bills being paid? It also warns of future stresses, for these are the webs of obligations of the next decade that circumscribe our freedom to act now. After all, we have to make the payment on the twenty-year mortgage today. These, then, are some characteristics of the Puerto Rican style of development—high growth of per capita income, high consumption levels, import dependence, and heavy reliance on external borrowing. This style can be seen throughout the Third World.

Perhaps we are inferring too much from but too few observations. We are presuming that the growing levels of product, income, consumption, and investment are all supported the same way, through imports. Clearly the reverse picture must also be considered: the creation of trade imbalances may be seen as the main *objective* of the economy, as evidence of the ability of the economy to export

TABLE 2.1
Economic Growth in Puerto Rico, by Decade, 1950–80

Growth Indicator	1950	1960	1970	1980	Percent change 1950–80[a]
Population (thousands)	2,200	2,340	2,710	3,184	45
Gross product per person (in constant 1954 dollars)	400	629	1,070	1,281	205
Gross product (millions of constant 1954 dollars)	879	1,473	2,901	4,077	364
Personal income	763	1,240	2,654	3,947	417
Personal consumption expenditure	774	1,261	2,649	3,962	415
Investment	127	336	902	724	470
Net sales to rest of world	−118	−312	−1,149	−1,474	1,149
Gross product by use (percent)					
Consumption	87.7	83.4	79.9	99.1	11.4
Government	11.4	13.0	16.3	20.6	9.2
Investment	14.7	23.7	31.0	22.1	7.4
Net sales to rest of world	−13.9	−20.0	−27.2	−41.9	28.0
Gross product by industrial origin (percent)					
Agriculture	19.4	10.1	3.4	2.7	−15.7
Construction	4.5	6.2	7.9	3.3	−1.2
Manufacturing	17.6	22.4	24.8	36.9	19.3
Service and trade	47.6	49.9	51.3	44.6	−3.0
Government	11.0	11.5	12.7	13.2	2.2
Employment (thousands)	596	543	686	753	26
Men/women employment ratio	2.67	2.66	2.21	1.81	−32
Income distribution (Gini coefficient)					
All income	.415[b]	.449[c]	—	.436[d]	5
Excluding food stamps and OASDI transfers	.415[b]	.449[c]	—	.466[d]	11

Sources: Puerto Rico Planning Board, *Economic Report to the Governor 1980; 1981; 1984;* Weisskoff, "Income Distribution and Economic Growth in Puerto Rico, Argentina, and Mexico"; Mann, "Economic Development, Income Distribution, and Real Income Levels: Puerto Rico, 1953–1977"; Puerto Rico Bureau of Labor Statistics, *Income and Expenditures of the Families 1977,* and *Employment and Unemployment in Puerto Rico 1982.*
[a]For gross product by use and by industrial origin, column refers to absolute change of shares.
[b]1953. [c]1963. [d]1977.

capital, to remit profits abroad now and in the future. The rise in living standards is a side payment, and the importing of consumer goods reflects the recycling of the cash flow, the return of the dollar to its creator, the exchange of labor and gifts for goods. The traditional sorting of the national accounts are actually upside down. The starting point might as well be net sales to rest of world, and investment is the current that flows between the U.S. and Puerto Rican economies and peoples. Personal income, once the top line, becomes the bottom line, the paycheck negotiated by the island's leaders—the cost for the use of this island and the conditions under which they play the game. This view, too, represents a unique style of development pioneered by Puerto Rico and now widely imitated with variations throughout the Third World.

The accounts, in summary, tell much and nothing. They give us measurements of concepts, which can be interpreted in a number of ways. We need to read more gauges.

Economic Performance, 1950–80: Shares of the Product

There are two conventional ways to slice the economic pie. One is to divide the gross product—the money value of all goods and services—according to its use (see table 2.1). This tells us how much of our annual paycheck is eaten at the dinner table (consumption), how much is spent on table and chairs (investment), and how much goes to maintain law and order (government). We also barter our fruits with our neighbor, who gladly, it seems, gives us limitless credit on the basis of our good name. This is the negative balance in the net sales to the rest of the world. Alternatively, the repartition of the product by industrial origin tells us how we spent our workdays: how much was produced by farmers (agriculture), bricklayers (construction), factory hands (manufacturing), merchants (service and trade), and officials (government).

Armed with the perspective of these categories, let us reapproach the economic record. In real terms, the economy grew continuously and without interruption from 1950 through 1980, as indicated by the rising gross product, personal income, and consumption expenditure.[8] Investment rose much more rapidly from 1950 to 1970 than the other categories and then fell from $902 million to $724 million in 1980. Since conventional theory tells us that investment is the motor of growth, it is surprising indeed that the economy has continued to grow.

The shares of gross product by use also indicate a major disruption somewhere between 1970 and 1980. Between 1950 and 1970, the shares all changed in predictable directions: consumption fell as a share of gross product, while the shares of government and investment rose steadily. By 1980, however, consumption had leapt to 99 percent of the total and the government share to 21 percent. The increase in the negative balance of net sales abroad provided the space in the accounts for the rise in domestic consumption. In summary, both the people and the state are consuming more as a proportion of the total in the recent decade, and supplies from abroad provide the balance for this elongated pattern.

The industrial origin of the product in table 2.1 tells us that from 1950 to 1970 agriculture declined steadily while construction, manufacturing, and trade all rose. From 1970 to 1980, however, the construction sector collapsed, services shrank, and the share of manufacturing increased even further.

The history of employment also shows a peculiar trend. From 1950 to 1960, the number of jobs actually declined, which alerts us to the connection between growth in that decade and the reduction of certain labor needs. From 1960 onward, however, employment rose steadily, although the net increase for the entire period falls short of the increase in population.

The decline of the men-to-women employment ratio indicates that relatively more jobs have been made available to women. The rise in the measure of income distribution (the Gini coefficient) from 1953 to 1963 and then its decline in 1977 indicate first a deterioration in equality and then a narrowing of the distribution in the later period. However, if we subtract the subsidies that represent the bulk of the poor's income, the Gini coefficient rises to .466, suggesting that the tendency toward inequality has continued in the productive sectors of the economy.[9]

In summary, the Puerto Rican economy has grown steadily in monetary terms and created more jobs in a different set of industries. Our model robot of the Puerto Rican economy must be programmed to do two feats: first, it must simulate the known record for the years 1950 through 1970. Second, the model must predict the surprising changes that took place during the 1970–80 period, especially the employment and income distribution measures around which our major economic questions revolve. Besides, for whom does the economy work? And who works the economy?

CHAPTER 3

Economic Performance and the Model

The Colonial Industrial Prototype

SEVERAL patterns emerge from our first glance at the Puerto Rican economy. We have noted that domestic savings has never been an important source of capital formation and that the economy has relied heavily on imports for consumption and raw materials. We have also noted that federal transfers have underwritten a significant share of the island economy. The computerized model of the Puerto Rican economy must encompass these characteristics, but in a general way. In selecting out the essentials of this structure, this model departs from the conventional view of a developing country, in which the local economy looks like a poor version of an industrialized economy with a larger agricultural sector tacked on. The conventional model then has the poor infant economy "grow," take on more industry, like its more developed brethren in North America and Western Europe.[1]

I hold, however, that Puerto Rico is actually the prototypical industrial colony, the archetypal case of the highest stage of development toward which many other Third World economies are moving. Its economy is open and dependent: open to both imports and exports; dependent on flows of foreign capital, government aid, and on the intangible methods, such as technology, consumption styles, and even wage levels for certain occupations.[2]

In the extreme case of the industrial colony, elements thought of as variables in a large, autonomous economy are severely constrained by laws, rules, or practices that link the colony to the larger economy. These economic links may have their origin in history, such as traditional channels for migratory labor. They may be legalistic, such as shipping rules, tax exemptions, and tariffs; or they may be political, such as government payments from the central state to the colony. The ties may be purely economic or market oriented: investments in search of low wages or cheap products in search of buyers. Put simply, what characterizes a colony is that it is on the receiving end of the stick, and from this vantage point, attempts to manipulate the relationship. Thus a native American reservation or the South African "homelands" are, in their purest form, reserves of labor and sometimes, to their chagrin, minerals. The economic development of these regions consists of bringing capital into their domain to combine with their labor, westernizing their lifestyles, broadening the world market for manufactured goods, and, the bottom line, extracting a higher rate of profit than would otherwise be available elsewhere.

A sense of social responsibility, once expressed crudely as *white man's burden* and more currently as *modernization,* has been the banner under which public funds are culled from the industrialized peoples to help their poorer brethren achieve higher material levels immediately—and also to lower private costs so that private enterprise might find a more hospitable and profitable climate.[3] Whatever the particular configuration of the social class alignments within the colony that tend to keep it in a subservient state, the basic structure I wish to analyze is similar: the economy is open and determined from abroad. These standard aspects contrast with the often large, autochthonous base, which is regarded as outside the money economy but somehow appended to it. It has been precisely the attraction of this, the backward sector, that has led Western countries in their quest for the integration of the "less developed" countries into the global economy.[4]

My model of the Puerto Rican economy comprehends the characteristic of dependency by setting by decree those variables that, from the point of view of the colony, appear determined outside the local economy. Investment, for example, is viewed as attracted from the United States and Europe as a result of the tax exemption of Puerto Rico's sales effort, not by slight differences in the profit rate. Government funds depend on the political climate in Washington, D.C., and the lobbying effort in Congress. Exports from Puerto Rico are seen as depending not on their prices but on the global economic condition of the industries whose branch plants are engaged in different stages of manufacturing in Puerto Rico.

The robot model then goes to work. Its structure, or machinery, consists of three main blocks of recorded circuitry (see figure 3.1): first, the record of who buys the finished goods, called final demand; second, the record of how things are made, termed the input-output structure; and third, the record of who the owners and

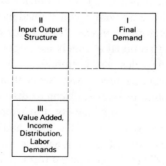

FIGURE 3.1
Three Blocks of Circuitry

workers are and how they are paid, called value added, income distribution, and labor demands. We shall examine each of these black boxes in a later chapter.

Given the historical records and our expectations for each of these blocks, the model first simulates production needed to meet final demand. Then it generates income to families at different earnings levels. These families spend their earnings according to historically given consumption patterns. This consumption in turn generates local demand, which in turn requires both imports and local employment. Employment, income and its distribution, and consumption are thus all endogenous to the model, that is, they are estimated within the model, and their final values are the object of our research quest. Their solution will vary as the exogenous variables—those elements determined outside the economy—are projected according to different guesses or strategies about the future. Productivity of different industries continues to change according to historical trends.

What we have just stated in the paragraph above can be seen simply in figure 3.2. However, employment in step 5 must be reconciled with the employment generated in step 2, and the production in step 4 must be related to production in step 1. Hence, the economy is not a simple linear sequence, but rather an intricate system of circles, feedbacks, swirling galaxies, with some major elements determined outside, like some of the elements of final demand, or drawn in from the outside, like imports (see figure 3.3).

Our robot model is designed to simulate the prototypical high-consumption behavior that seems to accompany rapid growth in the developing countries.

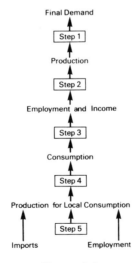

FIGURE 3.2
Economic Steps

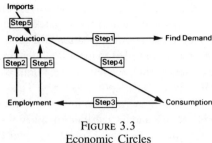

FIGURE 3.3
Economic Circles

Concretely, this is done by augmenting the detailed input-output structure in two directions to include, first, a range of consumption patterns varying by income level, and second, a range of income levels generated by different industrial sectors (see figure 3.4). The model was calibrated for 1970, and then set in motion in a static, robot-like walk on seven paths of projections until it reached the 1980 mark. The basic paths included three in a balanced trajectory, in which the elements of exogenous demand continued to grow altogether (that is, "continue with the same formula"); two emphasizing domestic construction ("build houses everywhere"); and two more emphasizing the growth of exports ("sell our products everywhere"). The results of these alternatives provide us with estimates of employment and income expected by 1980. These ranged from a pessimistic

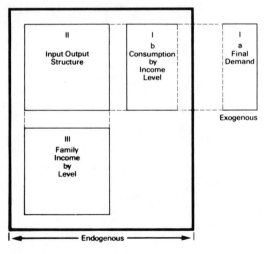

FIGURE 3.4
The Colonial Industrial
Prototype

estimate of 800 thousand jobs for the slow-growing balanced economy to 1.4 million jobs for the rapidly growing balanced economy. The other forecasts fell between these extremes (see figure 3.5).[5]

The projections themselves also presented clear warnings, especially with respect to the distribution of occupational needs. "The most significant change," the investigator had written of those estimates,

is reflected in the sharp decline in the share of laboring men . . . and a somewhat smaller decline in the share of managerial men. Both of these compositional changes are associated with the continued deterioration of the agricultural sector. . . . All programs reveal the relative decrease in male relative to female employment opportunity. . . . These results point to the likelihood of continued out-migration of substantial numbers of unemployable male laborers, despite the rise in overall employment. All the straight-line projections except the 10 percent balanced growth program imply a demand for labor that could easily cope with a 3 percent annual growth in the labor force. However, should the Puerto Rican industrial rate slow, especially, with a downturn of the U.S. economy, or should the mix of new industries be considerably less labor demanding than the industries previously promoted, or should the first generation of high-employment factories leave Puerto Rico for other low-wage, tax-exempt islands, then the actual achieved employment for 1980 is likely to fall far short of the optimistic projections [summarized in table 3.1 in the present volume]. At the time of this revision . . . all three of these effects are acting as brakes on net job

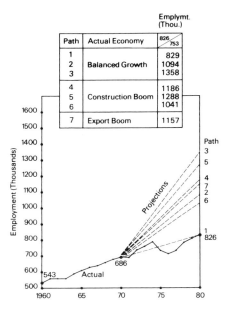

FIGURE 3.5
Alternative Growth Paths, Actual and
Projected Employment, 1960–80

TABLE 3.1
Seven Economic Growth Paths for Puerto Rico

Growth Indicator	Actual 1970	Projections for 1980						
		Balanced Growth			Construction Boom		Export Boom	
		Slow	Medium	Fast	Slow	Fast	Slow	Fast
Overall exogenous demand (annual growth rate)	12.7[a]	10.0	12.7[a]	15.0	12.7	12.7	12.7	12.7
Construction investment (annual growth rate)	16.7[a]	10.0	12.7	15.0	16.7[a]	20.0	12.7	12.7
Export demand (annual growth rate)	11.6[a]	10.0	12.7	15.0	12.7	12.7	11.6[a]	14.0
Employment (thousands)	686	829	1,094	1,358	1,186	1,288	1,041	1,157
Employment (percent increase)	—	20.8	59.5	98.0	72.9	87.8	51.7	68.7
Men employed (percent of total)	72.2	68.5	68.5	68.4	69.3	70.1	68.7	67.9
Women employed (percent of total)	27.8	31.5	31.5	31.6	30.7	29.3	31.3	32.1
Men/women employment ratio	2.6	2.2	2.2	2.2	2.3	2.4	2.2	2.1

Source: Weisskoff, "Income Distribution and Export Promotion in Puerto Rico"; and Puerto Rico Planning Board, Economic Report to the Governor 1981.
[a]Historical annual growth rate 1963–70.

creation; and, with the deepening recession in North America, Puerto Rico's return migration swells the ranks of the unemployed and augments the natural growth of the labor force.[6]

But these predictions were not entirely accurate either. The recession in the United States did deepen, and the Puerto Rican industrial growth rate slowed. New plants attracted to the island were more automated and employed fewer workers than the plants that were leaving Puerto Rico. But the out-migration never occurred on the scale that the decay of the productive structure implied. The unemployed were given a new lease for continued residence in their homeland when a billion dollar food stamp program was extended to Puerto Rico.

The Forecasts and the Economy, 1980

Having looked briefly at how the model was constructed, we are now prepared to compare the actual 1980 economic performance to the 1980 forecasts that were made in 1972. Of the seven different paths (see figure 3.5), the economy actually most approximated the slow-but-balanced growth scenario (path 1). Expressed in 1980 dollars, the projection of gross product per capita overshot the actual product by 12.2 percent (see table 3.2). Personal income underpredicted the actual, due most probably to the rise in federal transfers, which are included in the calculation of income but excluded from the product. The forecast of personal consumption exceeded actual consumption. Each of these aggregate forecasts represents less than a 1 percent annual deviation from the actual figure on an annual basis. Predicted employment for 1980 in the pessimistic path 1 scenario overestimated the actual historical employment by four-tenths of 1 percent, approximating with surprising accuracy the increase of employment during the decade.

In 1983, however, the Puerto Rico Department of Labor revised its historical estimates of employment for the period 1971–80 on the basis of the 1980 United States Population Census. These estimates reflect a significant reduction in employment throughout the decade. The model's predicted employment overshot these newly revised estimates by 10 percent, still a respectable margin for a decade projection.[7] The forecast for the 1980 occupational distribution correctly emphasizes the decline in the share of male employment, but in the actual economy the importance of women in the work force rose by more than was predicted. Within the declining male category, the projected shares of professional and managerial men are lower than the actual, in contrast to the projected shares of clerical workers, salesmen, and operatives, which are greater than the actual. Among women, the model also slightly underpredicted the full extent to which the actual share of professional, managerial, clerical workers, and operatives rose. In other words, the economy in 1980 actually provided more of these categories of jobs for women than was forecast.

In summary, the model's least optimistic forecast for the 1980 Puerto Rican economy closely resembles the overall actual 1980 employment situation, with the

TABLE 3.2
Actual and Projected Economic Indicators for Puerto Rico, 1980

Growth Indicator	Actual	Projected	Percent Difference
Gross product per person (in 1980 dollars)	3,479	3,902[a]	12.2
Gross product (in thousands of 1980 dollars)	11,074	12,424[a]	12.2
Personal income (in 1980 dollars)	10,932	9,557[a]	−12.6
Personal consumption expenditure (in 1980 dollars)	10,976	11,961[a]	9.0
Employment (in thousands)	826	829[a]	0.4
Revised	753[b]	—	10.1[b]
Employment percent increase 1970–80	20.6	20.8[a]	0.2
Revised	9.3[b]	—	11.5[b]
Distribution of employment[c] (percent)	100.0	100.0	—
Men	63.3	68.5	5.2
Professional	7.8	5.9	−1.9
Managerial	8.9	8.5	−0.4
Clerical	4.6	6.4	1.8
Sales	4.6	6.9	2.3
Craft	11.9	12.6	0.7
Operative	10.1	11.4	1.3
Service	6.8	7.5	0.7
Labor	8.2	8.6	0.4
Not reported	—	0.7	0.7
Women	36.6	31.5	−5.1
Professional	8.0	4.5	−3.5
Managerial	2.1	1.2	−0.9
Clerical	9.3	7.1	−2.2
Sales	2.0	1.3	−0.7
Craft	0.4	0.5	0.1
Operative	7.7	9.3	1.6
Service	6.8	6.8	0.0
Labor	—	0.2	0.2
Not reported	—	0.7	0.7
Men/women employment ratio	1.8	2.2	0.4
Income distribution Gini coefficient			
All income	.436	—	—
Excluding food stamps and OASDI transfers	.466[d]	.466	0.0

Sources: "Income Distribution and Export Promotion in Puerto Rico"; Puerto Rico Planning Board, Economic Report 1981; 1984; Puerto Rico Bureau of Labor Statistics, Employment and Unemployment in Puerto Rico, Report E-36; Mann, "Economic Development, Income Distribution, and Real Income Levels: Puerto Rico, 1953–1977"; Puerto Rico Bureau of Labor Statistics, Income and Expenditures of the Families 1977.
[a]Projections originally calculated in 1970 prices were inflated to current 1980 prices using implicit price indexes.
[b]Revised in 1983 on basis of 1980 U.S. census.
[c]Totals may not sum due to rounding. Projections of employment by occupation correspond to calendar year; actual figures to fiscal year 1979–80. Managerial category includes farmers and farm managers, laborers include farm laborers and foremen. Last column indicates absolute difference between percentages.
[d]1977.

exception that it underestimated the relative importance of the professional and managerial occupations for both sexes and of clerical positions for women; it overestimated the importance of women in sales, the importance of men in sales and clerical positions, and of both sexes as operatives. The model proved to be correct in predicting the decline in employment of men relative to women, but fell short of describing the degree to which women would displace men.

The model predicted a widening in the distribution of income to families, that is, a rise in the level of inequality, as suggested by an increase in the Gini coefficient from a measured .449 in 1963 to a forecast .466 for 1980. The Gini coefficient actually recorded for 1977, the year of the most extensive study, was exactly .466, for income excluding the major federal subsidies, the same as the value of the forecast. Since the model was directed at measuring the distribution of only those incomes that flow from the productive parts of the economy, the forecast is comparable in concept to this coefficient. The Gini coefficient for the society as a whole is lower (.436) and indicates a higher level of equality once the transfers are included. We expect this, since food stamps and old-age benefits are intended to raise the living standards of the very poor.

To conclude, the model's forecasts for 1980 for the least optimistic path have proven to be surprisingly accurate for the aggregate indicators, such as national product, income, and consumption. The forecasts of employment and income distribution have shown themselves to be extraordinarily close to the historical values for 1980. Perhaps errors within the model compensated each other, or the economy cooperated with the forecasters. In any case, the coincidence of the forecast and actual performance, while not itself a validation of the model or of its assumptions, does encourage us to look more deeply into its components and the other lessons we have learned from its construction.

CHAPTER 4

The Microcircuitry of the Model

IN THE PRECEDING chapter, we examined briefly the major blocks in the economy and the forecasts for 1980 that the working model produced. But what is within the black boxes?

Taken out of context, dissected, and analyzed under the economist's microscope, the sample slices from each box (the blocks of figure 3.1) appear formless and lifeless, an endless listing of numbers and recipes, statistical definitions and equations. But fitted together, they take on an added dimension and another significance. In this chapter, we shall examine the broad accounting framework, which is the structure of the model. Then we shall examine some of the slices in isolation and reassemble the parts in a new way.

The Social Accounting Framework

Let us begin with block I, final demand, which supposedly reflects the end and purpose of all economic activity. As noted earlier, final demand can be regarded in two ways: it may be divided according to use by household consumers, C, investors, I, the government, G, and net sales to rest of world, or exports minus imports, $X - M$ (see figure 4.1). Final demand for Puerto Rico in 1980, expressed in 1954 dollars, totalled \$4.1 billion (or \$41 hundred million) and was divided as shown in figure 4.2.

Alternatively, final demand may be divided according to the origin of the product. For the purpose of illustration, all economic activity may be seen as originating in the three main sectors: agriculture, A, manufacturing and construction, M, and service, trade, and government, S (see figure 4.3). The \$41 hundred

| C | I | G | X-M |

FIGURE 4.1
Final Demand by Use

C   I   G   X-M

| 40 | 8 | 7 | -14 | =\$41 |

FIGURE 4.2
Final Demand by Use
with Dollar Values

24

A
M
S

FIGURE 4.3
Final Demand by Origin

A	1
M	16
S	24

$41

FIGURE 4.4
Final Demand by Origin
with Dollar Values

million gross product for Puerto Rico in 1980 was divided by sector of origin as shown in figure 4.4.

The classification of final demand according to both use and sector of origin contains the data that compose block I of figure 3.1, a checkerboard of square cells, a rectangular pizza sliced horizontally and vertically (see figure 4.5). Hypothetical values for the detailed cells might be as shown in figure 4.6, with zeroes indicating that no transaction occurred in that category.

Block II of figure 3.1, input-output structure, is similarly an accounting of how

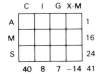

	C	I	G	X-M	
A					1
M					16
S					24
	40	8	7	−14	41

FIGURE 4.5
Final Demand by Use
and by Origin

	C	I	G	X-M	
A	9	0	0	-8	1
M	14	8	1	-7	16
S	17	0	6	1	24
	40	8	7	-14	41

FIGURE 4.6
Final Demand by Use and by Origin
with Hypothetical Dollar Values

the value of goods flowed among different branches of industry before final sale (see figure 4.7). The agricultural sector, A, sells wheat, an intermediate product, to a bakery in the manufacturing sector, M. The wheat is then baked into bread and delivered by truck by the service sector, S, to final demand for home consumption. The value of the wheat (say, $0.08), the manufactured bread (say $0.45), and the truck services (say, $0.05) are all sold to a family for $0.88, the cost of labor, machinery, and stockholders' return amounting to $0.30. If, however, we were to

FIGURE 4.7
Movement of Goods between Sectors

stand first at the gateway to each sector and count the value of all the intermediate materials as they left each sector and then stand at the entrance to the kitchen table and count the value of the final bread, the total would be $0.58 + 0.88 = $1.46 (see figure 4.8). Economists call the $0.58 worth of ingredients intermediate demand, and the flowing relationship between the *A, M,* and *S* sectors (values of wheat, baked goods, and trucking) is said to compose the input-output structure. The national accountant subtracts out the cost of materials ($0.58), recording only the value of the final bread, $0.88, as national product. The input-output accountant double counts the materials and the finished product and calls it total sales.

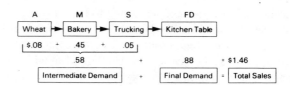

FIGURE 4.8
Movement of Goods between Sectors
with Hypothetical Dollar Values

The wheat-bread-shipping chain may be viewed as the economic recipe for making bread, and may be constructed from the historical money values of bread deliveries, not their physical quantities (see table 4.1). Since the payments to the workers and owners plus the depreciation of the machinery, collectively called value added, total $0.30, the cost of all the inputs is $0.88, equal by definition to the value of the final sale. Value added can be thought of as the only newly created value of the whole process, as the other ingredients—wheat, baking, and service—have already been assembled in their respective sectors. They are thought of as floating in the system.

But how are wheat, baking, and transport service themselves produced? What are their recipes? These too, require their individual brews of intermediate inputs

TABLE 4.1
Economic Recipe for Making Bread

Ingredient and Sector	Amount in Dollars
Wheat (agriculture)	8
Baking (manufacturing)	45
Transport (service)	5
Wages, profit, depreciation (value added)	30
Total	88

TABLE 4.2
Recipes for Wheat, Baking, and Transport

	Amount in Dollars				
Ingredient and Sector	*A* Corporation	*M* Corporation	*S* Corporation	Final Demand	Total Sales
Wheat (agriculture, *A*)	1	8	0	1	10
Flour and chemicals (man-ufacturing, *M*)	4	45	23	16	88
Trucking (service, *S*)	2	5	1	24	32
Wages, profit, depreciation (value added, *VA*)	3	30	8	41	—
Total inputs	10	88	32	—	130

and freshly added value. Let us say that the historical data collected during a $10 million wheat harvest shows the use of $1 million worth of hybrid seed, $4 million worth of chemicals and fertilizers, $2 million worth of trucking services, with $3 million left as farmers' wages, profits, and rent. Let us suppose that the historical recipe for all truckers for their year's activity is $23 million worth of gas and oil, $1 million worth of subcontracting from one trucker to another, and $8 million for wages, profits, and depreciation (see table 4.2).

If we regard each sector as being dominated by a single large corporation—the *A* Corporation, which produces all the wheat and seeds, the *M* Corporation, which manufactures all the flour, chemicals, fertilizers, and gasoline, and the *S* Corporation, which operates all the trucks, then each recipe can be considered as representing the consolidated business account of each of the major branches of the economy. A simplified flow chart of the whole bread-making process is shown in figure 4.9. The seed-to-table steps are undertaken sequentially by the *A*, *M*, and *S* corporations, respectively, and the finished product is sold to the consumer as final demand. Is such a flow chart also a good representation for the entire economy? Let us look closer.

We know that the *A* Corporation needs its raw materials: hybrid seed from a seed farm it also owns, fertilizers and chemicals purchased from the *M* Corporation, and trucking service purchased from the *S* Corporation. Although most of the wheat is sold to the baking subsidiary of the *M* Corporation, some grain is also sold

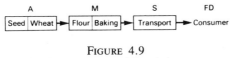

FIGURE 4.9
Simple Movement of Goods between
Corporate Sectors

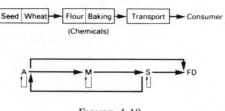

FIGURE 4.10
Simple Flows of Goods between
Sectors with Feedback

to consumers who grind their own flour and bake their own bread. The bakery and fertilizer subsidiaries of the *M* Corporation also purchase transport service. The flow chart becomes more complicated (see figure 4.10).

The accounting of all these complicated-looking flows is arranged for us in a neat format in table 4.2. Reading down the columns, we learn the ingredients for each of the corporations. The final demand column tells us the composition by sector of origin (borrowed from figure 4.4 and table 2.1). The bottom line of each column tells us the total value of all the ingredients.

Reading across the consolidated cookbook of table 4.2 gives us even more information, for here we find a list of each corporation's customers during the year. We learn, for example, that of the $10 million total sales of the *A* Corporation, $1 million were transactions within the company from the hybrid-seed farm subsidiary, $8 million were made to the *M* Corporation as wheat for baking, and $1 million was made to consumers as whole-wheat berries. Likewise, the *M* Corporation sold $4 million to the *A* Corporation, $45 million to its own branch plants (probably fuel from its gasohol division and chemicals for its bakeries), $23 million of fuel to truckers, and $16 million directly to consumers. The *S* Corporation, which owns a fleet of taxis and buses as well as trucks, sold some services to the *A* and *M* corporations, but for the most part, did its business directly with consumers.

A simple table can tell us the "secret" accounting formula for each branch of the economy and reveals the "secret" sales record of each industry to every other industry. Like any double-entry system, the vertically listed values of the ingredients, or inputs, must equal the horizontally arranged values of sales, or outputs. Final demand, which is the value of sales only to the consumers, is equal to value added, which is the sum of their incomes. In other words, consumers can spend only as much as they make, according to this accounting system. They earn $41 million as employees, owners, and landlords of the three corporations, and they spend $41 million on the products of the three companies.

All the recipes accounted for in table 4.2 may now be illustrated as flows of dollar values attached to the commodities and services produced and exchanged

TABLE 4.3
Accounting of Commodities and Services from the Three Hypothetical Corporations
to Consumers

Input	A Corporation	M Corporation	S Corporation	Total Intermediate Demand	Final Demand	Total Sales
Material	7	58	24	89	41	130
Value added	3	30	8	—	—	—
All	10	88	32	—	—	130

between the major sectors (see figure 4.11) and the inputs summarized (see table 4.3). Final demand of $41 million is but a fraction of the total sales in the entire economy. Intermediate materials and services, that is, sales from one corporation to another, amounted to $89 million, or more than twice the final demand of $41 million.

The circular flows shown in figure 4.11 are due in part to the complexity of the production process. If growing grain, baking bread, and carrying it to market were all carried out as one continuous operation by one tribe of worker farmers, then this tribe's single account might be much simplified (see figure 4.12). In such a case, the internal circuitry of that single tribe, while unknown to us as outside observers, is custom to the farmer workers. In other words, each production unit, no matter how simple or integrated, has its own internal bookkeeping system in a similar format, whether it is explicit or not.

To recapitulate, the black boxes of blocks I, II, and III of figure 3.1 can now be viewed as the trace values of a crossword puzzle worked out historically by the

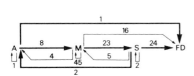

FIGURE 4.11
Complete Flow of Goods between
Sectors with Dollar Values

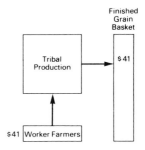

FIGURE 4.12
Three Blocks of Circuitry
for a Tribe

corporations (see figure 4.13). But what is the basis for this circuitry? In the following sections we shall examine the underlying microcircuits and then reassemble the blocks and see to what use the integrated circuitry might be put.

The Basic Unit

The microcircuit that underlies all economy is the basic production process, in which workers combine their labor and raw materials and with the assistance of machinery or tools create a product at the farm or shop (figure 4.14). The product then must be distributed, sold, or transferred to another process, where it enters as

A. The Black Boxes

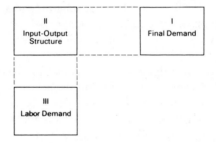

B. The Accounting Summary

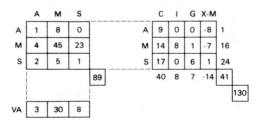

C. The Circuits

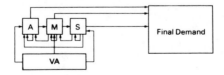

FIGURE 4.13
Boxes, Accounts, and Circuits

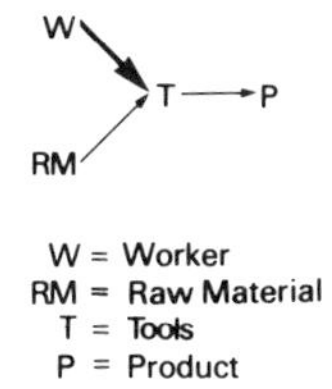

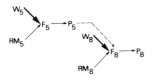

W = Worker
RM = Raw Material
T = Tools
P = Product

FIGURE 4.14
The Basic Production
Process

P_i = Wheat
F_i = Factory

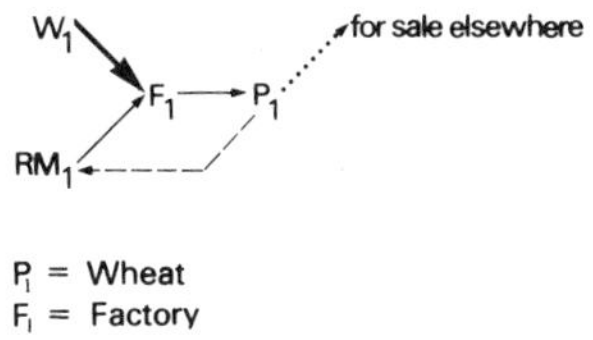

FIGURE 4.15
The Basic Production Process with
the Product as Raw Material

another raw material or machine. Or the new commodity may be consumed as a finished product. A farmer might preserve part of his crop as seed and sell the rest of his crop (figure 4.15). Or, a more complicated case, a tool and die maker might produce machinery for his own factory and for other plants (figure 4.16). Yet another case is that of the worker who consumes some of his own product, the rest being put in inventory, exported abroad, and sold to the government (figure 4.17).

All three cases above are variations on the single process, sketched in figure 4.14, of the worker with the raw materials and tools producing a new thing or service. Depending on the complexity of the economy, all of production can be depicted as a web of interlocking processes (figure 4.18). Much as wheat (product 1) can be used to make flour (product 2) and eventually bread (product 3), it can be used also for the fermentation of whiskey (product 4). Just as the chain of production links different sectors of the economy with each other through production, workers too become related. Farmers, millers, bakers, and brewers are cousins and depend on one another. This they quickly discover when, for example, factory 3 closes in bankruptcy and, as a consequence, the others also face collapse— unless factory 4 can absorb all of farm 1's production. The processes are linked even more closely, as the workers, factories, and raw materials are all consumers of each other's products (figure 4.19). This linear chain is actually a series of circles, spirals, and helixes of differing shapes, sizes, and complexities.

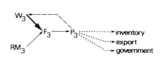

P_i = Machinery
P_8 = Tractor

FIGURE 4.16
The Basic Production Process with
the Product as Capital Good

P_i = Bread

FIGURE 4.17
The Basic Production Process with
the Product as Consumer Good

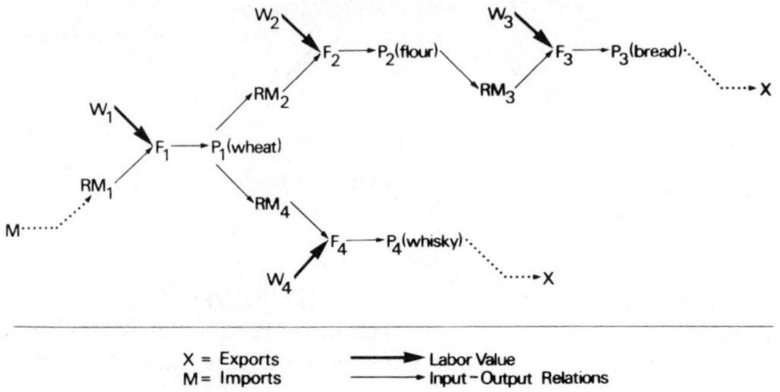

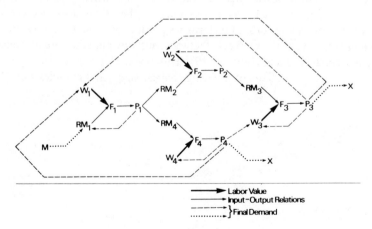

X = Exports
M = Imports

→ Labor Value
→ Input–Output Relations

FIGURE 4.18
The Webs of Economic Relationships

Why is it important to chart these circuits? What difference does it make? Once the circuits are known for an economy, then it may be possible to anticipate the consequences of different policies upon each branch of activity. For example, what would happen if exports were doubled or if imports were cut off? In the former case, we could trace the industries that would prosper most, and in the latter case, we could pinpoint the most strategically affected industries and anticipate their needs.

All this might appear hopelessly confusing and involved, but economists, rather than concern themselves with the individual flows (which is the domain of business and the consumer), have been long preoccupied with sorting and summing

→ Labor Value
→ Input–Output Relations
→ } Final Demand

FIGURE 4.19
The Webs of Economic Relationships,
Including Final Demand

these flows with an eye toward improving the wealth of their nation. In this task, the national accountant and social statistician have given names and numbers to the grand sums of each of these elements. The total of all payments to workers and owners is our familiar value added. The input-output structure refers to the flow of materials from one factory to another. And national product is the sum of all final sales to consumers, domestic and foreign.

We have already examined these as global categories and the way they fit together. We have noted, too, that the black boxes are really composed of webs of wires, confusing only to the casual observer, who would be similarly confounded by a visit to the switching station of the local telephone company. Schematically, the economic accounting system is no more than a gigantic jigsaw puzzle. What remains now is to show some alternative uses for and details of our versatile network.

CHAPTER 5

Games Economists Play

IN THIS CHAPTER, I shall rearrange the economic circuitry, complete the accounting system, and describe the innovations that were first introduced in the model. Then we shall play some games with the blocks, asking questions of them and assigning tasks.

The national economy must be seen as a closed circuit, with exports serving as the opening or connection to other economies (figure 5.1). (We will consider imports in a moment). Or the blocks may be slightly rearranged, placing value added at the starting point of production (figure 5.2).

The blocks themselves are composed of many cells, metaphors for the aggregations and separations of the microcircuits. The value added block is composed of the payments to different types of workers and owners. The input-output block consists of all the production recipes, and the final demand block is the two-way classification of the national accounts (figure 5.3). The usual presentation of the classic input-output system is inverted in figures 5.2 and 5.3 to emphasize the importance of value added as the focal block of the economy. It is the living matter of the economy, the origin of the value-creation process and the residence of labor

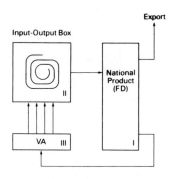

FIGURE 5.1
The Traditional Closed
Circuit

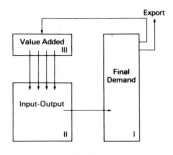

FIGURE 5.2
The Closed Circuit
Rearranged

34

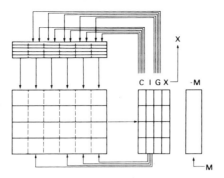

FIGURE 5.3
The Circuitry Detailed

power. Three major innovations or extensions have been introduced into this basic model, each dealing with one of the three major blocks. Each innovation is described below.

Model Innovations: Final Demand and Consumption

In our model, it is not sufficient to view consumption simply as the summation of all household purchases, the classic C of the national accounts. More important are the specific patterns by which families of different income levels spend their earnings on the full array of products and services. These patterns depend on custom, social class, physical location, and other factors, as well as income, and it is presumed that they describe the underlying and continuing spending behavior for each type of family.

Usually it is business people and market analysts who are most concerned with the specification of consumption patterns. For our purposes, however, the measurement of these expenditure patterns makes it possible to anticipate and plan for the more general consumption needs of the total society, such as the national demand for food, clothing, and recreation. The study of consumer behavior is based on sample surveys of thousands of families. The spending patterns of these sampled families are conventionally summarized in a simple statistical relationship between total spending and the amount spent on a product.

The classic relationship between total spending and the amount spent on food, for example, has generally been found to be a gradual tapering curve. This states simply that if a family's total spending doubles, say, from one hundred to two hundred dollars a week, then its purchases of food rise, although by a lesser proportion. In this case, spending on food rises from forty to seventy dollars (figure 5.4).

The relationship between total spending and spending on a so-called luxury

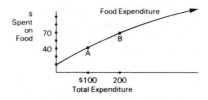

FIGURE 5.4
Engel Relationship for Food

commodity, for example, automobiles, might be quite the opposite. As income doubles, families spend an increased proportion of their budget on the luxury (figure 5.5). For example, a family spends thirty dollars of its hundred-dollar budget on its automobile. However, if its income were to rise to two hundred dollars, then the family would spend a hundred dollars, or half its weekly budget, on its vehicle. The study of these consumption patterns, named Engel curves after a nineteenth-century investigator, lies at the heart of the Puerto Rico model, since their detailed specification allows us to predict with greater accuracy the precise needs of the population.

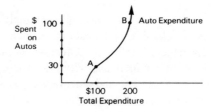

FIGURE 5.5
Engel Relationship for Luxuries

Model Innovations: The Import Matrix

A second innovation of our model deals with the three-dimensional nature of the input-output structure. Until now we have presumed that the material ingredients for our economy were all readily available from local production, but block II is actually the icing of a two-layer cake. The two underlying levels are, first, the locally produced ingredients and, second, the imported ingredients (table 5.1).

The input-output block depicted in figure 4.13 may be thought of as a crossnumber (rather than crossword) table, which is the summation of the two underlying levels. Figure 5.6 shows the second layer, the foreign component of each entry. For example, of the four-dollar sale of manufactured goods to agriculture, two dollars' value consisted of imported goods. Furthermore, seven dol-

TABLE 5.1
Recipe for Growing Wheat

Ingredient and Sector	Amounts		
	Domestic Agriculture (A_d)	Imported Agriculture (A_m)	Total (A)
Seed (A)	1	0	1
Fertilizer (M)	2	2	4
Trucking (S)	2	0	2

lars of the eight-dollar sale of agriculture to manufacturing (wheat to bakeries) consisted of imported goods. For an open economy, this import matrix contains the single most important piece of strategic information for evaluating economic policy, as we shall soon see.

Model Innovations: Value Added

The third innovation in the model involves the extension of the value added matrix in two directions. The value added block is conventionally composed of the summation of subcategories, such as wages and salaries, profits, depreciation, and taxes paid by each industry. We, however, are interested in how these are distributed to the families of different income levels. The agricultural sector, for example, may generate low wages to many laborers and high rents to a few large individual landlords. Manufacturing, on the other hand, may generate high salaries to its workers and moderate returns to its owners. Service may distribute its value added to white-collar professionals at middle-income levels.

Each industry, then, may be seen as generating a characteristic pattern or a distribution of incomes, which can be expressed as a series of cells or "earnings recipes," according to the income class of the families (figures 5.7 and 5.8). Similarly, each sector may be seen as requiring a characteristic recipe, or pattern, of the different occupations. Agriculture, for example, demands more laborers;

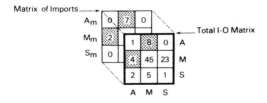

FIGURE 5.6
The Import and Total Input-Output Matrices

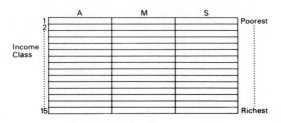

FIGURE 5.7
The Distribution of Value
Added to Families

service, more professional and clerical workers (figure 5.9). Instead of aggregate totals, the value added is now composed of castes of employees and owners, classified by their income levels and associated with their occupations. People can move into and out of these job and income positions, changing their income in accordance with their job description.

Each branch of economic activity produces a characteristic trace, or stream of incomes and jobs. What I have done is decipher these patterns, unscrambling each one, sector by sector, and then reattaching each distribution individually to the particular sector that gave rise to it. The individual patterns are then reassembled into the total society—but under different experimental conditions. For example, in 1960 the economy was actually a mixture of three different sectoral patterns,

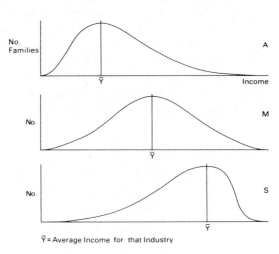

FIGURE 5.8
Sample Patterns of Income Distributions

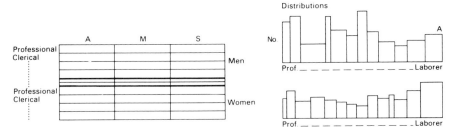

FIGURE 5.9
Sample Patterns of Occupational Distributions

each accounting for a significant share of national income. By 1980, however, the *A* sector had virtually disappeared, and the *M* sector grew enormously, their sizes and shapes both changing. In the model, I measure these changes and apply them to many alternative scenarios. What if agriculture had not disappeared? What if manufacturing had not grown? What then would the overall society have looked like? These might-have-beens have been popularized professionally in counterhistorical investigations and in children's stories as well.[1]

The assumptions that underlie input-output recipes are well known, as their critics are always ready to point out.[2] The fixed circuitry of relationships among technology, income distributions, and job assignments presume a continuity of the existing substructures in an economic world in which these very blocks seem to change daily through inventions, automation, and wage negotiation. Even the specification of the consumption patterns presumes that people will continue to behave as they have in the past. All these assumptions about the fixed circuitry can be altered as we receive new information about technology, income distribution, and consumption habits, and make allowance for these changes. Furthermore, by comparing blocks from one decade to the next, we can measure just how much national change was due to the alteration within a given block of the economy. The complete model is simply the reassembly of the three blocks in all their detail (figure 5.10).

Economic Scenarios

The model will be used to test out different economic scenarios, plays whose script is known but whose final conclusion is not. The first scenario is the promotion of the country's exports abroad. This is the classic strategy of a small country that has long depended on the sale of sugarcane or tobacco and seeks to strengthen its economy by selling more sugar or more tobacco. The increased exports necessitate a greater work force directly in these industries, and also in those sectors that indirectly supply the exporting industries with their raw materials, for example,

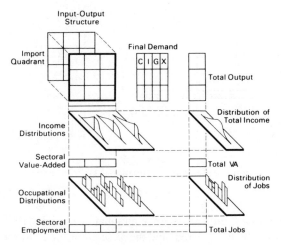

FIGURE 5.10
The Total System

fertilizers and insecticides. As exports expand, new farm workers are employed, and it is assumed they spend their income, or value added, in a manner similar to the farm and factory workers of past years (figure 5.11).

A second strategy, import substitution, is the reverse of export promotion. If the world demand for the nation's exports were to fall, then the earnings from the sale of sugar and tobacco would be insufficient to cover the cost of importing, for example, wheat, television sets, and automobiles. To replicate this crisis, I ask the model to shut down both the flow of imports and exports and redirect resources toward producing directly for the needs of the population. The agricultural sector grows food for local consumption, not staples for export. Factories are built that will assemble autos and television sets—and make all the components as well.

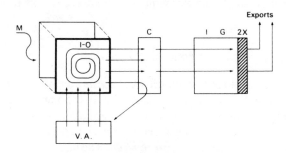

FIGURE 5.11
The Strategy of Export Promotion

Import substitution has been used by a number of nations supposedly to free them from the constraints imposed by the balance-of-payments crises precipitated by the failure of traditional export earnings (figure 5.12).[3]

Import substitution carried to the extreme would lead to isolationism and autarky, requiring a major reorientation for countries that have been historically integrated into the world economy. It may be more realistic to have the model trace substrategies of import substitution, say, food self-sufficiency, or to design a program of selective import substitution of basic necessities or luxury goods. These programs can be wired into the model to test for their indirect effects.

For example, a program to import substitute food would trigger the creation of more employment directly in agriculture and indirectly in manufacturing (chemicals and fertilizers, tractors and fuel) and services (trucking and railroad transport, tractor repair, and crop insurance). The production of these indirect manufactures and services in turn would require further production of their own inputs and create further employment. The fuels for the tractor and truck services may be made from grain, and the production of more grain requires more chemicals, and so on along and around the chains of relationships until all the circuits are completed and the country produces its own food.

I shall replicate one further scenario, the Robin Hood model. In this scenario, the rich will be taxed and the poor given subsidies in such a way that there are no longer poor or rich. All end up with the same income. But then the model faces another problem. If Robin Hood is successful in making the society egalitarian, then how will these now-equal people consume? Will they consume like the old lower class but buy higher quality goods? Will they behave like the old upper class, buying as the rich once bought, but now with a reduced income? Or will they take on the spending patterns of the old middle class, whose income all the families now enjoy under the Robin Hood scenario? The model will test all these possibilities.

For all of these scenarios, the part of the block of final demand that contains investment, government, and exports (I, G, X) is fixed at the outset on the basis of

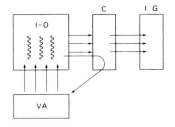

FIGURE 5.12
The Strategy of Import
Substitution

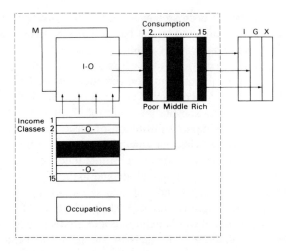

FIGURE 5.13
The Robin Hood Scenario with Different
Expenditure Patterns

our expectations of those components described in chapter 3. All the rest of the model (figure 5.13) is then free to work itself out. This working out provides us with the final, or equilibrium, solution of jobs, income, consumption, and intermediate goods that the economy produces, in order to deliver the final demand (investment, government, and exports) predicted for a given year in the future.

All this requires imports and capital. Where do the imports and the capital and newly trained labor come from that could satisfy instantaneously all these needs? Since we are dealing with a colony with access to the industrial world, we assume that such an economy is able to attract needed capital by selling bonds (which it does) and to attract skilled labor by offering high salaries for the needed occupations (which occurs). Nor do imports necessarily have to balance exports (the usual balance of trade) for each year, since a trade deficit can be compensated by changes in interest rates, by transfer payments, or by increasing indebtedness and the expectation of future repayment.

These, then, are the basic scenarios that I will play out on the blocks of our model. And the liberties taken in constructing our model give us more space to explore the consequences of the alternative economies.

CHAPTER 6

The Economy That Might Have Been

As IN ALL good experiments, the procedures performed with the model led to strange and unexpected observations. In this chapter I shall report these confounding results and explain the contradictions to which they give rise.

The working hypothesis that underlies the entire model-building exercise, from beginning to end, was the drive to compute the Robin Hood scenario described in chapter 5. It was my hope to show scientifically that taxing the rich and rewarding the poor would in fact be better for all: the poor would benefit directly, as they would buy more things and services with their new income and not hide the money in their mattresses. More goods would be produced in factories and farms, more people would be put to work, and more profits would be received by the owners. What the rich would lose initially through stiff taxation would soon be earned back many times over through the growth of their industry. Such was the vision that guided this enterprise.

The very first experiment performed by the model after all the historical data was assembled naturally was to simulate the Robin Hood scenario. The rich were taxed and their wealth given to the poor, but the economy showed no change! Then the poor were taxed and their money given to the rich, a Robin-Hood-in-reverse scenario, and still there was no change! What was happening? Surely we would expect that our sensitive robot model, so carefully assembled, would react when jolted in one direction and then in another! Why was there no economic response to such extreme changes in policy?

As any Caribbean schoolchild could have told us, the type of economy we are studying is wide open to the rest of the world. Both poor and rich spend their money on imported goods. Even local products are made with imported materials, processed on imported machinery, and repaired with imported parts. In both the Robin Hood and Robin-Hood-in-reverse scenarios, the typical consumer basket was filled with different items, one with apples and the other with a Mercedes. But both were filled with imports. The expected feedback on the local production was never realized.

As a starting point for all further experiments, then, the economy had to be closed and, by fiat, these import leakages reduced. Otherwise, any domestic policy would be overwhelmed, washed out as it were, by the flows to the international system. As a first step, the economy was returned to its 1963 starting point, an arbitrary but statistically convenient benchmark, and then made to walk through its actual growth path to 1970. This guided walk, called calibrating the model, simulated the export promotion scenario that Puerto Rico actually pursued. In replicating this route, it was presumed that technology, capital, and skilled labor were instantly imported or otherwise provided, as indeed was the case.

The second step was to return the robot model to its 1963 starting point once again. The model then walked through an alternative import substitution scenario, but this time a few of its open-trade doors were closed. Since the colony is not legally in control of its own tariffs, this could be done in practical terms by raising excise taxes on imports as superfluous luxuries.[1] The economy, however, is so penetrated by imports, much like a wedge of Swiss cheese, that several such programs of import substitution had to be contemplated.

Consumption was the first candidate. Working forward from 1963, it was decreed that 20 percent of all imported consumer goods were to be produced locally, and local industries producing such goods would be given low-cost loans to help get them started. Such a policy would reduce, for example, the sale of imported frozen chicken that was being marketed in competition with fresh domestic chicken. A second step went even further. Local poultry still was being fed imported grain and imported medicine, and the increased sale of domestic fowl had the consequence of increasing imports of the needed ingredients. Therefore, a policy was put into effect whereby both household demand and intermediate demand would be reduced by one-fifth by means of appropriate taxes on imports and subsidies for local production.

What were the results of all these experiments? Under the export promotion scenario, which the country actually followed from 1963 to 1970, employment rose by 18 percent and income by 77 percent! This is the familiar golden goose story (see table 6.1). If, however, households had been encouraged to shift their consumption away from imports to local things and services by 20 percent, then the model shows that employment would have risen by nearly 28 percent and income by 96 percent! An import substitution policy of intermediate demand would have led to the further growth of employment by 21 percent and income by 28 percent. The effects of import substitution suggest, moreover, that more men would have been employed relative to the results of the actual export-promotion campaign.

By means of these experiments it was possible to observe the effects of the two polar directions of economic growth, the competing export promotion and import substitution scenarios. Both yielded high incomes and more jobs, one relatively more work opportunities for men, the other relatively more work opportunities for women. That more opportunities were opened up for women in the export promotion scenario implies that men were left jobless and migrated, seeking work abroad and drawing their families into the emigrant streams to the United States. The import substitution scenario, maintaining the dominant male job structure, might

TABLE 6.1

Results of Eight Development Scenarios in Puerto Rico, 1963 and 1970

Scenario	Employment		National Income		Men/Women Ratio	
	Thousands	% Change	Millions $	% Change	Total	% Change
Export promotion						
Actual, 1963	606.2	—	2,454	—	3.3	—
Calibrated, 1970	715.2	18.0	4,350	77.3	2.6	−21.2
Import substitution by 20% local goods						
Household consumption only	774.2	27.7	4,695	96.3	3.3	0.0
Household consumption and intermediate demand	900.1	48.5	5,498	124.0	3.4	3.0
Import substitution with equal income redistribution						
Peasant life-style	881.1	45.3	5,486	123.6	3.9	18.2
Bourgeois life-style	892.5	47.2	5,439	121.6	3.5	9.1
Elite life-style	896.5	47.9	5,421	120.9	2.9	−13.8
Import substitution 100% of household consumption and 90% intermediate demand	919.3	51.6	5,452	122.2	3.5	9.1

have cut down on this type of migration, and imbalances in employment opportunity, that is, the economic disenfranchisement of women, could have been attacked directly through legal means.

The economy, now partially closed under the import substitution policy, was ready to receive the Robin Hood scenario. The mechanics of this scenario were all relatively easy to implement: the rich were taxed, the poor subsidized, and every now-equal citizen received the average income of the country. But what would the average citizen buy with his or her average income? To test out the effects of different consumption patterns, all citizens were given alternately one of three ration books, much like a passport, in which different menus of things and services were listed.

The first ration book lists all the items that the formerly poor used to buy (call it the peasant life-style). Since the total budget available to the average family to buy this menu is considerably greater, the new average family improves its quality of living by buying more of the same items and in the same proportions as the formerly poor had purchased. The second ration book contains the items that the former middle class used to buy (call it the bourgeois life-style)—now available to all the families at the new average income. And the third ration book lists the things and services of the former upper class (call it the elite life-style), replete with services and appliances, but cheapened in order to bring all these tastes within reach of the average citizen's budget. The Volkswagen replaces the Mercedes, an electric fan instead of an air conditioner, the local clinic and public beach for the private doctor and the country club. In all three Robin Hood ration plans, all the families still receive the same average income, but the model measures the direct and indirect effects their differing life-styles exert on the economy, on the number of jobs, and on the income ultimately generated.

The results are shocking. The imposition of the peasant life-style on the closed import substituting economy would have, by 1970, led to the creation of 881 thousand jobs and a national income of five and a half billion dollars (table 6.1). This employment represents the fewest number of jobs relative to the other ration-plan life-styles. The elite life-style would have created 897 thousand jobs, an increase of nearly 48 percent over the 1963 base, compared to the 45 percent increase of the peasant life-style! The total income of the elite life-style would have been but 121 percent above the 1963 base, while the peasant life-style would have led to an increase in income of 124 percent. The elite life-style creates relatively more jobs for women.

Herein lie four surprises. First, the peasant life-style writ large leads to relatively fewer jobs than the elite life-style. Second, there is a contradiction between job creation and income creation, as the ration plan that generated the highest income results also in the lowest employment. Third, all three Robin Hood scenarios result in both lower employment and income than a straight import substitution program in which no attempt is made toward egalitarian earnings! Fourth, when import substitution is pushed to its extreme and all consumer imports are directly prohibited except for some critical intermediate materials and no redistribution is attempted, then employment is the highest of all, but the income generated falls within the same range as the other scenarios.

All these observations are contrary to expectations. It turns out that the peasant market basket requires less labor than that of the upper class, whose overwhelming demand for services leads to the employment of more people—teachers, doctors, bankers, barbers, and so on. The lower class buys processed food and light appliances, which are produced in factories and do not lead to the creation of many new jobs. However, the material-intensive nature of these roundabout processes generates more complex flows of income between sectors. The elite life-style, on the other hand, requires more direct services, but once the service is delivered, its impact on production and income is limited.

It is these mixes of things and services that distinguishes the two life-styles and results in the contradiction between high income, which is achieved by the things-dominated life-style, and high employment, which is achieved by the service-dominated life-style. This is also consistent with one of the observations of the classical economists, that the production of commodities under capitalism tends to create a society that encounters difficulties employing all its people, although the theoretical reasons for this observation are much debated.[2] It is no secret that as a developing country moves from a society based on agriculture, handicrafts, and local services toward modern industry, it faces a perpetual employment crisis.

In examining the results of the model, we have also uncovered other hitherto hidden characteristics of the economy. (We must remember that each scenario may be taken as representative of the paths that real countries have attempted, replicated here in slower motion and with more detail.)

First, we have discovered that redistributing income without closing the economy can lead to heavy losses as funds are used to pay for imports. (Such was the recent experience in Jamaica.) Second, if an import substitution program is put into effect, and income is redistributed toward raising the incomes of the lower classes, the resulting economy may lead to relatively low employment. This gives rise to the national problem of what to do with people who had been employed in those sectors that the wealthy, who have now lost their fortunes through heavy taxation, had once patronized. Such a country must be prepared to deal with the disenchanted unemployed, whose former positions as gardeners, waiters, bank tellers, and domestic servants have disappeared, when the new factories that produce for the thing-dominated culture fail to provide an equal number of jobs. But the reverse is also true: the elite life-style generates more jobs in response to the surge in demand for service workers, but there will be a slower growth of national income. In other words, the living standard of the nation when it follows this higher-quality life-style will be less than it would have been by following the peasant life-style!

These observations have both reactionary and revolutionary implications. Reactionary, because we have discovered the stabilizing force inherent in upper-class consumption, which makes its change so difficult. As a country's top strata grows, for example, and sets an example of jet-set living, a kind of Robin-Hood-in-reverse scenario, then the economy proves able to absorb considerable labor from the farm and provide these migrants with income-earning opportunity. But the inequality that follows may trigger reform movements, as radicals attempt to effect a redistribution program through taxes and subsidies, which itself brings on economic difficulties. Here policy must negotiate between the contradictory goals of creating employment and generating income.

That the simple egalitarian life-style would lead to a relative scarcity of jobs was at first disappointing. The investigator, an impassioned yet objective scientist, had set out to demonstrate that adoption of the peasant life-style nationwide would in itself release a developing country from economic stagnation, replicating the programs of redistribution that have occurred in China and Cuba. However, the model's testimony (as a former Chilean economics minister subsequently pointed out to the investigator), is basically correct.[3] The upper-class consumption pattern in its modified egalitarian form is the desirable one. It is that pattern that revolutionaries and reformers try to obtain for all the people—the elite life-style market basket put within the reach of the entire population. And that basket *is* replete with services—health, recreational, educational, personal, and travel, for example—services formerly thought of as luxuries. The model warns us that as the reformers attempt to deliver such a basket to large sectors of the populace, they will encounter contradictory objectives between the increased need for human labor and a national income less than what might otherwise be, as the conservative critics will be quick to point out. This is especially clear in comparing the economy under any of these egalitarian schemes to the economy with no income redistribution—that is, more jobs and more income are generated when the differences between the social classes are preserved.

It cannot be overemphasized that all these results stem from a unique set of experiments performed on a unique economic structure. I have uncovered no general law for all times and all economies. But what has been found for this economy may be expected as well for similar economies. Brazil is not Puerto Rico, but some of its characteristics are parallel. Cuba, Nicaragua, Jamaica, Grenada, and Haiti are all structurally similar to Puerto Rico. How are all these economies similar, and how does Puerto Rico represent the prototypical developing nation? We shall examine these questions in chapters eleven and twelve.

II

The Specific Setting

CHAPTER 7

The Economics of the Puerto Rican Problem

EACH DISCIPLINE—actually an ideology for analysis—grapples with reality and arrives at its own conclusions. The economist looks at Puerto Rico, its history, its present condition, and cannot help but be confused. By all the usual standards of economic progress, Puerto Rico has, as the expression goes, made it. Yet something is also amiss.

The Success of the Economy

The conscious goal of the Puerto Rican development ideology since the 1950s was to create a better life for its inhabitants in physical and material terms. By its own terms, it has indeed succeeded. The record of Puerto Rican growth reads like the ideal for every aspiring Third World country: life expectancy raised from forty-six to seventy-four years; all major diseases eradicated; water and sanitation extended to every hamlet; an almost totally literate population; mass construction of housing, schools, and hospitals; extensive training of physicians; thousands of new roads paved and maintained (see table 7.1) Along with these objective accomplishments has also come the modern life-style based on the automobile, the telephone, and electrical power; and with these also tens of thousands of auto accidents, serious industrial pollution, the decline of traditional industry, and the conversion of the island into an international weekend resort and a traveler's way station.

The conflicts over its "success" are seen within and without Puerto Rico. On the one hand, the island seems like the crossroads of North-South relations, the midpoint of the transition from "backward" colony to industrial nationhood. On the other hand, Puerto Rico is regarded by many as an insignificant speck in the Caribbean, hardly a sovereign country, a people who developed so quickly that neither political nor material adaptations could be made.

Furthermore, the real and much-cited accomplishments for the country as a whole cover up a gross unevenness in the distribution of those accomplishments within the island. This is not to say that all the people, from rich to poor, from city to mountain, have not done extraordinarily well—all have. But the egalitarian and democratic ideal of the leadership has always been explicit, and this necessitates

TABLE 7.1

Measures of Economic Success in Puerto Rico, by Decade, 1940–80

Measure	1940	1950	1960	1970	1980
Life expectancy (years)	46	61	67	72	74[a]
Literacy of population over 10 years (%)	68.5	75.3	83.0	89.3	91.3[b]
Teachers (1,000)	6.3	8.7	13.2	21.8	30.6
Registered motor vehicles (1,000)	27	61	180	614	1,035[c]
Maintained roads (1,000 kms.)	2.4	3.6	4.7	5.9	6.4
Gasoline sales (1,000 gals.)	—	—	167	408	681
Traffic accidents (1,000)	—	—	27	60	80
Telephones (1,000)	17	35	83	319	693
Construction permits (1,000)	—	6.1	9.4	12.5	6.3
Cement sales (1,000 94-lb. bags)	—	—	15.7	33.4	29.5
Sugar production (1,000 short tons)	1.0	1.3	1.0	0.5	0.2
Tourist visitors registered (1,000)	—	58	207	735	823
Passengers to Puerto Rico (1,000 arrivals)	—	137	643	2,033	2,742
Electricity consumed (1,000 kwh.)	—	423	1,667	6,495	11,121
Electricity authority customers (1,000)	—	176	409	691	978
Water authority customers (1,000)	—	117	257	530	832
Persons per physician	—	—	1,130	758	534
Hospital beds (1,000)	—	11.5	12.2	11.9	12.1

Source: Puerto Rico Planning Board, *Socio-Economic Statistics 1980* (San Juan, n.d.).
[a]1977.   [b]1976.   [c]1979.

that the record be matched up occasionally with those ideals as well as with the record of the United States.

In comparison to the United States, much has been done and much remains to be done. Puerto Rico's per capita income has been less than half that of the United States, with one quarter of its total population economically active compared to nearly 45 percent for the United States. Puerto Rico's rate of population increase is nearly three times that of the United States, and the rates of birth and of infant mortality about one-and-a-half times. Among Puerto Rico's seventy-six *municipios,* which correspond to the American township, the uneven distribution of its proudest accomplishments indicates that many people have been left behind (see table 7.2). According to census data of 1970, nearly two-thirds of the families were living on income below the United States poverty line, ranging from 34 percent in the most prosperous township to nearly 90 percent in the poorest *municipio.* The median level of schooling was nearly seven years countrywide, but this varied from four years in the poorest to eleven years in the most prosperous *municipio.* And so the record continues: uneven literacy, school enrollment, access to physicians, birth rates, death rates, infant mortality, and housing conditions. Preliminary runs of 1980 census data show some improvement in the levels of these social characteristics, but the unevenness persists. These are tolerable symptoms, frills, the conventional economist argues, which will all be worked out with time. My analysis looks differently at the economy.

TABLE 7.2
Measures of Economic Success in Puerto Rico, 1970

Measure	Average	Municipalities by performance		
		High	Median	Low
Families below poverty line (%)	64.3	34.2	71.2	87.8
Schooling completed (years)	6.9	11.1	5.3	3.8
Literacy of population over 10 years (%)	89.2	96.0	87.0	80.1
School enrollment (% of 5–14-year-olds)	—	91.5	82.8	74.7
Persons per physician	701.0	291.0	3,195.0	15,461.0
Birth rate (1,000 inhabitants)	24.8	18.7	26.2	32.8
Death rate (1,000 inhabitants)	6.7	2.8	6.7	9.6
Infant mortality	28.6	10.1	27.8	54.4
Houses "inadequate" by census (%)	—	7.4	30.1	57.5
Houses with electricity	—	100.0	93.6	79.4
Houses without sanitary facilities (%)	—	9.2	55.8	82.0
Houses without running water (%)	—	1.4	18.5	46.6

Source: Puerto Rico Planning Board, Standard of Living of the Municipalities (based on 1970 census), n.d.

The "Successful" Economy Reexamined

The problem with the Puerto Rican economy is that it consumes but does not produce. It has not always been this way. Puerto Rico today is a working museum of past economies. Knowledge of the history enables us to understand what those earlier epochs were and thus to read today's signals more clearly.

The present Puerto Rican economy holds vestiges of at least three former economies. The oldest was the self-sufficient economy, in which farmers raised their own food staples, fashioned some handicrafts, traded their surplus, or grew special export commodities for cash sale. This economy was supported by an international "putting out" system, the most prominent branch being the needlework trades. Home-based crafts were made for export, specifically with imported materials supplied by the trader, or jobber. We still find remnants of this economy in the mountains.[1]

A second economy was the plantation, a large-scale organization directed by local or foreign capital, usually for the production of an export staple. The plantation sometimes combined advanced industrial technology, for example, the processing of the sugarcane, with the most basic labor skills, for example, cutting the zafra, or harvest, by hand. A wide range of crops also were produced on capitalist plantations, such as tobacco, coffee, coconuts, and cotton. We find today some large farms (plantations is not an especially endearing term) still operating, and many remnants of the older economy survive in worker-patrón relations and plantation attitudes. The plantation era, both on the coast and in the mountains, is but thirty years in the past.[2]

The third economy was the industrial factory, highly promoted since the 1950s, and the cornerstone of Operation Bootstrap. The factory brought the worker from the farm and home into centralized workplaces and provided new machinery: sewing machines rather than needles in the case of the needlework trades; drill presses and lathes rather than hammers and machetes for the farmhand turned factory worker.[3] Since the population was primarily rural, the early factories were scattered throughout the countryside, and many abandoned industrial zones can be seen today throughout the island. Vestiges of the work force remain.

The modern version of these factories of the fifties is the superfactory, itself more like the sprawling plantation/sugarmill of the early twentieth century. The superfactory, however, employs relatively few people, since it is more fully auto- mated and uses the latest technology. Its choice to locate in Puerto Rico was dictated by the logic of the tax exemption offered by the U.S. Treasury and the global profit-maximizing strategy of the multinational corporation. Should that strategy shift or the external incentives be altered, then the plants too will shift, as the failure of the petrochemical complex has shown. The superfactory will seek other locations, just as the garment and shoe industries have in the past. The factory segment of the present economy, then, is constantly in a state of transition. New plants open and others leave. Puerto Rico has become an offshore island continually in search of floating capital.

The fourth economy, which encompasses the earlier forms and undermines them, is the welfare society. As a colony, Puerto Rico has always survived by extracting some elements of welfare from its foreign dominators: from Spain in the nineteenth century and from the United States in this century. Welfare should be distinguished theoretically from social investment. The former supports daily life; the latter supposedly provides capital for better living, such as water and hospitals, or it lowers industrial costs, such as electric power or port facilities.

It is difficult to speak of grants or transfers, which are the forms of welfare, as one-way transactions. If, under the Spanish, repressed wages and controlled farm prices kept the peasant's living standard at subsistence, giving the intermediaries and traders large profits, then is it not naive to speak about a grant to the local economy from the imperial treasury. Such transfers are but partial returns of the value created but not appropriated by the colonial farmer.[4] And if the grower was able to share in the good times, then the grant to the colonial administration reflects their incapacity to tax the peasant directly. Instead, the Crown taxed the exporter and returned to local bureaucrats a fraction of what had been taken from the peasant originally.

In this century, transfers are most clearly seen in the remittances of emigrants to their homes, enabling their island-based families to continue living in the absence of comparable work there. At times, the U.S. government has contributed directly, as in the food distribution and work programs of the New Deal. In the early fifties, an anthropologist noted the effects of the life-styles of returning veterans in a small mountain town: men who could live without working by virtue of their income from having served in U.S. armed forces.[5] But as other entitlement programs have been extended to Puerto Rico, almost the entire island has come to qualify for remedial payments. Rights of citizens, the politicians explain cynically, a partial return for the years of low sugar prices and low factory wages. But the empire never settles its debts that generously. There is another transaction being carried on somewhere else.

The Symptoms of the Puerto Rican Problem

In the early days of development economics, the conventional wisdom attributed a country's poverty to the fecundity of its people. Overpopulation, they called it. After all, was it not obvious that fewer people could live better on the same resources? This logic, compelled by the ability to perform long division, justified the early programs of population planning and birth control. In Puerto Rico, the population problem, as it has become known, was alleviated by the escape valve of mass migration to the United States.[6]

The point here is that, despite occasional neomalthusian rhetoric in Puerto Rico today, the statistical picture suggests that overpopulation cannot lie at the heart of the economic problem. The trebling of product per person from four hundred dollars to thirteen hundred dollars during a thirty-year period when population rose barely 45 percent simply does not support the contention that the superfluity of people explains the current difficulties of the economy (see table 2.1). Besides, economic growth, conventionally defined, has continued nonstop.

Something else was happening on the employment front. The statistical picture shows that the fraction of all adults working or seeking work (labor participation rate) declined from 53 percent to 43 percent between 1950 and 1980. In other words, by 1980, more than a majority of the adult population had dropped out of the formal work force (table 7.3).[7] And of the fraction who sought work, never less than 10 percent, and by 1980, 17 percent, were unable to find jobs. By 1980, nearly two-thirds of the adult population were not working formally for pay, an increase from 54 percent in 1950.

Was the rise in the nonactive labor force due to increased enrollment in high school and the number of elderly? Has the decline in the labor force been concentrated in specific age or sex groups, for example, the return of women to the home and out of the work force? To investigate these hypotheses, let us use another source of labor statistics. According to U.S. census data—which differ somewhat from the Puerto Rican Labor Department surveys for the same years—the overall participation rate fell from 52 percent in 1940 to 38 percent in 1970. Much of this change was due to the decline in the male participation rate (table 7.4). Among women, only the teenage participation rates declined, due, as with men, to increased school attendance. Altogether, 55 percent of adults between the ages of eighteen and sixty-four years were not working in 1970. This contrasts with 60 percent of the entire adult population (table 7.3). Both estimates point in the same

TABLE 7.3
Employment by Sector in Puerto Rico, by Decade, 1940–80

Measure	1940	1950	1960	1970	1980
Employment (%)					
Labor participation rate	52.20	53.00	45.20	44.50	43.30
Unemployment rate	15.00	12.90	13.10	10.30	17.00
All nonworking adults	55.60	53.80	60.70	60.00	64.10
Industrial origin of net income (%)					
Agriculture	34	26	13	4	4
Manufacturing	14	19	28	33	41
Service	52	55	59	63	55
Employment structure (%)					
Agriculture	45	36	23	10	5
Manufacturing	23	23	25	30	25
Service	32	41	52	60	70
Income per worker relative to economy-wide average (1.00)					
Agriculture	0.74	0.70	0.57	0.44	0.80
Manufacturing	0.62	0.85	1.10	1.07	1.64
Service	1.64	1.35	1.14	1.06	0.79
Homogeneity index	40.00	28.00	20.00	12.00	32.00
Public debt relative to GDP (%)	—	—	—	0.35	.63
Import coefficient (%)	—	46.40	54.00	53.50	74.00

Source: Puerto Rico Planning Board, *Economic Report to the Governor 1981* and *1983*.

direction: a high if not exaggerated degree of internal dependence, based on the declining participation of men in the work process and the low, if rising, participation of women.

The age groups available for the labor force for 1980 are not strictly comparable to the other years. Nevertheless, the share of active men continued to decline and the share of active women continued to rise for the basic working-age population (those between sixteen and sixty-four years of age).

Analysis of the productive structure of the economy indicates an important "twisting" among major sectors and some kind of gradual and then almost cataclysmic change occurring beneath the surface prosperity. The decline of income originating in agriculture parallels the decline of employment in agriculture, as the shares of income and employment in both manufacturing and services rose (table 7.3). However, from 1970 to 1980, the share of manufacturing income rose while the share of its corresponding employment fell, suggesting a radical improvement in what economists call productivity, or a shift to more capital-intensive industries. The reverse trend can be observed in services. This twisting, or reversal of the sectors, suggests that manufacturing has become the more privileged activity and services has become the employer of last resort.

TABLE 7.4

Labor Force Participation by Sex and Age Group in Puerto Rico, by Decade, 1940–80

Group	Participation of Group (percent)				
	1940	1950	1960	1970	1980
Men in labor force[a]					
14–17 years	30.9	20.6	12.9	7.8	18.9[b]
18–24 years	84.1	72.0	67.0	51.3	58.1[c]
25–44 years	93.5	84.6	88.4	78.7	73.7[d]
45–64 years	88.1	83.3	82.5	66.8	44.9[e]
65 years and over	51.1	44.9	27.6	20.3	12.4
Women in labor force[a]					
14–17 years	22.3	13.3	5.6	3.6	13.0[b]
18–24 years	32.0	28.1	27.5	30.4	37.4[c]
25–44 years	26.4	25.4	27.5	34.4	39.6[d]
45–64 years	19.0	15.8	17.2	18.7	13.9[e]
65 years and over	7.9	4.8	3.9	3.0	2.8
Labor force 18–64 years					
Men	89.3	80.9	81.6	68.3	59.5[f]
Women	26.7	24.0	24.8	28.9	32.6[f]
Nonworking 18–64 years	—	50.5	51.5	55.4	56.8[f]

Sources: U.S. Census Bureau, Census of Population 1960; 1970; 1980.
[a]Working or seeking work.   [b]16–19 years.   [c]20–24 years.   [d]25–54 years.   [e]55–64 years.   [f]16–64 years.

When the income per worker in each sector is compared to the national average, we see that this reversal of sector productivities flies in the face of the longer-term trends. From 1940 to 1970, the income per worker in industry relative to the economy-wide average rose steadily, while the average income in services during the same period had been falling. In other words, differences among sector productivities were being reduced, as summarized also by the decline in the homogeneity index. Between 1970 and 1980, however, manufacturing became the privileged sector, and the average income in services fell below the national mean. The homogeneity index rose to 32, indicating an increase in the level of sectoral disparity similar to that experienced in 1950—only the positions of services and manufacturing had become transposed.

Two further changes deserve comment. First, the gross public debt as a share of gross domestic product rose from 35 to 63 percent during the 1970s, indicating heavy mortgaging of the island's future. Yet with a decline in the productive base and increase in the share of nonworking adults, how and who will pay the future interest? Second, the degree of openness of the economy, as indicated by the share of merchandise imports to the gross product, increased from 54 percent in the 1960s to 74 percent by 1980. This rise in imports indicates a further reliance on foreign commodities for consumption, investment, and raw materials for processing for export.

Puerto Rico by 1980 had become little more than a way station economy, a transfer for business activity, with a Caribbean flair. As in the early twentieth century modern navies needed coaling stations in the Pacific, today modern industrial economies need offshore enclaves to refuel their value. The coaling station has become the military-industrial colony, with, however, three million U.S. citizens residing there. But how can such an "unproductive" place possibly produce profits, the traditional prize?

The simple answer is that the production of value reaped through Puerto Rico originates in both the Puerto Rican and the American labor forces. Puerto Rico is but the geographical expression, a convenient location through which the value passes.[8]

The basic production process sketched originally in figure 4.14 is played out partially in Puerto Rico and partially elsewhere. The webs of economic relations delineated in figures 4.18 and 4.19 are spread between Puerto Rico and the United States by means of sea and air transportation. The basic relationship in which workers operate on imported raw materials with imported machines to produce products for export takes on almost totally international dimensions. The workers themselves purchase imported things and services, and profits attributed to the imported capital are remitted abroad. The catch, however, is that the wages and profits, that is, the income generated by this international process within the boundaries of Puerto Rico, do not cover the expenses of the population. Two further transactions complete the bookkeeping: public transfers and subsidies are pumped into Puerto Rico—and people are pumped out. The complete formula is: commodities, capital, and transfers in; products, profits, and people out. The

TABLE 7.5

Social Accounts of Puerto Rican Economy, Selected Years, 1940–83

Year	Total Imports[a]	Total Exports[a]	Investment[a]	Non-Remitted Profits[a]	Remitted Profits[a]	Public Transfers[a]	Net Out-Migration (thousands)
1940	259	261	34	137	—	—	—
1947–49	1,337	916	319	715	33	—	146[b]
1950–59	7,459	5,713	1,896	3,143	394	555	461
1960–69	17,872	11,669	4,916	4,649	1,854	977	78
1970–79	34,205	20,041	7,915	5,840	6,640	5,975	86
1980–83	15,477	10,323	2,019	2,965	7,121	4,270	104
1947–83	76,350	48,662	17,065	17,312	16,042	11,777	875[c]

Sources: Puerto Rico Planning Board, Economic Report to the Governor (various years); Puerto Rico Planning Board, Puerto Rican Migrants: A Socio-Economic Study (San Juan: 1972). (For an enlightening discussion of out-migration data see ibid, "A Note on the Reliability of Net Passenger Movement on a Measure of Net Migration," pp. 47–60. See also U.S. Census Bureau worksheets of corrected airlines reports.)
[a]Millions of 1954 dollars.   [b]1940–49.   [c]1940–83.

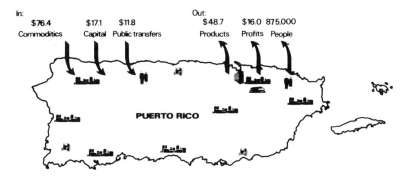

FIGURE 7.1
The Revolving Door: Social Accounts for Puerto Rico, 1947–83
(billions of 1954 dollars)

social accounts provide us with an idea of the magnitudes (table 7.5 and figure 7.1).

I calculate conservatively that, from 1947 to 1983, Puerto Rico imported $76.4 billion worth of goods and services and exported $48.7 billion, the difference corresponding to public and private transfers and loans. I estimate that from 1947 to 1983, $17.1 billion invested in Puerto Rico has given rise to $33.3 billion in net profits, of which $16.0 billion has been remitted. Public transfers and grants have amounted to $11.8 billion. The bottom line, of course, is the other real export, human beings, conservatively estimated at some 875 thousand people during the forty-three-year period. This Puerto Rican diaspora is but a hint of the total human cost that is the other side of the profitable paradise.

In short, the U.S. public underwrites the Puerto Rican people, while U.S. corporations shift profits through their Puerto Rican plants and back to the United States, tax free. The Puerto Rican family then buys its consumption needs, which consists for the most part of imported goods, shifting its public grant money back to the U.S. private sector. As its own economy decomposes, Puerto Rico becomes the revolving door for funds flowing from the American public back to the American corporation and from the multinational company back to itself to avoid taxes. Puerto Rico has become a geographical laundry for corporate profits to avoid federal taxes. Meanwhile, these corporations employ only a token Puerto Rican work force. The rest of the island's people live peaceably on welfare or not so peaceably in the ghettos of America's industrial cities.

CHAPTER 8

The Decade of Economic Cataclysm: Food Stamp Savior Comes to Puerto Rico

WE HAVE SEEN a number of symptoms of a basic transformation in Puerto Rico in the 1970s: radical changes in the sectoral productivities, large-scale and premature retirement of the work force, rising unemployment and economic dependency, and the increase in remitted profits and the attraction of public transfers. All this has grown out of the mid-decade crisis. The year 1975 represents the inflection point of the economy and coincides with the worst year of the economic recession and the arrival of the food stamp program in Puerto Rico.[1]

It may be an exaggeration to claim that food stamps have altered the entire face of the island. I will argue that it has certainly salvaged the productive structure—and has also led to its further decay. The largest single federal program ever directed to the people of Puerto Rico, food stamps were introduced quickly throughout the island from September 1974 to January 1975, "like a hurricane relief expedition," according to one federal official. Seen in historical perspective, the food stamp program in Puerto Rico arrived at a critical juncture in the island's development. Extended almost casually to Puerto Rico after fourteen years of experimentation in the United States, unintended for a small economy and unadjusted for the different circumstances of the Puerto Rican people, food stamps have served as the rescue operation for the entire commonwealth economy. A bankrupt island government, pursuing a growth strategy of giving tax holidays to new corporations and to its own wealthy, simply turned to the federal government to feed a majority of its population.

Food stamps have underwritten the consumption of the majority, stimulating a perverse type of prosperity in all sectors of the island, a prosperity mistakenly ascribed to other policies. Food stamps have been detrimental to native agriculture by triggering a reduction in the supply of labor and shifting the demand for food toward imports and away from native crops. The enormous flow of funds—first as stamps redeemed through the banking system and since July 1982 as cash—has bloated demand deposits, the local money supply, and consumer credit. This contrasts strikingly with the absence of any real increase in productive activity on the island.

In this chapter, I shall outline the potential effects of food stamps in an open, colonial economy with a considerable rural population. I shall then analyze the empirical results of food stamps on consumption, prices, labor, and agriculture, and conclude by outlining a solution to the excessive dependence. Only in recognizing the full extent of the damage that food stamps (or, in the words of one observer, occupation money) is currently doing can the path be sought toward reconstructing a new economy.

Food Stamps in a Small Economy

A small, island society has characteristics of both an open and closed economy. It is closed in the narrow geographic sense, as the capital city also serves as the single entry point for imported consumer goods. Exclusive suppliers distribute merchandise throughout the island, and retailers, recognizing their common interest, tend to charge the same prices. In a small society, shopping around makes no sense at all.

The island economy is also open in that almost all final goods, raw materials, and machinery are imported. Any increase in demand for goods can be satisfied quickly by ordering more from the outside. Since the island does not produce what its people need, any increase in the effective demand for goods, especially for food, is not likely to be reflected as demand for locally produced goods and hence creates no new local jobs, except those needed to handle the imports, like dockworkers, truckers, and shopkeepers. Any increase in cash transferred to the poor exerts a very small multiplier on the local economy. On the contrary, there may even be highly undesirable effects of large inflows of cash. If a share of consumer needs is met through the noncash economy, especially in rural areas where exchanges between growers and neighbors, gift-giving, and home production of food are common, and other needs, such as medicine and housing materials, are met in the cash economy, then the equilibrium between these two segments may be easily disrupted.

When a massive supply of free money (food stamps) comes into such a small, island economy overnight, the economic effects are straightforward. First, the new purchasing power becomes expressed as market demand and possibly an increase in flow of new goods, expecially food, if the supply of imported goods into the open economy proves to be elastic. If importers respond somewhat lackadaisically, they may let stocks run down and prices rise. Especially in the rural and remote areas, we might expect both an increased flow of new goods and an increase in profit margins. As in any small society, all apparently benefit. The poor consumer, the local grocer and supermarket, the supplier, and the monopolist all take a cut of the food stamp dollar.

The next step in the chain is a bit more complicated. According to established procedures, the retailer or wholesaler accepts coupons for merchandise, deposits the coupons in his bank account, and then eventually writes a check based on this deposit to pay his creditors. In actuality, there are more possiblilities, and it is these that mark the distinction between an economy that receives a subsidy in kind, as in free commodities, and one that receives a subsidy in cash, as in free money.[2] Retailers, for example, accept food stamps for the full range of items in their store, say, food, liquor, and tools.[3] Rather than deposit their stamps in the bank, they may find it more convenient to pay their suppliers directly in food stamps. When, however, a mechant needs real cash, he must rely on a clearing house, or currency exchange, where "coupon money" can be cashed in for "green money"—at a discount and with no questions asked.

The rapidity with which food stamps circulate among users is also of critical importance. This turnover may be quite high if recipients and merchandisers alike treat stamps as "hot money." If, however, consumers hoard excess stamps, then their velocity could be quite low. In any case, coupon money circulates with its own characteristic velocity, supplementing the supply of green money. Since the total value of money, defined as the product of the quantity of money and its velocity, is thought to be equal to the total value of goods and services—the usual monetarist equation—it follows that any addition to the money supply or any change in its velocity will also exert an impact on the quantity of goods and services sold, or on the general price level.

Monetarizing the Economy

Thus the entire economy becomes monetarized. The poor, the rich, all alike, become liquid, to use the banker's term. With new money flowing into and out of even the poorest pockets, everything takes on the characteristic of a commodity. Labor exchange is at once converted into cash. The economy inflates, and the money-scarce economy now becomes a money-rich economy.[4] Although food stamps can be used like money, they are inferior to green money. At some point, coupon money confronts and must be converted into green money. This is the job of the banking system. The food stamp program has had the net result of channeling $800 million of costless, risk-free government money through the local banks, creating a costless float than can be lent out to other customers. It also ties the business of food retailing into the local banking industry.

On the surface, all this appears innocuous enough. The banks are merely exchanging the stamps for green money supplied to them by the Government Development Bank from the New York Federal Reserve Bank. But, the local banks actually also create money by lending their cash on hand (which is how food stamps are classified) and by having customers deposit loans from other banks. Both cash and demand deposits can then be lent out again, keeping up to the legal reserve.[5] The banks, appearing as neutral food stamp redeemers, are actually thrust into a position of handling $800 million more in cash at no cost to themselves! But whom can they lend to—on an island of failing industry and an indigent population?

Enter the financial intermediaries and loan companies, offering easy terms for purchases of automobiles and jeeps, appliances and furniture. A population formerly too poor to acquire the panoply of consumer devices and facing little prospect of earned income from productive sources accepts the consumer loan and enters what W. W. Rostow has called "the stage of high mass consumption." Hooked on the American style of living financed through credit—a common phenomena when more goods are around than real purchasing power—the food stamp family faces a minor liquidity crisis when the monthly payments come due. Again, food stamps come to the rescue, for here again they can be cashed in on the black market for green dollars.

Thus food stamps finance the whole network of this prosperous pauper colony. From the poor households to the retail store through the intermediaries and to the banks, expanded many times over and recycled back as consumer loans to the same indigent, food stamps form the basis of a new specie, which interlocks with the normal specie, bloating the economy with quasi money and credit and filling it with imported paraphernalia and the services required to promote, finance, distribute, and repair them.[6]

Disincentives to Labor

It is often alleged that food stamps affect the supply of low-wage labor by creating what economists call a disincentive to work. The conventional argument, as applied by the critics of the U.S. food stamp program, takes the view that human nature is inherently lazy and prefers, as they put it, leisure and consumption to backbreaking, poorly paid menial labor.[7]

But surely it is irrational for human beings to work for nothing. With rising prices of goods, it may seem indeed pointless to work for a few cents an hour washing cars only to see the local grocer mark up the wholesale price of imported merchandise by 100 percent and earn a living by merely opening crates and turning over the goods. Small family farmers, faced with low wholesale prices for vegetables and livestock and high costs of fertilizer, sprays, and feeds, abandon the land and buy imported rice, beans, and meats with the specie received (they are told) by virtue of their right of U.S. citizenship. Meanwhile, factory labor, whose wage had customarily been regulated and periodically negotiated, continues to demand yet higher wages to cope with higher prices. The casual or service worker, unable to break into this privileged sector, withdraws even further, dropping out of the labor force, (refusing to "participate"), or by registering as unemployed. Hence, we observe the contradiction of a rising wage (the supply price of those who do work) and at the same time a rise in the number and percentage of the unemployed.

It may be somewhat incongruous for an economy to experience both an increase in consumer demand and a degeneration of the conventional labor supply. A black market exists for converting food stamps into green money to meet the monthly payments. But black marketeering in food stamps hardly satisfies all the cash needs of a population that has acquired on credit a car, a TV, a stereo, factory-made furniture, and heavy appliances, as well as a low-interest mortgage. If cash is earned and reported, then the recipient's food stamp status is jeopardized. But if no income is obtained, then the family is barred from the world of modern consumerism, and the objects purchased may be reclaimed by the finance company.

The Emergence of the Underground Economy

Where does the needed cash come from? The real economy offers few new jobs every year. The government tries to create jobs, but these are of short duration and pay only partial salaries because of the attempt to spread federal monies as far as possible. Cash income must come from the clandestine, or underground, economy. This economy exists side by side or slightly sheltered by the normal economy, touching the real economy at different points and boosting it, thus aiding the recovery of the real economy.

The underground economy is that name commonly given to the system of informal arrangements by which a laborer agrees to perform a task and is paid under the table in order that his or her poverty status not be jeopardized. The accepted wage in this economy may be—and usually is—lower than the legal minimum and, like any labor market, depends on the number of workers and the desperation with which they bid against one another. The result is a vast pool of informal labor ready to work for cash. In this economy, the income multiplier may be very high indeed, until dollars are lost through the import leakage.

This clandestine economy merges with the real economy in many ways. Even if, for example, a house is being constructed entirely with informal labor, the construction materials must be bought from the formal economy, and the whole operation may be financed by a loan from the Farmers' Home Administration. The house built clandestinely but financed in public then goes above board for its electricity, water, and furnishings.

The existence of this informal economy explains the contrast between Puerto Rico's image of destitution—low incomes and high unemployment—and the superficial consumer prosperity observed throughout the island. In this sense, food stamps are at once cause and solution: to qualify for food stamps, workers earn income underground, even if at lower wages. At the same time, food stamps provide the liquidity for the bank loans to finance consumer purchases, which drive the workers to need further cash and yet more underground activity. While other government agencies provide mortgages for the purchase of land and materials, the commercial bank again is ready with financing to stock the home with the required appliances and furniture. The food stamp "solution" is thus a desperate spiral that surrounds and sucks up the real economy with the fantasy-laden turbulence of fast-moving money and profit, giving the impression of a real economic prosperity based, ironically, on coupons or cash distributed by the U.S. Department of Agriculture and underwritten by the U.S. Treasury.[8]

CHAPTER 9

The Decade of Economic Cataclysm:
The Economic Record

To WHAT EXTENT does the economic record support the contention that food stamps have been the external device that rescued the Puerto Rican economy from the recession of 1974 and in so doing has altered the direction and style of development?

As the magnitude of the program has been so great, there is no single indicator of the true impact of the subsidy. Many different measures must be consulted to trace the program's effect on the economy. Food stamps represent a new motor of development, changing the source of growth from private investment in manufacturing and public investment in infrastructure to the federal treasury.[1] The impact of these transfers can be more clearly evaluated if the 1970s are divided into two periods. The first five-year period corresponds to the old strategy of growth through industrial invitation, and the later one, 1976–80, corresponds to the era of federal programs. The third period, 1981–83, provides the most recent information about the current period (table 9.1). During the early years of the decade, personal disposable income grew more quickly than in the later years, the period in which transfers have come to represent nearly 18 percent of disposable personal income. The $80 million of net transfers to Puerto Rico in 1970 grew to $200 million by 1973, trebled again by 1975, exceeded $1.7 billion by 1980 and $2.2 billion by 1983. The search for federal funds had become big business.

As other federal programs were extended to Puerto Rico, the food stamp share of transfers declined. In 1976, food stamps comprised nearly 70 percent of transfers. By 1980, they accounted for less than half, and by 1983 little more than a third. The share of the population receiving food stamps rose from 48 percent in 1977 to 58 percent by 1980.

Inflation, Migration, and Labor Participation

Was the new disposable income transferred to Puerto Rico spent on food or on other consumer goods? Was the new purchasing power absorbed by rising prices, or were more goods imported at constant prices? To answer these two critical questions we must turn to the aggregate statistics of the period, and the empirical

TABLE 9.1
Transfers to Puerto Rico, Selected Years, 1950–83

Year	Disposable Personal Income[a]	Net Transfers[a]	Transfers in Personal Income (%)	Food Stamps[a]	Food Stamps (% of Transfers)	Population Using Food Stamps (%)
1950	638	63.4	9.9	—	—	—
1960	1,334	46.6	3.5	—	—	—
1970	3,565	80.1	2.2	—	—	—
1971	3,990	129.7	3.2	—	—	—
1972	4,476	159.6	3.6	—	—	—
1973	5,065	215.0	4.2	—	—	—
1974	5,683	249.8	4.4	—	—	—
1975	6,480	631.3	9.7	388.4	61.5	27.8
1976	7,265	1,085.1	14.9	754.8	69.6	51.1
1977	7,770	1,245.5	16.0	802.1	64.4	47.7
1978	8,554	1,451.5	17.0	879.0	60.6	49.3
1979	9,357	1,569.7	16.8	821.2	52.3	54.2
1980	10,333	1,726.1	16.9	812.1	47.0	58.4
1981	11,432	1,864.0	16.3	860.1	46.1	56.0
1982	11,969	2,196.1	18.3	895.9	40.8	52.8
1983	12,009	2,224.7	18.5	775.0	34.8	47.9
1971–75[b]	5,139 (12.7)[c]	227 (59.3)[c]	5.0	—	—	—
1976–80[b]	8,656 (9.8)[c]	1,416 (26.8)[c]	16.3	813.8 (6.2)[c]	58.8	52.1
1981–83[b]	11,803 (5.2)[c]	2,095 (9.0)[c]	17.7	844.7 (−1.1)[c]	40.6	52.2

Source: Puerto Rico Planning Board, Economic Report to the Governor 1979, 1980, and 1983.
[a]Millions of current dollars.
[b]Average annual amounts for the period.
[c]Average annual growth rate.

66

record is ambiguous. The national account price deflators for food consumption rose by 25 percent in 1974 and 18 percent in 1975, stabilized for the next four years, and then jumped a full 12 percent by 1980 (table 9.2). Thus it is difficult to discern a clear connection between food stamps and the global food price index.

Were the increases in food prices caused by rising import prices? There is some evidence for this, since import prices rose by an even greater percentage than food prices. This imported inflation can be then seen as having filtered through food and all consumption expenditures, but there is no reason to expect the inflation to be registered entirely in the food markets. The regular and less erratic increases in the gross product deflator reflect the degree to which the rest of the components of the economy (investment, government, and exports) are insulated from the more volatile sectors (personal consumption and imports).[2]

The arrival of food stamps may have been helpful in reversing the flow of population to the United States and in thus increasing population growth. Puerto Rico lost 46,500 people in the 1970–75 period and only 10,900 in 1976–80. These numbers, however, are of such small magnitude, given the vast flows of people in both directions, that any conclusion regarding the impact of food stamps on migration must be treated with great caution. In the absence of food stamps, however, a collapsing Puerto Rican economy of the mid-seventies might have sent even greater numbers of people to the United States.[3]

The coincidence of the initiation of food stamps and the deterioration of the general work situation is more obvious. From 1974 through 1976, the labor force participation rate fell from 44 to 42 percent, and the unemployment rate rose from 12 to 19 percent. Thus, the total proportion of adults not working due either to their departure from the labor force (inactive) or the inability to find jobs (unemployed) rose from 61 to 66 percent from 1974 to 1976. In the most recent period, 1980–83, the participation rate declined once again from 43 to 41 percent. Unemployment rose steadily in these years from 18 to 23 percent, and the share of nonworking adults reached nearly 69 percent in 1983, the highest in the postwar period.

To summarize, an increase in import prices coincided with rising food prices in the initial years of the food stamp program, but prices continued to rise erratically in the second half of the seventies. The rate of migration slowed and reversed itself in the late seventies, with food stamps possibly keeping people on the island. The decline in labor force participation and the rise in unemployment confirm the deteriorating work situation and the absence of productive activity.

The Import Structure

An examination of some of the other structural features of the Puerto Rican economy suggests the reversal of some long-term trends by the mid-seventies and a possible resumption by the early eighties. Food expenditure as a proportion of total consumption fell from 36 to 23 percent between 1950 and 1970, a trend experienced in most developing countries. However, food expenditure rose to 26

TABLE 9.2
Impact of Food Stamps on Puerto Rico, Selected Indicators, 1950, 1960, 1970–83

Year	Annual Growth Rate				Population (thousands)	Annual Migration[a]	Labor Force Participation (%)	Unemployment (%)	Adults Not Working (%)
	Food Consumption Deflator	Personal Consumption Deflator	Import Deflator	Gross Product Deflator					
1950	—	—	—	—	2,200	—	53.0	12.9	53.8
1960[b]	2.6	2.6	1.9	2.9	2,340	—	45.2	13.1	60.7
1970[b]	3.5	2.5	2.2	3.6	2,710	—	44.5	10.3	60.1
1971	5.4	4.1	3.4	5.7	2,742	-2,500	44.6	11.3	60.5
1972	6.2	3.3	4.0	4.3	2,835	23,600	45.1	12.0	60.2
1973	4.2	3.6	2.5	2.0	2,868	-37,100	44.6	11.8	60.7
1974	25.1	11.3	31.2	7.1	2,878	-25,000	44.4	12.3	61.1
1975	17.9	14.0	20.3	7.0	2,908	-5,400	42.3	15.4	64.2
1976	5.9	7.5	6.4	3.4	2,982	36,200	41.6	19.4	66.4
1977	0.0	3.6	4.8	3.2	3,047	-4,600	44.9	20.0	64.0
1978	5.9	4.7	5.8	5.0	3,100	-20,300	44.8	18.8	63.6
1979	6.7	5.2	9.6	5.8	3,140	-6,100	43.7	17.5	63.9
1980	12.3	12.1	16.3	7.9	3,184	-16,100	43.3	17.0	64.0
1981	12.4	10.2	13.0	8.8	3,232	-10,500	43.2	17.9	64.5
1982	3.0	5.7	5.0	7.4	3,261	-33,300	41.8	21.7	67.3
1983	2.2	3.1	5.0	4.5	3,265	-44,400	41.0	23.4	68.8
1971–75	11.4	7.2	12.3	5.2	1.4	-46,400	44.2	12.6	61.3
1976–80	6.1	6.6	8.6	5.1	1.8	-10,900	43.7	18.5	64.4
1981–83	5.9	6.3	7.7	6.9	0.5	-88,200	42.0	21.0	66.8

Sources: Puerto Rico Planning Board, *Economic Report to the Governor 1979, 1980,* and *1983;* U.S. Census Bureau, *State Estimates.*

[a]Negative sign indicates net departures. No sign indicates net arrivals.

[b]Entries for 1960 and 1970 are average annual growth rates for preceding decades.

TABLE 9.3
Structural Changes in Puerto Rican Economy, Selected Years, 1950–83

Measure	1950	1960	1970	1971–75[a]	1976–80[a]	1981–83[a]
Consumption (percent share)						
Food consumption/all consumption	36.1	30.3	22.8	23.8	26.1	24.0
Food imports/food consumption	37.4	37.1	36.0	45.6	45.6	38.1
Local food mfg./food consumption	17.6	15.8	18.9	16.1	15.5	22.2
Local agriculture/food consumption	55.2	38.8	18.9	17.2	13.3	13.1
Local food intermed./food consumption	—	—	—	21.1	25.6	26.6
Food imports/consumer imports	51.6	42.9	36.1	41.3	46.1	42.1
Food imports/all imports	25.5	17.3	12.2	15.5	16.0	13.1
Consumer imports/all consumption	26.2	26.1	22.7	25.4	25.6	21.3
Consumer imports/all imports	49.9	40.3	33.9	37.5	34.6	30.5
All imports/gross product	46.4	54.0	53.5	55.7	73.7	69.5
Consumption/disposable income	103.8	104.8	105.1	103.6	105.7	106.0
Domestic income (percent share)						
Agriculture	25.6	13.2	4.4	4.4	3.3	3.1
Manufacturing	19.2	27.7	32.5	33.9	38.8	41.0
Service	55.2	59.1	63.1	64.8	57.8	55.9
Employment (percent share)						
Agriculture	36.5	23.0	9.9	7.6	5.4	5.0
Manufacturing	22.5	25.2	30.4	30.3	25.5	23.7
Service	41.0	51.8	59.7	62.1	69.1	71.3

Sources: See table 9.1.
[a]Annual average.

percent by the 1976–80 period and has stabilized around 24 percent most recently (table 9.3).

How was this increased proportion of food demand met? Direct food imports as a share of food consumption rose from around 36 percent to nearly 46 percent for the entire decade and in the eighties has fallen to 38 percent. Local manufactured food supplied about 16 percent of demand between 1971 and 1980, and its share increased to 22 percent in the early eighties.[4] These two sources, local food manufacturing and food imports, replaced local agriculture, whose share of total food expenditure fell from 55 to 13 percent between 1950 and 1983.[5] With the decline of local agriculture, it appears that local intermediaries absorbed at least a quarter of the food trade.

Another change was the reversal of a long-term trend in the decline of food imports as a share of all consumer imports. Between 1950 and 1970, food imports fell from half to a third of all consumer imports. By the end of the seventies, however, the food share had risen to nearly half of all consumer imports and began to decline in the early eighties. The evidence suggests that with the demise of local agriculture, the consumer is importing a sizable fraction of food relative to other consumer goods, and an increasing share is being processed in Puerto Rico. If there had once been a division of the market between local tropical food and imported temperate-climate food, that market boundary is disappearing, and with its disappearance a deepening dependence on imported food.

Consumer imports during the entire period represent only a quarter of all consumption expenditure due to the importance of local services and high markups, and this share has fallen in the 1981–83 period. The share of imported consumer goods relative to total imports declined in an economy in which all imports relative to gross product rose from 1950 to 1980. In the early eighties, both fractions have fallen due to general economic difficulties. The relative decline in consumer imports to all imports means simply that more raw and intermediate materials are being imported and processed for consumption or for reexport. But since both food and other consumer imports are increasing in absolute terms, and the share of imported food to total food consumption was rather constant at 46 percent throughout the decade 1971–80, the picture is now complete: Puerto Rico is importing higher values of raw materials, as described in the model (and which I have elsewhere called the import enclave).[6] Direct imports satisfy nearly half of the food needs and a quarter of all consumption needs. That these ratios have fallen in the 1981–83 period indicates that there is some closing of the economy to direct imports and an increase in local food processing and intermediaries.

Since aggregate consumption has always exceeded disposal income by some 4 to 6 percent, no local net savings or investment has accrued. The open, importing economy has satisfied its voraciousness for consumption through exporting products, importing capital, and more currently, by seeking transfers, gifts, and grants.

Internally, the structure of productive capacity has also changed. The share of agricultural value and employment fell. The share of manufacturing value rose throughout the period, and manufacturing employment rose at first and then fell to nearly the original share in 1960. This indicates a higher level of earnings in the later years for those employed in manufacturing. Finally, the decline in the share of income generated in the service sector and the rise in its employment suggest a decline in the earnings per person, or, more accurately, the spreading of low-paying public-sector jobs to a broader share of the work force.

Imports as a Key Variable

Imports lie at the heart of the undoing of the local economy. How is it the local economy could grow when everything comes from abroad? The answer lies in the markup and how the seller spends his profit. It is true that imports drive out locally made products, especially when financed by a general consumption subsidy of such magnitude as the food stamp program. This has led to the creation of a commercial pauper mentality, in which the majority seek even more subsidies while the minority sell the goods.

The irony is that there is a small share of imports to which local value can be conveniently and effortlessly attached and therefore collected. Value is also created and exported in the industrial sector. But the wages and profits made and spent in Puerto Rico quickly leak out, paying for imported food, housing materials, hardware, clothing, durables, and so on. The markups on these imports remain in Puerto Rico and claim their share of the consumer's dollar:—importers, transporters, advertisers, wholesalers, and retailers all take their wages and profits. Domestic circulation of this markup continues, diminishing as it is spent on imported commodities. That this value added may be considered locally generated, of course, is no less a sign of dependence. In fact, as importing margins rise, a greater share of services and commerce are classed as domestic, although they are fully attached to the imported purchase. Without the import, that local value added would disappear instantaneously.

Conclusions

The transformation of the Puerto Rican economy during the period from 1940 to 1980 duplicates a normal growth trajectory that characterizes many developed countries during their early years of industrialization. However, the Puerto Rican experience shows the excesses of a development path totally oriented toward and dependent on the larger industrial economy to which it has become appended. Indeed, the recent phase of this growth trajectory demonstrates the precariousness, if not emptiness, of the industrial export strategy that neglects other aspects of development.

The Puerto Rico case shows the dead-endedness of the export promotion strategy. With each swing of the business cycle or change of temperament in Washington, short-term solutions have been sought. To this day, the question of the limits of the strategy for long-term economic development remains unchallenged and its alternatives unexamined. On the contrary—and with a certain irony—the Puerto Rico model as a positive example of "how to do it" is now coming back into vogue and currently is being resuscitated as the successful path for the development of all poor or decaying regions, from the Caribbean Basin initiative to the industrial tax-exempt zones (urban enterprise zones) for the inner cities of the United States.[7]

An air of false prosperity pervades Puerto Rico: gross product in real terms has continued to rise as increasing levels of imports are sustained by fresh purchasing power using federal funds. Much of this "prosperity" also is financed by heavy borrowing by the commonwealth. The availability of these loans gives the impression of confidence and a flashy superstructure within which private borrowing is also carried out on levels far in excess of the real producing power of the economy.

Beneath the superficial prosperity, the labor situation is truly alarming. Only by massive transfers and a two-way emigrant stream can the working fraction support a total population of over three million people. By 1983, 67 percent, or nearly 1.5 million adults, were not working. This situation represents a steady deterioration of the entire labor picture in Puerto Rico since 1950.

Puerto Rico, then, presents two contradictory pictures. To the industrial developer, Puerto Rico is still the example of the power of tax-exemption to pick an economy up by its bootstraps, modernize itself, and raise wages and material living standards.[8] To others, Puerto Rico shows the absolute limits of the strategy of industrialization by invitation: after thirty years of an uninterrupted tax holiday, the island is little more than a vast labor reserve, potentially explosive but tranquilized since 1976 by nearly one billion dollars yearly in food stamps plus other federal transfers. To critics, Puerto Rico remains a colony, a ward of the U.S. Treasury, a conduit for tax-exempt profits for multinational companies, an island with no tax base of its own and little productive activity directed to meeting the needs of its population. Locked politically into fruitless haranguing about political status and with no economic alternatives forthcoming, Puerto Rico has, in the last analysis, pursued a two-fold strategy: one, encouraging mass emigration, a form of economic exile, for a large part of its population rendered surplus by the decline of agriculture; and two, for those who remain at home, providing a life dependent on federal subsidies. Neither the plight of the Puerto Rican emigres in the ghettoes of the United States or the current labor situation in Puerto Rico says much for the success of the Puerto Rican economy.[9]

In summary, Puerto Rico has been both object of and witness to a rather bizarre scenario. Third World countries in pursuit of capitalist development usually experience a decline in their agrarian sectors, but supposedly commercial or industrial activity absorbs the farm migrants. In Puerto Rico, also, agriculture has declined with great speed, but the noise that would accompany such destruction has been muffled by unlimited emigration or bought off with food stamps and loan programs.[10] A small fraction of adults find highly remunerated work in private manufacturing and the public utilities, but most officially employed adults work for token wages in services, trade, and public sector jobs. The Puerto Rican variant on the typical developing scenario suggests that the last or highest stage of dependent industrialization is the welfare colony.

CHAPTER 10

The Other Side of Paradise: Puerto Ricans
in the United States

THUS FAR in our analysis, we have learned that the goose that lays the golden eggs has, in recent years, been requiring periodic shots of synthetic growth hormones. We have focused on the machinery that has produced wealth without work. And that is precisely the point: the populace of a place and their livelihoods have become divorced from one another.

The neoclassical economist exclaims at once, "Of course, that's what you would expect. With wages fixed by law and not the market, there can be no full employment. Let wages fall to reach their competitive level and then you will find full employment." But the global market has never been suspended, and in Puerto Rico this market has effectively cleared the land of its people. Had the nearly one million emigrants remained, by 1980 Puerto Rico would have been a nation of five or six million people.

Another Measure of Puerto Rican Success

Another test of the success of Puerto Rican development is how the emigrants have fared in the United States. The neoclassical economist exclaims, "Much better, of course, than in Puerto Rico as they were living, or how they would have lived had no one emigrated." This position is the result of no brilliant analysis, for by standard measures an emigrant has only to get on the plane from San Juan to New York and walk through the electrified gates of the Consolidated Cigar Corporation in the Connecticut Valley and instantly his income trebles. But the lucrative wage and the stock of goods the migrant acquires are but indexes of the transition the migrant faces.[1]

Ways of viewing this leap from one society to another fall into three categories: a literature of assimilation, a literature of protest, and a literature of stagnation. The literature of assimilation sees the Puerto Rican migration as the same as earlier waves of immigrants. With time, this view holds, American society will absorb these people and provide them with livelihoods. The tide is irreversible, and only patience, time, and understanding are needed.[2] By virtue of a mere plane ride, the emigrant problem becomes a U.S. problem, compartmentalized into a variety of approaches, such as language, schooling, and social services.[3] The literature of protest is the antiassimilationist view, an outcry against the exploitation and the disadvantages that the Puerto Rican faces in America. It is an angry, compassionate literature, striking out at the society that thrusts these people out and at the society that sucks them in.[4] The literature of stagnation sees emigration as evidence of a permanent culture of poverty. The emigrant may be moving in physical space, but his or her mind-set perpetuates attitudes that inhibit assimilation, and the economic structure reinforces these attitudes.[5]

Some Data on Puerto Ricans
in the United States

How well have Puerto Ricans done in the United States both in absolute terms and relative to other groups? How has their economic position changed during the decade? And how well have the returned emigrants done? Rarely cited data from the Census Bureau provide us with some statistical evidence to test the polemic and apologetic literature on emigration.

We find Puerto Ricans in the United States to be a young population composed of more single men and more divorced adults than in either the U.S. population or the Mexican American population (table 10.1). The Puerto Rican population in the United States almost totally lives in urban areas. In terms of the acquisition of education, the picture is more complicated. Nineteen percent of Puerto Ricans twenty-five years and older have only a rudimentary education. Only 30 percent have completed high school. These statistics are consistent with the crisis of the inner-city school systems, the problems of bilingual education, and mass teaching of the ghetto populations.

Income figures also give disturbing signals. Puerto Rican males earn less than the average U.S. male but more than the Mexican American male. Puerto Rican women, however, earn *more* than the average U.S. female and a great deal more than the average Mexican American woman. Puerto Rican family incomes, however, are much lower. The apparent contradiction between relatively high individual earnings and low family income is no real contradiction: Puerto Rican families have a greater percentage of female heads of households and fewer earners per family than the average U.S. family and the average Mexican American family.[6] Income distributions are shown in figure 10.1. The Mexican American distribution shows higher percentages of families in the low-income ranges. The Puerto Rican distribution follows a very different shape, with a heavy concentration of families in the three-to-six-thousand-dollar intervals and another concentration between seven and eight thousand dollars.

The employment data for Puerto Ricans in the United States indicate a lower participation rate for both Puerto Rican men and women. The unemployment rate

TABLE 10.1

Educational, Income, and Other Characteristics of Puerto Ricans Living in the United States, Mexican Americans, and Total U.S. Population, 1975–76

Characteristics	Men[a]	Women[a]	Total[a]
Median years of age			
Puerto Ricans in U.S.	17.8	21.8	19.4
Mexican Americans	19.4 (0.97)	20.2 (1.08)	19.8 (0.98)
U.S. population	27.6 (0.65)	29.7 (0.73)	28.6 (0.68)
Percent unmarried			
Puerto Ricans in U.S.	40.3	27.0	—
Mexican Americans	36.2 (1.11)	27.2 (0.99)	—
U.S. population	36.3 (1.11)	27.1 (1.00)	—
Percent living in cities			
Puerto Ricans in U.S.	—	—	97.3
Mexican Americans	—	—	67.7 (1.44)
U.S. population	—	—	76.2 (1.28)
Percent of 25-year-olds and over with 5 years or less of school			
Puerto Ricans in U.S.	—	—	18.7
Mexican Americans	—	—	24.2 (0.77)
U.S. population	—	—	3.4 (4.92)
Percent of 25-year-olds and over with 4 yrs of high school or more			
Puerto Ricans in U.S.	—	—	29.8
Mexican Americans	—	—	32.5 (0.92)
U.S. population	—	—	64.1 (4.65)
Median income, persons with income (dollars)			
Puerto Ricans in U.S.	7,055	3,889	
Mexican Americans	6,154 (1.15)	2,682 (1.45)	
U.S. population	8,379 (0.84)	3,079 (1.26)	
Family income (dollars)			
Puerto Ricans in U.S.	—	—	7,629
Mexican Americans	—	—	9,498 (0.803)
U.S. population	—	—	12,836 (0.594)

Source: U.S. Census Bureau, *Current Population Reports 1976,* Series P-20.
[a]Figure in parentheses is ratio of Puerto Rican emigrants to the other group.

for Puerto Rican men was more than twice the U.S. rate and also higher than that for Mexican Americans. The unemployment rate for Puerto Rican women also exceeded that for U.S. women and Mexican American women. Relative to the U.S. population, more Puerto Rican men work as machine operators, laborers, and as service personnel, and fewer as professional, salesmen, or craftsmen. Puerto Rican women are more likely than other women to be craftsworkers and machine operators (table 10.2).

In summary, the most striking characteristics of the employment distributions are the overwhelming concentrations in the operative classes (read factory hands) for both men and women and in the service category for men (read dishwasher,

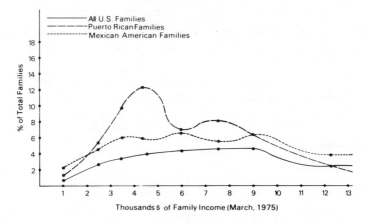

FIGURE 10.1

Comparison of Family Income Distribution for All Families of
Puerto Rican, Mexican American, and All-U.S. Origin, March
1975. *Source: Current Population Reports,* Series P-20, no. 290,
February 1976, table 23. For income intervals greater than $1,000, a
horizontal distribution was assumed within the interval midpoint.
This applies only to the intervals < $2,000, $5–6,999, and $10–
14,999 plotted above.

guards, cabbie). The low shares of Puerto Ricans as craftsmen and clerical women
may be suggestive of the racial and educational barriers in entering areas of higher
earning potential.

Characteristics During the Decade

Some data are available that permit us to test the "progress" of the Puerto Rican
population in the United States during the seventies.[7] Despite caveats of noncom-
parability, we infer from the annual population surveys a slight increase in the
years of schooling completed (table 10.3), rising unemployment (table 10.4), and
cyclically moving incomes with no clear trend (table 10.5). The Puerto Rican
population in the United States had been growing at an average annual rate of 3.9
percent (table 10.6). The median age for males remained between eighteen and
nineteen years and for females between twenty-one to twenty-two years.

The data on educational achievement suggest either wide cyclical swings or a
changing sample base. The proportion of adults who had completed minimal
schooling declined between 1971 and 1976, and the median number of years of
schooling completed for both men and women shows a steady increase during the
same years. Nevertheless, by 1975, the majority of Puerto Ricans living in the
United States had completed the freshman high school level.

TABLE 10.2
Employment and Occupational Distributions of Puerto Ricans Living in the United
States, Mexican Americans, and Total U.S. Population Aged Sixteen Years and Over,
March 1975

Characteristics	Puerto Ricans in U.S.	Mexican Americans		All U.S.	
Men[a]					
Population (thousands)	423	1,939	(0.218)	72,061	(0.006)
Labor force (thousands)	311	1,547	(0.201)	54,900	(0.006)
Labor force (percent)	73.5	79.8	(0.92)	76.2	(0.97)
Unemployed (percent)	19.3	12.2	(1.58)	8.9	(2.17)
Distribution of employment					
Professional	9.1	7.6	(1.20)	15.1	(0.60)
Sales	4.0	2.6	(1.54)	6.1	(0.66)
Clerical	8.0	5.0	(1.60)	6.8	(1.18)
Craft	11.2	18.3	(0.61)	20.1	(0.56)
Operative	28.9	28.1	(1.03)	17.5	(1.65)
Labor (not farm)	9.4	14.2	(0.66)	7.0	(1.34)
Farm labor	1.4	7.7	(0.18)	1.6	(0.88)
Service	20.5	10.4	(1.97)	8.8	(2.33)
Women[a]					
Population (thousands)	549	1,982	(0.277)	79,453	(0.007)
Labor force (thousands)	184	835	(0.220)	36,495	(0.005)
Labor force (percent)	33.5	42.1	(0.80)	45.9	(0.73)
Unemployed (percent)	14.7	11.9	(1.24)	9.5	(1.55)
Distribution of employment					
Professional	10.4	6.2	(1.68)	16.2	(0.64)
Sales	3.5	5.4	(0.65)	6.9	(0.51)
Clerical	26.3	28.2	(0.93)	35.3	(0.74)
Craft	5.9	1.5	(3.93)	2.4	(2.46)
Operative	28.7	25.3	(1.13)	11.3	(2.54)
Labor (not farm)	1.0	1.9	(0.53)	1.0	(1.00)
Farm labor	1.1	1.1	(1.00)	0.7	(1.57)
Service	21.6	28.3	(0.76)	21.9	(0.99)

Source: See table 10.1.
[a]Figure in parentheses is ratio of Puerto Rican emigrants to the other group.

The trends in family and personal income suggest that the gains in income have
been highly cyclical. In 1971, the median Puerto Rican family lived at income
levels 61 percent of the U.S. median; this fell to 59 percent of the U.S median by
1975. Personal income for Puerto Rican men rose from 81 percent to 84 percent of
the U.S. median from 1971 to 1975, while the median personal income of women
fell from 130 to 126 percent of the U.S. median.

Employment data suggest fluctuation and instability. Participation rates vary by
11 percent and unemployment rates vary by 12 percent. Occupational distributions
suggest rising representation by Puerto Rican women in the professional, clerical,
and service classes and a falling share in the operative category. The shares of

TABLE 10.3

Education of Puerto Ricans Living in the United States, 1971–76

Characteristic	1971	1972	1973	1974	1975	1976
Percent with 5 years or less of school						
25-to-29-year-olds	9.2	6.4	4.9	—	—	9.4
45-to-64-year-olds	34.2	33.1	27.9	—	—	27.4
Total, 25 years and over	23.8	20.3	15.6	—	—	18.7
Percent of 25-year-olds and over with						
4 years of high school or more	19.8	23.7	26.0	—	—	29.8
Years of school, 14-year-old and older						
Men	8.7	9.3	9.5	9.7	9.5	—
Women	8.5	8.8	9.4	9.5	9.5	—

Sources: U.S. Census Bureau, *Current Population Reports 1971–76,* Series P-20.

TABLE 10.4

Employment of Puerto Ricans Living in the United States Aged Sixteen Years and Over, 1971–76

Year	Thousands	Percent in Labor Force	Percent Unemployed
Men			
1971[a]	379	68.6	9.5
1972[a]	432	67.4	8.8
1973	395	78.0	11.1
1974	394	75.1	8.6
1975	423	73.5	19.3
1976	453	66.5	14.3
Women			
1971[a]	481	25.8	10.8
1972[a]	469	23.7	17.8
1973	472	31.8	6.3
1974	483	33.7	9.8
1975	549	33.5	14.7
1976	561	30.5	14.0

Sources: See table 10.3.
[a]Fourteen years old and over.

Puerto Rican men in the operative and laboring categories fell and the share of men in services rose.

No clear trends are obvious from these data. The occupational composition may be stable, but the implied gains in personal earnings are counterbalanced by changes in family composition, a decline in educational levels, high employment, and low participation. Indeed, there is nothing in the six-year picture to suggest a

TABLE 10.5

Income of Puerto Ricans Living in the United States, 1971–76 (current dollars)

Characteristic	1971	1972	1973	1974	1975	1976
All families	6,011	6,210	7,163	6,779	7,629	7,291
Two-person families	—	5,390	6,951	7,203	7.279	—
Three-person families	4,609	5,365	7,234	6,529	6,698	—
Four-person families	5,718	—	6,886	6,544	8,391	—
Men	5,396	5,613	5,931	6,197	7,055	6,687
Women	2,955	2,784	3,374	3,593	3,889	3,837

Sources: See table 10.3.

TABLE 10.6

Population and Age of Puerto Ricans Living in the United States, 1971–76

Characteristic	1971	1972	1973	1974	1975	1976
Population (thousands)	1,450	1,519	1,548	1,547	1,671	1,753
Men	655	754	732	717	765	—
Women	795	765	816	830	906	—
Median age (years)	—	—	—	—	—	19.6
Men	17.8	16.8	18.1	18.9	17.8	—
Women	20.9	20.2	19.2	20.4	21.9	—

Sources: See table 10.3.

steady or encouraging progress in income or status of the Puerto Rican people in the United States.

Concluding Speculations

It will come as no surprise that the people who compose America's poorest colony also compose the poorest subpopulation within the United States. If emigration had not been an option, and the two million or so Puerto Ricans now living in the United States had remained in their own land, would that island today be super-populated? or would some solution have been developed other than mass steriliza-tion and exile?[8]

Nevertheless, emigration has come to be regarded as the solution to the eco-nomic problem, redefined as a population problem. People in the Caribbean have traditionally skipped from island to island, depending on the economic fortunes and the need for labor. However, the big leap from island to mainland, be it from Puerto Rico to New York or Kingston to Liverpool, tends to be irreversible both geographically and culturally. The migrant rarely returns, except to visit; and he or she takes on characteristics of the poverty subculture within the industrial society.

The economic connection between the developing, backward island and the squalid ghetto existence must be made perfectly clear. It is not the Puerto Rican family that, in its fecundity, brings backwardness to its homeland and, in its poverty, brings dereliction to the inner city. On the contrary, this backwardness and dereliction are the effects of the economic collapse of the colonial economy, which barely a century ago was starving for labor. The decay of the inner city is also the effect of industrial stagnation.[9] Ghetto conditions in the South Bronx and London are the flip side of Caribbean poverty. The summertime race riots and rebellions, which have become rituals in the industrial cities, are also the other side of the political and economic repression in the colonies, the far side of the island paradises.

Migration, for the modern economist, is nothing more than a gimmick, as we discovered in our model-making exercise. How is the predicted number of jobs to be reconciled with the population that needs work? Rather than face the dilemma of an economy that cannot employ its own people, the economist relies conveniently on migration to siphon off the surplus, nothing more sophisticated conceptually than an overflow drain in a bathtub. Once outside the developing country, these people, the emigrants, cease being a problem for the local economy. The dimensions of the Puerto Rican diaspora, however, with three million on the island and at least two million in the United States, is of another magnitude. And as long as the homeland exists, the possibility of movement in both directions continues. To the economist working in the United States, Puerto Rican emigration is merely another minority flow to be absorbed by the services, crafts, and farms. To the economist working in Puerto Rico, emigration is seen as the final solution.

The real challenge is the reverse: to develop a country with all its people intact— to accept the population as the basic resource and to define the task that would use this resource wisely. Material resources—mineral deposits, land, foreign capital—then would become tools for the population. This is the opposite of current thinking, wherein population is regarded as redundant because the needs of the mineral extraction, land tilling, or factory operations do not call for so many hands.

History teaches us that a labor-surplus area with a redirection of purpose can become labor scarce overnight.[10] The recent history of the Caribbean is the reverse swing of this cycle: it is the metropolis that is in need of cheap labor, which can be obtained as livelihoods in the colony are undermined. This the metropolis does, not with armies but with mass-produced products and food. Whole houses, called trailers, are imported, and with the disappearance of the native forests, the poorest live under the refuse of the industrial debris—corrugated tin, wood planks, and metal scraps. Not all industry waits on the mainland for labor to come its way. Footloose factories move to the colony to avail themselves of cheap labor, low taxes, and unregulated consumption of water and air. Still, too few jobs are created, since that is only incidental to the corporation's objectives. Nor is their produce intended for the consumption of local workers and their families.

Emigration, then, becomes the traditional solution, nothing more than a stream of people speaking another language and possessing only agricultural and manual skills seeking to make a living in the industrial cities of America. The literature is filled with the trauma of the adaptation to the work, to the culture, the weather, the sheer brutality of survival in the brick and asphalt jungles. (See table 10.7 for comparisons of the work experiences of Puerto Ricans who have not left the island with those who have emigrated and then returned to Puerto Rico.)[11] Nothing has prepared the emigrants for the parachutist's leap they are about to take except enticing stories of wealth and the labor contractors' ballpoint pen.[12] Today's challenge is to reintegrate the returned migrant, if not to call all the migrants home, to build with their skills a new economy that does not require the perpetual expulsion of its people under the guise of successful economic development.

TABLE 10.7

Employment Statistics of Returned Puerto Rican Emigrants and Puerto Rican Nonemigrants, 1968

Characteristic	Working Men		Working Women	
	Nonemigrants	Returned Emigrants	Nonemigrants	Returned Emigrants
Age (years)	37.8	32.6	32.0	27.2
Jobs held	9.7	18.4	4.3	8.8
Industries worked in	3.3	5.8	1.9	3.6
Locations worked in	2.6	5.6	1.8	3.6
Quarters worked	36.6	35.2	40.1	37.8
Sector (% distribution)				
Agriculture	16.7	18.0	0.7	4.6
Construction	12.6	20.5	—	—
Manufacturing	17.7	16.7	37.8	50.6
Commerce	14.7	9.6	12.9	9.2
Service	5.7	4.2	9.2	3.4
Government	19.1	13.6	29.9	16.1

Sources: Puerto Rico Planning Board, *Two Studies of Puerto Rican Labor Mobility,* vol. 1, *Labor Mobility among Social Security Covered Workers in the Puerto Rican Labor Force* (San Juan: 1974); and *A Comparative Study of the Labor Market Characteristics* (San Juan: 1973).

III

The General Setting

CHAPTER 11

Puerto Rico as Prototype: The Intellectual Background

The Conventional Wisdom

THE CONVENTIONAL wisdom today among political observers is that Puerto Rico is a special case—an American territory, a unique commonwealth linked in an exemplary relationship to the United States. Its economy is but a regional annexation, so the argument goes, and ought not be compared to other developing nations. Likewise its political status ought not be reviewed by the United Nations. Since modern economics ignores this territorial subtlety at times, the conventional wisdom among economic analysts cites Puerto Rico's successful record of uninterrupted economic growth as proof that it is indeed the exception: that only by wholesale integration with an industrial metropolis can a small, island country prosper. Since this is the very opposite direction that newly independent colonies are moving in, the conventional wisdom concludes that the experience of Puerto Rico is best ignored.

The inverse of this reasoning is that Puerto Rico's experience can be applied to the other Caribbean nations. Due to the variety of European colonial intrusions, these states are in a disharmonious competition with one another. Latin America tends to disown the Caribbean as a sister region. Languages and passports block exchanges between Caribbean neighbors who live a short raft ride apart. It is a convenient ideological shortcut to view these nations and their economies as fragments of some irrational puzzle, their societies as either staunch allies or communist agents, and the only unity as being imposed by the U.S. Navy.

Many Caribbean intellectuals from other countries would remove Puerto Rico from even this fractionated context. They do not see Puerto Rico as a sister society with a similar history and rarely stop in San Juan on their periodic trips to their respective metropolitan assemblies. Only work-hungry migrants from the other islands risk their lives to swim ashore to Puerto Rico, for once there, an illegal alien finds easy passage to New York and the American labor underground. Perhaps due to its colonial status or to the opulent life-style of its population relative to the other islands, Puerto Rico barely retains any identity as a Caribbean island. In social-economic space, Puerto Rico lies somewhere south of the Bronx,

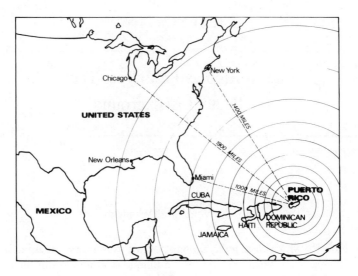

FIGURE 11.1
Socioeconomic View of Puerto Rico's
Place in the Caribbean

FIGURE 11.2
Politico-Military View of Puerto Rico's
Place in the Caribbean

north of Disneyworld, west of Appalachia, and east of Samoa (see figure 11.1).
However, in politico-military space, Puerto Rico is a significant part of the Caribbean entity (figure 11.2).[1]

The alternatives to the conventional wisdoms present quite a different picture.
Puerto Rico, first of all, is no special case at all. Its experience of economic
development both qualitatively and quantitatively is relevant for the rest of the
Caribbean and, indeed, for other small, open, densely populated countries. The
similarities and differences among these small nations, such as market size, resource base, reliance on foreign capital, colonial histories, and political power, are
but variations on a basic economic theme. They also form a class of country that is
on the fringe of, but not fully integrated with, major industrial powers. Within this
class of small, open, fringe countries, the economies of the Caribbean have had
strikingly similar experiences, and it is in this context that Caribbean patterns takes
on real meaning.

Within the Caribbean, Puerto Rico is not exceptional for its growth, diversifica-
tion of exports, reliance on tourism, out-migration, currency stability, and commonwealth status, because these all bear similarities to other colonial territories
that have their own agreements with industrial powers. Puerto Rico is exceptional
only in the quantitative sense of having pushed a particular development strategy
to the extreme, a strategy guided by pragmatic elements in both the United States
and Puerto Rico. The great past success of Puerto Rico shows the limits, not of the
special case, but of the general case, since that island has traveled the farthest in
the shortest time on this particular path. The net result of the forces that push from
within and pull from without are not dissimilar from those forces acting on the
entire class of small, open, densely populated countries.

Although the experience of Puerto Rico is especially relevant to Latin America,
the Latin American structuralist model, so very important in analyzing the short-
comings of the import substitution strategy there,[2] has scarcely been applied in the
Caribbean, for several reasons. Until recently, Caribbean economists have not
found that particular strategy relevant. Moreover, economic ties and intellectual
traditions lay historically with the European and North American powers, not with
their Southern Hemisphere neighbors. The New World Group in Kingston focused
on models thought to be applicable for the Commonwealth Caribbean, models of
integration and specialization, dependency and mineral-based growth. The Latin
American economies were large and expansive, with diversified markets, and it
appears that Latin American economists, especially the CEPAL School in Santiago, came to regard the Caribbean, at best, as somewhat numerous statistical
appendages to the industrial metropoles. Meanwhile in Puerto Rico itself, San
Juan economists were busy taking their intellectual cues from Cambridge and New
Haven. In all these cases, from Santiago to Port of Spain, the idea of a Caribbean
economy was not seriously pursued. Yet a unity may be seen between the inwardly
oriented import substitution strategy carried out in Latin America and the outwardly oriented export promotion strategy pursued in the Caribbean. This unity is

consummated in the transnational corporation and facilitated by many Third World countries, which fall over themselves in their desire to replicate with other industrialized nations the economic arrangement that Puerto Rico "enjoys" with the United States. The arrangements sought by these countries (Jamaica, Mexico, Turkey, Spain, South Korea, Algeria, and Ireland, to name a few) touch a whole variety of policies in which Puerto Rico has pioneered, such as attracting branch plants, awarding tax holidays, and arranging for migrant labor.

In the remainder of this chapter we review some of the intellectual vogues that have put Puerto Rico either out of or into the Caribbean. This discussion has implications in evaluating the relevance of the model to these traditions. In the chapter that follows we then examine some of the quantitative data relevant for the identification of Puerto Rico as a prototype for developing countries.

Puerto Rico as a Nontype

It is the fashion among economists concerned with developing countries to discount the experience of Puerto Rico as worthy of study or emulation. Having widely praised Puerto Rico's progress in the 1950s and early 1960s, these economists now turn elsewhere for their model countries. Its rapid and long-term growth is wished away as a thoroughly atypical case, as the super (and thereby inimitable) success, according to the very criteria that once held Puerto Rico as the exemplary or prototypical case.[3] Others claim that Puerto Rico represents the worst in a certain style of development. By becoming just another subregion of the United States, Puerto Rico has lost its relevance as a national economy.

Because the failings of the Puerto Rican path are glaring and well known (they range from high unemployment to human rights violations), the development establishment may well find it convenient to minimize the Puerto Rican experience and look elsewhere for less extreme and less prominent examples. Despite its fall from grace as a worthy academic subject, many elements stemming from the Puerto Rican experience operate in a real way throughout the rest of the Caribbean. The business community, having learned from the Puerto Rican environment, has come to expect, and has received, similar treatment by other islands.

It is Puerto Rico's "unique politico-institutional relationship to the U.S." and a "vital source" for growth that lies at the root of the argument for dismissing Puerto Rico as a "model for Caribbean small-state development," according to Ben Stephansky, former executive secretary of the United States–Puerto Rico Commission on the Status of Puerto Rico.[4] He concludes, "This relationship . . . [a customs union, a common currency, ample budget for public expenditures, fiscal autonomy and flexibility, access to capital markets, a secure legal framework] . . . is not transferable." Yet Puerto Rico's experience has changed the Caribbean by demonstrating "that the Caribbean species of the small state, beset by the characteristic constraint of small size, limited resources, monoculture, overpopulation, and low level of human achievement, was capable of development and not doomed to eternal backwardness constitutes a psychological break-through for the whole region."[5]

The "psychological breakthroughs" and "demonstration effect" of Puerto Rico have worked in two ways: first, other Caribbean governments and politicians search for material improvement within their own setting, anxious to imitate their neighbor's success at riding the economic tiger, yet ignore the lesson of the already devoured; and second, transnational enterprises try to avail themselves of other low-wage, profitable, island opportunities and, like the tourists, discover the value of island-hopping. Nor is Puerto Rico's relationship to the United States unique, for its programs have been duplicated under a variety of arrangements both with other countries and with the United States.[6]

Stephansky's conclusion that "both Puerto Rico and the Caribbean region could pursue their own paths of development without each other"[7] is true only as a reflection of the apparent isolation of the many nations from each other. But they all interact with their respective metropolitan power. Simply by its being, and being successful, Puerto Rico serves as a model for Caribbean development.

Puerto Rico as Prototype

Puerto Rico had not always been regarded so equivocally. W. Arthur Lewis, the author of what was to become known as the labor-surplus model, had seen Puerto Rico's export promotion campaign as the correct strategy for the small, densely populated islands. He had written as early as 1951, "What should be done is to try to persuade existing suppliers with established channels in Latin America, to open factories in the islands to supply their trade. . . . It is what Puerto Rico is doing, in its invasion of the U.S. market, and it is one of the outstanding lessons of the Puerto Rican experience."[8]

He continues, "There is no reason why the West Indies should not succeed in getting the very small share of these markets, which is all that is needed to put the islands on their feet. Puerto Rico shows that it can be done" (p. 33). Further, "Although her wage level is much higher than that of the British island, she is exporting a wide range of manufactures to the U.S. What Puerto Rico and the countries of Europe . . . can do, the British West Indies can do also" (p. 35). Clusters of industries that hung together and used one another's products would locate together in the Caribbean. "Industries are like sheep," he writes. "They like to move together." And, changing metaphors, "for once the snowball starts to move downhill, it will move of its own momentum and will get bigger and bigger as it moves along" (p. 36).[9]

Lewis preferred manufacturing rather than the extractive sectors, and praised the tripartite wage-setting procedures established in Puerto Rico. "That a policy of inducements does not conflict with protection of legitimate interests is amply illustrated by Puerto Rico. In that island, minimum wages are fixed by law for practically every trade, with a thoroughness unknown to the British islands, and at a much higher level. . . . All that is required is a sense of proportion" (p. 39). Lewis proposed a colonial development corporation on the model of PRIDCO (Puerto Rico Industrial Development Corporation), with offices in London and New York. "The British islands do not have far to look if they want to study the technique of industrialization. For, on their very doorstep lies Puerto Rico, whose Industrial Development Company is a most intelligent model of what is required. . . . Where is the money to come from? [PRIDCO] . . . has had appropriations amounting to $24 million with which it has worked wonders" (p. 50).

Lewis concludes, "Some key is needed to open the door behind which the dynamic energies of the West Indian people are at present confined. The key has obviously been found in Puerto Rico, where the drive and enthusiasm of a people hitherto as lethargic as the British West Indian warms the hearts, and inspires confidence in the future . . . put hope, initiative, direction, and an unconquerable will into the rest of their affairs. And this is the hardest task of all" (p. 53).

Puerto Rico as the Antimodel

As the 1960s and 1970s unfolded, however, practice consistent with the optimism of Lewis' early insights was becoming increasingly difficult. William G. Demas recognized the importance of Puerto Rico on the rest of the English-speaking Caribbean, but he criticized the going policies candidly for their assumptions, behavior, and the "omitted" variables.[10]

Demas was wary of the dangers of dependence and private foreign investment, the limited opportunity for import substitution and economies of scale, external vulnerability, and the dangers of Keynesian economics applied to an open economy. "What is the real meaning of self-sustained growth in a satellite economy?" he asks. Having raised this central question, he backs off, "I must confess, I do not know." Citing Hoselitz's concept of "satellitic pattern of growth," a concept that incidentally never did catch on among North American economists, Demas continues, "I would rather consider them as a case of highly open economies with 'the capacity . . . to adjust . . . to the needs and opportunities of the countries surrounding them.' "[11]

While unwilling to offer a fundamental critique of the system as a whole, Demas in his later work criticizes Puerto Rico's style of development, especially in his nonprofessional and more polemic writings: "It is possible for a small Caribbean island to achieve a relatively high per capita income and become 'prosperous' by literally selling-out its national patrimony to unscrupulous foreign investment and permitting the introduction of tax havens, casinos, free ports and numbered bank accounts . . . a highly artificial pseudo-prosperity . . . not by any stretch of the imagination . . . 'economic development' . . . not internally-generated self-sustaining and soundly-based economic growth, full employment and an attitude of independence and national self-reliance and self-respect."[12]

Two separate traditions have been derived from the writings of Lewis and

Demas. The British Caribbean has given rise to many concrete studies of integration and dependence, corporate imperialism and the influence of the multinationals, fragmentation and decision making, plantations and colonialization.[13] A second tradition has taken quite a different turn. Stimulated by Lewis on the British Caribbean and Reynolds on the American Caribbean,[14] and thus derived from the experience of the smallest of nations, the labor-surplus model has become generalized and embellished and finally applied to the People's Republic of China, the largest of all nations.[15] The consequences of the dominance of this tradition has been that words like dependency, colonialism, and the multinational corporation have virtually no place in mainstream economics in the United States.

What then is the lesson of Puerto Rico to the U.S.-trained economist? In one branch, those trained in dual, or labor-surplus, economics, Puerto Rico must be ignored, generally with some reference to the unique political arrangement.[16] A second branch of mainstream economics counts Puerto Rico, like many other countries, as but another small, industry-oriented economy like Jamaica and Haiti, Bolivia and Paraguay, Norway and the Netherlands.[17] Whether Puerto Rico is treated as an aberrant observation, as in the first branch of mainstream economics, or as just another series of observations homogenized with the rest of the developing world, the net effect is identical: the experience of Puerto Rico, indeed of the Caribbean as a unit, is ignored.

The Caribbean as Prototype

Other disciplines do not seem quite as perplexed as modern economics does by the existence of the Caribbean as a viable or meaningful region. Frank W. Knight, a historian with the sensibilities of an econometrician, writes, "The major assumption is that while the separate units pass through the same general experience, they do so at different times—hence comparisons of the Caribbean should be systadial rather than synchronic."[18] In his "examination of fragments," which forms the history of the Caribbean, Knight touches other themes as relevant to Puerto Rico's modern history, although they are drawn from the early experiences of Haiti, the Dominican Republic, Cuba, and the British West Indies. The chronic absenteeism of plantation proprietors may find its modern analogue in the transnational corporation. The willingness of the European powers in the nineteenth century to accommodate representative political arrangements within a neocolonial economic setting may be analogous to the present proliferation of commonwealths. Other repeating themes include the adeptness at imitating the "mother" country's culture, the use of general funds to subsidize the "profits of a few," not to mention the readiness of international capital and its armies to intervene or to blockade, as, for example, in 1800 in Haiti and in 1960 in Cuba.[19]

On contemporary Puerto Rico, however, Knight cuts through the rhetoric. "The Puerto Rican 'Operation Bootstrap,' " he writes, "once highly hailed, proved eventually to have more style than substance."[20] He is correct, of course, only if the operation is to be judged in terms of its original polemics. Seen in a different perspective, however, it was actually quite successful—as the economic side of a political alliance between the island's ruling families and the colonial administrator. Its goal was never to achieve economic improvement for all the Puerto Rican people, but rather through some transformation of the economic base together with armed repression, its goal was to undermine the nationalist appeal and end the overt colonial status of the island. This kind of "modernizing alliance," carried out most successfully in Puerto Rico, differs in degree, "but not in kind from the neighboring states of the Caribbean . . . with the notable exception of Cuba."[21]

If the Caribbean is indeed a natural and relevant unit of analysis for the historian, the political scientist, the anthropologist, the businessman, the journalist, the travel agent, then why not for the economist?[22] We turn now to review those qualities that unite Puerto Rico and the developing world, especially the other Caribbean economies.

CHAPTER 12

Puerto Rico as Caribbean Prototype:
The Statistical Background

Puerto Rico as the Prototype Labor-Surplus Economy

THE KEY to understanding the tremendous diversity among developing countries, especially in the Caribbean, is a mental fabrication, the labor-surplus, model.[1] In this economic model, a developing country is seen as consisting of two main sectors, the traditional or backward sector and the modern or industrial sector. In the traditional sector, workers use rudimentary tools, the contribution of each worker is low, and a worker can leave a job without measurably affecting the output of the entire farm or shop.

The modern sector is all that the traditional is not. Its modern factories, surrounded by green lawns and high barbed-wire fences, employ relatively few, highly paid workers. This sector produces many of the same commodities as the traditional sector but more efficiently, using a fraction of the labor. The traditional farm produces corn with hoe and machete; the modern plantation uses chemical sprays and tractor-combines. The traditional craftsperson fashions shoes and belts in small shops, using hammer and awl; the factory extrudes plastic shoes, while assembly lines stitch the pieces together. The street vendor and neighborhood markets sell a few products daily; the supermarket and department store magically stock their shelves at night, and an employee is hardly to be found, except at the checkout counters.

In each branch of manufacture and commerce, the modern way fixes on the traditional technique, competes with it for a place in the market, and eventually defeats it. The workers in the traditional sector then face a dilemma. Forty years cultivating tobacco on his plot hardly qualifies the sharecropper for a place on an assembly line making baseball bats. Hawking wrist watches on the street is poor training for a sales position in Lord and Taylor's or Gonzalez Padin's. As the traditional sector collapses, the displaced workers must seek new jobs. But where to go?

The labor-surplus model offers a refreshing prospect, which lies at the heart of the Western idea of economic development. The modern sector employs workers at a wage higher than the going wage in the backward sector. The profits of these modern companies are reinvested in industry. Capital accumulates in the modern sector, and new jobs are created as new factories and stores, mines and hotels are opened. New lands are cleared, swamps are drained, airports constructed. All this needs labor, especially in construction and manufacturing. Finally, the traditional sector disappears, and its workers are either retired or fully absorbed in the modern economy. This is the vision that underlies all of development policy, from the Alliance for Progress to the current Caribbean Basin initiative: the notion that the growth of the modern, highly productive sector will be able to absorb all the labor released as the traditional occupations are destroyed.

The four variants on this model have to do with the nature of the traditional and modern sectors. The most prominent backward sector is usually agriculture, the production of subsistence crops using ageless techniques and knowledge. The traditional sector also includes all kinds of crafts, from spinning and weaving to jewelry making, and the sales of products in fairs and wandering caravans.[2] In many countries, the modern sector may have long replaced one branch of the traditional activity, leaving others totally intact. The intact activities usually are regarded as curious and charming by tourists and business people on holiday. It is ironic that the sympathetic industrialist and trader who visit these remaining enclaves and who purchase their souvenir crafts are, in fact, financing their vacations with the earnings gained by their own market's triumph and the destruction of the livelihoods of these quaint peoples! The nonsurvivors become busboys in the local hotel and wage workers in the big city factory. Such are the ironies that connect the developing and industrial worlds.

The sugar plantation on many Caribbean islands long ago forced the settler farmer into proletarian cane cutting or slave overseeing, but on other islands, the hilly uplands still harbor the remnants of the self-sufficient cultivator and craftspeople.[3] Thus, the traditional and modern sectors may still coexist side by side in certain societies. Development is nothing more than the defeat of the traditional when confronted with an aggressive and expanding capitalism.

What we see throughout the developing world is the unevenness with which the model operates. Not all the labor expelled from the traditional occupations can be picked up readily in the expanding modern sector. The canecutter goes to the provincial town and then on to the capital city. There he builds his shack of debris culled from garbage dumps and industrial refuse. His wife begs bread from his more fortunate cousin, scavenges it from the street, or steals it from the rich. Husband or wife, man or woman, may be recruited to do work abroad, in the factories or farms of America or Europe depending on the arrangement his government makes with foreign migrant programs, which are always looking for cheap labor. Or he may swim across a river or float on a raft in search of economic livelihood.

The four variants of the model have to do only with the nature of the modern sector and the ultimate use of its product. The modern activities may be the new mines opening up, say, bauxite or copper, manganese or diamonds. It may be

PHOTOGRAPH 12.1
After a day's work, migrant apple pickers share drinks with
visiting students inside a hog barn used as a dormitory during
the harvest season in Winterset, Iowa.

PHOTOGRAPH 12.2
Sprawling San Juan replaces the cane fields with parking lots, office buildings, and
new housing. Looking northwest from the new federal office building.

modern factories using the latest machinery, modern farms employing the latest tractors and airplane-borne sprays and seeds; or a high-rise tourist zone built around a beach or mountain resort. These models—mineral extraction, manufacturing, agroexporting, and tourism—are activities of the modern sector. If the products are exported, then the economy is said to be outwardly oriented. If the markets are internal and the modern sector produces commodities or foods that were once imported, then the model is said to be import substituting. Most economies are mixtures of all these variations—they have some mines, modern plantations, a tourist resort, and an exporting factory zone. Some of its products are designed for local consumption and some for export.

Puerto Rico is the clearest example of the labor-surplus economy that has passed through all its stages and has elements of all its variants. It is the purest form of the model, and from Puerto Rico's experiences we learn the ultimate failings of the model. Having provided for employment in factories oriented to both export and local use, in tourist zones, and on modern farms, Puerto Rico has reached the limits of modernization. It has built the roads and ports and electrical networks, trained technicians, and provided mass housing for its workers, and still there is insufficient work in its modern sector.

The slums of the South Bronx are filled with the traditional sector residuum of Puerto Rico, to use Alfred Marshall's term, just as the slums of Liverpool are filled with those who fled the collapsing traditional sectors in Jamaica and the barrios of Los Angeles with fleeing Mexicans. These international concentrations of misery are nothing less than evidence of the failure of the labor-surplus model. The people then appear as a "problem" for the industrial country, as "boat people," as "illegal aliens," "undocumented workers," or in the Puerto Rican case, as "fellow U.S. citizens," all economic exiles.

This then is the model. Traditional agriculture collapses, sometimes with the assistance of modernization and foreign aid, sometimes under pressure from imports. The modern sector is built with foreign capital, and the products of the modern sector are exported. Profits earned in the modern sector are exported too, and because not enough jobs are created, the people also are exported. The formula, then, that summarizes the failure of the labor-surplus vision, is the export of people, profits, and products.

Immediately, the neoclassical economist intervenes. "No! The model is a success. It's the economy that is a failure! The policies these nations have pursued, especially Puerto Rico, have all impeded the natural operation of the model. They encourage supermodern technology and fix artificially high wages. If only they followed the classical policies I have been prescribing, then the model would surely work!"

So, according to the mainstream economist, hundreds of nations are all pursuing wrong policies on a correct path: build the modern sector, let agriculture collapse, use foreign capital to accelerate capital formation, repress wages, export the products, and pay off the foreign investor. If there are surplus workers (workers *made surplus* by the process), then blame them as overreproducers, prescribe the appropriate birth control program, and export them, too. Nor does suppressing wages seem to stimulate employment, as imported machinery is not easily adapted to absorb more workers. Low wages result in higher profits, perhaps, and a lower standard of living for the laboring people, a development that makes emigration even more rewarding.

Despite the rosy promise of the model, tension grows throughout the developing world. Rebellions occur, and the industrial countries become alarmed and talk about political instability and immaturity in the excolonies. Two courses follow. First, the industrial country sends emergency aid in the form of food (for hungry people whose own land the market has made uneconomic to farm) and in the form of new roads (which facilitate the invasion of modern products into the remotest regions, destroying the remaining crafts and helping people migrate even faster to the big cities and eventually abroad). As the aid proves insufficient and misguided, and if the world price for the traditional export dips a few cents, the unstable economy goes into a crisis, and a second course is followed. The industrial country is asked for a different kind of emergency aid—money, arms, military training, and, as a last resort, troops—and economic conflict turns into armed conflict, the consequence of the failure of the economic model.

"But how could a *model* fail," retorts the neoclassical economist, "when it is clear that it is the *economy* that is failing?" To say the model is still viable in the face of the economic record is like the doctor who, confronted with the corpse of his patient, keeps insisting that the operation was a success.

I hold simply that the labor-surplus model is no model at all. It is an antimodel, a model of what should not be done and how not to do it. And the leading example of this failure is, of course, America's "showcase in the Caribbean"—Puerto Rico with its four-thousand-dollar per capita income, twenty-five hundred factories, and tremendous hotel complexes—which the rest of the developing world, especially the Caribbean, is trying to imitate. Puerto Rico, the most advanced model, the most successful case of Caribbean development, verges on bankruptcy. Nearly 60 percent of its people live on food stamps, and farmlands are virtually abandoned. Puerto Rico is an island of three million inhabitants with another two million of its citizens—once agricultural people—living under the most miserable conditions in America's cities. This, then, is what the "showcase" promises for the rest of the developing world and the Caribbean.

How is this possible? What are the essential elements of the model that are missing that have led the economist so far afield? The reason for the failure of the model is that certain qualities of the nature of the developing country are simplified out of the model. Those qualities have to do with the openness of the Caribbean to trade and technique, the size of country, the density of the population, and its proximity, in economic space, to an industrial nation. Puerto Rico is representative of the class of such states, the outstanding prototype of the failure of the antimodel.

PHOTOGRAPH 12.3
Los Caños, an abandoned sugar mill in
the Arecibo River Valley, Puerto Rico.

PHOTOGRAPH 12.4
Harvesting sugar cane in Havana Province, Cuba, using oxen, tractor, crane,
and cart.

Openness, Size, and Density

Of all the world's countries, Puerto Rico ranks fourteenth in openness to trade, as measured by the sum of imports and exports relative to gross domestic product (table 12.1). The fifteen most open small states are all associated with a metropolitan power and all have populations of less than five million. Seven are Caribbean. Of open nations with less than a million hectares of land, Puerto Rico ranks ninth. And of these small, open economies, Puerto Rico is the sixth most densely populated. When population density is considered relative to farmland rather than total land size, Puerto Rico ranks fifth, and in terms of potential food production, sixth.

How do the qualities of openness, size, and density, affect the workings of the Lewis model? The degree of openness indicates exposure and orientation to world markets, or at least toward the principal trading country. The dependence on imported capital, by introducing labor-saving machinery, might lessen employment possibilities. Economists represent this by a kinked transformation curve between labor and capital (curve $b'a$, figure 12.1). The poor, less-open society may experience relatively easy substitution between labor and capital (curve $a'a$). Thus, openness may imply a transformation of the conventional transformation curve!

Such export-orientation suggests that employment is determined by the state of the international market demand for its products, not by its own local demand. Openness also implies the vulnerability of local products to international products, undermining domestic production, such as crafts or manufactures for local use, and short-circuiting the growth of a domestically oriented industry.

How should the size of the country affect the model? Small population coupled with low income indicate a limited market, making it difficult for local industry to realize economies of scale, encouraging specialization in a single crop or industry, and implying dependence on a large, industrial country. But there is nothing inherent in such dependence; it is merely the consequence of the historical formation of these countries. They are small as the result of specific colonial wars and policies. In the Caribbean, European powers struggled over each island, carving up the map. Curaçao, Barbados, and Puerto Rico became construct economies, that is, made for specific trades and highly linked to a metropolitan power for that purpose. As that purpose—say, sugarcane or tobacco—plays out its historical cycle, the island, now attaining political independence, must fare for itself.

Population density indicates yet another dimension of the model—the depth or quality of the market, how quickly it may be saturated with new products, and how easily organized its labor market may prove to be. A densely populated country may exert more pressure on the land and at the same time offer a ready work force for agriculture or manufacturing. A dense population dwelling in valleys or in cities may prove more efficient for the delivery of social services and housing as well as for military security, compared to the same population spread more widely over a large land area.

TABLE 12.1
The Fifteen Countries Most Open to Trade, Some Characteristics, 1975

Country	Openness[a]	Associated Metropolitan Power	Population (thousands)	Land (thousand hectares)			Population/Land Ratios		
				Total	Farm	Potential Farm	Total	Farm	Potential Farm
Netherlands Antilles	592	Netherlands	238	96	8	8	2.50	29.8	29.80
Singapore	241	United Kingdom	2,248	58	9	13	38.80	249.8	172.90
Hong Kong	198	United Kingdom	4,225	103	11	22	41.00	384.1	192.00
Malta	163	United Kingdom	329	32	14	14	10.30	23.5	23.50
Barbados	138	United Kingdom	245	43	33	37	5.70	7.4	6.60
Belize	133	United Kingdom	140	2,280	49	1,082	0.10	2.9	0.10
Swaziland	129	United Kingdom and S. Africa	361	1,720	165	1,617	0.20	2.2	0.20
São Tomé and Príncipe	128	Portugal	80	96	30	31	0.80	2.7	2.60
Guyana	126	United Kingdom	791	19,685	845	17,401	0.04	0.9	0.05
Trinidad and Tobago	125	United Kingdom	1,006	513	157	394	2.00	6.4	2.60
Gabon	121	France	521	26,767	126	26,445	0.02	4.1	0.02
Mauritania	120	France	1,283	103,040	1,000	55,389	0.01	1.3	0.02
Mauritius	119	United Kingdom	899	185	102	171	4.90	8.8	5.30
Puerto Rico	116	United States	2,902	886	200	658	3.30	14.5	4.40
Surinam	107	Netherlands	422	16,147	45	14,505	0.03	9.4	0.03

Source: United Nations, *Yearbook of National Accounts Statistics 1975*; Food and Agricultural Organization, *Production Yearbook 1976.*
[a]Exports plus imports divided by gross domestic product.

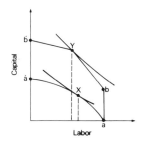

FIGURE 12.1
Transformation Curves between
Labor and Capital

The Caribbean as Prototype

Most Caribbean countries are small and open. The low densities of places like Belize and Surinam (see table 12.2) disguise their true land scarcity. Density as measured by the ratio of population to arable land places them on a par with China and India.

Cuba is the most populated Caribbean country and third largest in physical size after Guyana and Surinam. Puerto Rico, fourth in population, is the richest on a per-person basis (table 12.3). In general, there is a rough inversion between wealth and size in the Caribbean, as the bigger countries tend to be the poorer ones. Part of the association between land size and poverty lies in the identification of the agricultural sector with poverty: in the small islands, this sector has collapsed and the farm workers have gone to other islands or to the metropolitan country; in the larger countries, agriculture is still being transformed.

The remainder of the economic record testifies to the great economic fluctuations throughout the Caribbean. During the 1960s, Puerto Rico's gross domestic product grew at twice the U.S. rate and faster than most economies throughout the world. During the 1970s, growth slowed to a crawl, a fraction of the U.S. rate. In the 1970s, Puerto Rico's population grew at the fourth highest rate in the Caribbean, although the absolute natural rate of population increase was the second lowest, and the absolute decline in infant mortality was the second highest in the Caribbean. These indicators point to Puerto Rico's inclusion as a somewhat progressive but ordinary member of the Caribbean. Its population density is high but not atypical. Its population growth, once held to be at the root of a neomalthusian dilemma, is now characterized by the lowest rate of net reproduction and infant mortality in the Caribbean, the fourth lowest live birth rate, and the third lowest death rate.[4] Indeed, to the extent that population growth was ever a problem, its

TABLE 12.2
Caribbean Countries: Trade Openness and Land Densities, 1975

Country	Openness[a]	Population (1,000)	Land (1,000 hectares)	Population/Land Ratios		
				Total	Farm	Potential Farm[b]
Barbados[c]	138	245	43	5.70	7.4	6.60
Belize[d]	133	140	2,280	0.10	2.9	0.10
Cuba[e]	48	9,481	11,452	0.80	2.6	1.20
Dominican Republic[f]	48	5,118	4,838	1.10	5.1	1.40
Guyana[f]	126	791	19,685	0.04	0.9	0.04
Haiti[e]	30	4,552	2,756	1.70	5.0	3.00
Jamaica[e]	77	2,029	1,080	1.90	7.8	2.10
Puerto Rico[e]	116	2,902	886	3.30	14.5	4.40
Surinam[g]	107	422	16,147	0.03	9.4	0.03
Trinidad and Tobago[h]	125	1,006	513	2.00	6.4	2.60

Sources: See table 12.1.
[a]Exports plus imports divided by gross domestic product.
[b]Includes permanent meadows, forests, and woodlands.
[c]1972–73.   [d]1973–74.   [e]1970–74.   [f]1970–75.   [g]1972–74.   [h]1964–68.

TABLE 12.3
The Caribbean: Gross Domestic Product per Person and Population, 1979

Country or Territory	GDP per Person		Population	
	Rank	Dollars	Rank	Thousands
Puerto Rico	1	3,749	4	3,360
Trinidad and Tobago	2	3,429	6	1,130
Martinique	3	3,249	10	320
Netherlands Antilles	4	2,567	12	240
Guadaloupe	5	2,398	9	320
British Virgin Islands	6	2,376	19	12
Surinam	7	1,999	8	370
Barbados	8	1,931	11	270
Jamaica	9	1,554	5	2,100
Dominican Republic	10	917	2	5,120
Belize	11	766	13	142
Antigua	12	713	17	71
Turks and Caicos islands	13	690	22	6
St. Lucia	14	588	20	12
Montserrat	15	566	21	10
Guyana	16	540	7	810
St. Kitts-Nevis-Anguilla	17	432	18	70
Grenada	18	410	14	110
Dominica	19	394	16	80
St. Vincent and the Grenadines	20	375	15	100
Haiti	21	278	3	4,830
United States of America	—	9,687	—	218,230
Cuba	—	—	1	9,690

Sources: United Nations, *Yearbook of National Accounts Statistics 1979; Demographic Yearbook 1979.*

connection either with economic growth or with the reproduction of a people has apparently been broken.[5]

One statistic points to a general problem underlying Caribbean societies: the difficulty of putting their people to work. Except for Haiti and Barbados, the share of the economically active population—that is, those over fourteen years old working or seeking work—never surpassed 31 percent. In Puerto Rico, only a quarter of this population was economically active. (One explanation of the low participation rates lies in the structure of Caribbean families. Traditionally, the man is sent forth as the wage earner, the woman remains in the home. But both prosperity and poverty force a change in that structure. In times of prosperity, the woman is drawn out of the home by high wages and career possibilities, and in times of poverty, the woman is forced into the work force out of necessity. This explains why Haiti, which is poor, and the United States, which is wealthy, experience the greatest proportion of adults in the work force.)

In terms of economic activities, Puerto Rico demonstrates the smallest agriculture and the largest manufacturing and service sectors. (table 12.4). The agrarian sectors of Guyana, Jamaica, and Trinidad also have been reduced, in strong contrast to Haiti and the Dominican Republic. But only in Puerto Rico has public administration picked up so much of the slack. Puerto Rico leads the Caribbean in its share of manufacturing, but Jamaica and the Dominican Republic have significant enclaves as well. To summarize, the variations and similarities of the Caribbean economies can be seen in their structures. Haiti is distinguished by

TABLE 12.4

Economic Sector, Average Annual of Gross Domestic Product, Six Caribbean Countries and the United States, 1975–79 (percent)[a]

Country	Agriculture	Mining	Manufacturing[b]	Construction	Trade[c]	Transport[d]	Other Services[e]
Dominican Republic	20	3	19	7	17	6	28
Guyana[f]	25	14	13	8	13	5	22
Haiti[g]	41	1	14	4	10	3	26
Jamaica[f]	8	10	20	8	18	6	30
Puerto Rico	3	0	37	3	18	6	34
Trinidad and Tobago[f]	3	41	15	6	14	7	14
United States	3	3	27	4	18	6	37

Sources: United Nations, Yearbook of National Accounts Statistics, various years.
[a]Totals may not sum to 100 due to rounding.
[b]Includes electricity, gas, and water.
[c]Includes restaurants and hotels.
[d]Includes communication.
[e]Includes finance, insurance, real estate, business and personal services, government, and defense.
[f]1975–77.
[g]1975–78.

its large traditional agricultural sector; Trinidad, Guyana, and Jamaica by their modern mining enclaves; and Puerto Rico by its large manufacturing and service sectors. The uniqueness of the Puerto Rican case lies not in its change from agriculture to manufacturing, nor in the rise of services and government, (for other countries are pursuing that same route), but rather in the absolute size of those sectors, its agriculture being the smallest and its manufacturing and service sectors the largest in the Caribbean. It is with some irony that Puerto Rico, in terms of proportions, has taken on the profile of the economic structure most similar to that of the United States.

CHAPTER 13

Failings of the Labor-Surplus Model

Omitted Variables and a Question of Direction

I HAVE ARGUED that Puerto Rico is prototypical of a class of small, open, densely populated societies. I have also argued that Puerto Rico has achieved the highest or most advanced phase of a certain style of development, which many other countries appear to be following with the expectation of similar achievement. However, we have also seen how the Puerto Rican economy has faltered, especially in recent years. This is an inevitable consequence of the structural nature of the economy, not merely a cyclical or temporary difficulty.

Moreover, the experience of Puerto Rico shows us how the model fails to explain the problem of employing its own people as the economy grows. The particular solution that Puerto Rico adopted, that of encouraging its citizens to leave the country, may be available to other fringe societies, depending on their arrangements with an industrial country and their own labor needs. But this alternative is generally not available. Instead, we find congested cities, housing shortages, and greater reliance on armed repression.[1] The pattern is so frequently seen around the world that one is forced to ask whether the model is correct but these countries have failed to fulfill its buoyant predictions or whether the model itself fails to describe the true course of events.

Having argued that Puerto Rico has pushed this style of development to its highest stage, I am now prepared to fit its experience back into the labor-surplus framework, for I believe it is the model, not the country, that went wrong. It clearly fails to comprehend certain real factors that are always present and that are critical to understanding and anticipating real events. Excluding these, simplifying them out of the model as insignificant details, has led to a model of limited usefulness.

The model presented in the opening chapters of this book, however, while lacking in storybook appeal—since it was presented as an extended accounting system—lays bare certain features of the economy that, in their statistical application, pinpoint the failings of the labor-surplus approach. I am suggesting that mine is a truer model, more complete and faithful to the basic structure of the x-rayed patient and, at the same time, more useful in understanding the structure of similar patients. There is less room for fancy and imagination in explaining the actual detail—in other words, how the numbers fit together. This is the essential step

105

between model making and model testing, a step that presents the observer with either a validation of the model or the discomforting prospect that the initial model should be scrapped. Such is the nature of scientific progress.

My one agreement with the labor-surplus model is its starting point. Labor does leave the traditional sector to seek employment in the modern sector. But from here on, the models part company. Higher wages in the modern sector may attract the impoverished peasant, but more important is the fact that efficiently produced farm imports and manufacturers drive traditional agricultural products and crafts out of the market. Nor can the small farmer resist successfully the market pressure for his land if it is close to an expanding plantation. The classic model also wishes away the historic role of internal commodity prices and the role of force in explaining the decline or rise of certain activities. There are at least seven other omissions: openness of the economy, colonial tradition, population density, market size, time, foreign profits, and domestic consumption needs.

Before going on to these and other omissions, we must consider another question. If the labor-surplus paradigm is so wrong, why is it still used at all? What is the secret of its attraction? The answer to this lies in its elegance, simplicity, and promise. Moreover, the empirical record for the longer period is only now becoming available. These data are more conclusive; we cannot blame the early pioneering economists for not knowing what is now known. Moreover, when the model was new, it was a positive force, for it offered a clear direction away from stagnant primary exports, like mining and staple crops, toward dynamic manufacturers. The labor-surplus vision was also easy to administer; it was doable. Its policy implications could be implemented, and market forces, it was thought, would build a modern economy.

Furthermore, Puerto Rico and other frontier economies had already done it. Here was an example to be seen and followed. The labor-surplus model also offered a manageable and immediate solution to the population problem—the seasonal or permanent emigration of workers, who could send back needed money and also relieve the pressure on land, food, and human services. The Puerto Rican prototype and its labor-surplus image offered another kind of promise in that the small, industrializing economy situated on the fringe of a metropolitan society could throw its chips in with the bigger economy, like hitching its future to an already-risen star. The instability implied in such a relationship (exemplified in the expression that when the U.S. economy catches cold, its "friends" come down with pneumonia) was thought better than being adrift in the Sargasso Sea.[2]

Variables to Be Included in the Model

At least seven areas are ignored by the labor-surplus model, variables that must be explained more comprehensively because of their importance. One is the openness of the economy as measured by imports, exports, and the balance of trade. Trade openness may imply a reliance on the production process, the ideological and living styles, and the capital of the industrial countries. It also implies strong links to the international capital market. Labor-saving machinery arrives continually to refresh the modern sector with new inventions: mechanized canecutters, automated mining equipment, computerized machine tools. Even obsolete machinery from an industrialized country has revolutionary implications for the developing country.[3]

Second, the classic model ignores the colonial tradition and the manner in which that tradition affects the present economy, especially in terms of its laws, history, and attitudes. The open countries are all former colonies; in fact, most of the Third World is composed of former possessions, protectorates, territories, or quasi colonies. It is ludicrous to pretend, as is often done by development economists, that these excolonies are merely poor versions of Britain or Japan and that they, too, will eventually pass through stages similar to those of the great powers. Those more successful were never governed by a foreign state power for long periods of time. The sovereignty of these small, newly freed states is tempered by conditions and arrangements left over from centuries of domination. We must know, in short, about nothing less than the nature of power in the open economy—the deployment of physical force as well as market force, and ultimately its stance on military intervention by its own or foreign armies.[4]

There are also subtle implications of a colonial tradition for tariff-setting and for attracting capital. Although a developing nation may erect a tariff wall to keep out unwanted luxury goods, its consumers might prefer a life-style based on imported goods like they saw colonial administrators enjoy. The use of domestic resources to produce these luxury goods behind a high tariff wall can lead to economic perversions, such as the rebottling of bulk imported hair coloring in Jamaica (labelled gloriously an import-substituting industry) and the importing of ground, bottled nutmeg in Grenada, the world's second major exporter of whole nutmegs. To attract capital, the excolony may feel compelled to provide a legalistic and ideological framework similar to its former colonizer, so that foreign capital might feel at home and operate efficiently. This bending over backward, which passes as forward-looking, might restrict a country's flexibility and innovation when circumstances demand it.

Third, a densely populated country does not necessarily mean the economy is unable to support its people. High density may deepen the market, even when purchasing power is low. High density forces and favors adaptations that encourage the very survival of the people, its language, its family ties and its society.[5] It also requires caution in adopting the land-use practices and life-styles of low-density countries: the large auto, the six-lane superhighway, the spacious suburban house, the asphalt parking lots, the sprawling factories and offices.

Fourth, the small absolute population does mean a country has a limited local market, and practices borrowed from countries with big markets all must be adjusted. If the going technology has led to the development of a single plant that can produce 20 percent of the world's need for penicillin, no local branch plant can produce for a small population competitively. The trick is to find those processes that can be done small and those products for which economies of scale are either unimportant or can be realized at low levels of production.

The actual course taken by many countries is exactly the opposite. Yielding to the argument of size, large factories are built precisely because of their position in the international, not local, division of the market. Hence, Puerto Rico is a major pharmaceutical producer for many companies which have located the world manufacture of certain products there to avail themselves of the tax exemptions. Medicines for the local market are imported. Agricultural techniques imported from the United States are also not adjusted to the realities of Puerto Rico's land, unlike traditional agriculture, which uses each piece of land efficiently.[6]

Fifth, time is a factor in the model. Is our judgment of the labor-surplus model too harsh? Are we not being too impatient? The model may, eventually show itself to be correct, and thirty years experience may not be enough to judge fairly. My position is that to these peoples, thirty years is time enough, and the daily stress is great. As earnings and material welfare at home deteriorate, people are forced to flee from the path of the bulldozer and tractor to make room for the high-rise apartment, the tourist resort, the extending dairy pasture, or they flee to seek a new place to practice their craft.

It is at this point that force must be considered in the model. The scenario goes something like this. Agriculture collapses, and the foundations of modern industry are built. The country buys food on the international market and pays for it by exporting a specialty commodity—copper, for example, or bauxite, or sugarcane. For some external reason, say a recession in the United States, a twist of the business cycle, or a rise in the price of oil, the price of copper or cane falls or the price of imported food rises. Scarcity raises the prices of locally grown food. The country lifts controls on food prices, and the people, already living on the brink of subsistence, rise up in protest. Police or military force is required to maintain control, and the tanks roll into the streets of the capital. Often these events are triggered by a political spark—an arrest, an assassination, a rebellion—but the underlying economic basis is the same.

If the government complies with the people's demands, it is viewed as demogogic or communist in Western capitals. If it takes a tough stand, it is viewed as tyrannical by the oppressed. In nondemocratic countries, the ruling class, caste, or family holds on for its very survival, which its industrial ally is called upon to support. Such was the situation in Nicaragua under Somoza, and in El Salvador, Guatemala, Haiti, Brazil, Chile, Argentina, South Korea, and countless other countries.

The solution is not to treat these cases as anomalies or, worse, to leave them in the domain of the political scientist. The solution is to accept the notion of force as an economic variable. For small, densely populated societies, the beginning phases of the development process, which the Lewis model so eloquently depicts, lead to gross and glaring inequalities.[7] Before these inequalities can be remedied, the society explodes, armed conflict begins, talking and negotiations stop, and the remedy becomes the liquidation of either side. In the words of the political economist, between equal right, force alone decides.[8]

In many colonies, armed rebellion led to independence (Kenya, Mozambique, Angola, Rhodesia/Zimbabwe). In other colonies, the struggle goes on underground and the battle lines are everywhere (Northern Ireland and Puerto Rico). In the latter cases, the political stance is unrelenting. "Out with the British." "Push the Americans into the Sea."[9] The intensity of the anticolonial movement, it is thought, will cleanse the homeland and lead to a new regime free to pursue its country's interests, especially economic interests, with the political triumph of the liberation movement as the empowering first step. In many cases, however, the political triumph has done little more than clear the stage for the Lewis model to begin. Thus impatience, not an indifference to time,[10] must be part of the economic model. People are hungry now, land is idle now, resources are scarce now.

Sixth, the role of foreign-owned profits earned in a country must be dealt with explicitly in the model. Profits and interest are, according to the present legal system, the just rewards of capital. Since the capital is international, then the profits and interest are international and will eventually return abroad. Thus, foreign ownership of capital sets up future claims, ties the hands of the present regime, and sets limits on the exercise of its own wisdom. At the same time, it embeds a country in the international capitalist community. Its indebtedness is a mutual obligation: the poor country won't be abandoned in spite of its fear of bankruptcy and occasional mismanagement, nor will it be permitted to abandon the collective capitalist ship or change its own specialized place. The developing country deepens its specialization in the same economic direction as in its colonial era. It returns to cane, to coffee, or to tobacco with even greater intensity. It opens new mines; it promotes the cultivation, sale, or refinement of drug-containing plants. Its economy hungers for dollars, and the quest for dollars leads even the virtuous to sell arms to petty dictators (and then to apologize for its flexible morality). New leaders fall into old patterns with new labels; they dig old ruts deeper.

CHAPTER 14

Consumption as a Subversive Activity

THUS FAR we have seen how the labor-surplus model emphasizes production. There is not enough exports, not enough capital, not enough employment. Work is scarce, we are taught, because wages are not low enough to encourage business to clear the market, and the technology of production is inappropriate to the resources available. However, there is a further aspect of final demand, consumption, that, as we shall see, offers another avenue of explanation of the problem.

The Dissociated Economy

In the traditional poor country, the upper strata consumes like the colonizers, imitating the French style or the British or the American. The lower class in a plantation town eat the produce sold in the company store, the mountain people adapt its traditions to what is available in its market, and the urban poor go to supermarkets and chain stores, where local eggs and city-raised chickens are sold along with baskets from China, German machetes, and American pots.[1] Thus the economy is dissociated—it does not produce the commodities that are consumed. The economy produces bauxite, but not aluminum pots and pans for its people. It produces highly priced work boots; the people consume inexpensive sandals made in Hong Kong. The link between consumption and production is met by imports, which are unlimited in variety, style, price, and quantity. Every necessity or whim can be satisfied, for a price, by the international market—codfish from Nova Scotia, rice from California, wood from Sweden. The open, dissociated society easily achieves a commodity-diverse life-style. The diversity includes goods of low quality—synthetic garments, inexpensive housewares, and used automobiles, and so these economies are part of the international recycling of commodities. In the extreme case, the only consumer goods made locally are services and some specialized handicrafts.

Normal economic flows are charted as in figure 14.1—neat boxes connected to one another through circular flows of value. But developing countries have hollow economies as shown in figure 14.2; local production is but a fraction of total production. And what we see is only a fraction of what is. Behind the boxes are flows of imported consumer goods, imported government grants and aid, import-

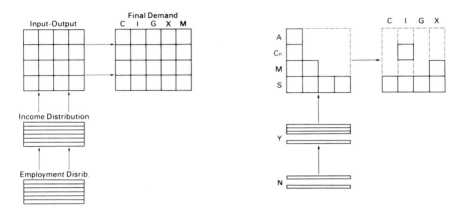

FIGURE 14.1
Normal Economic Flows

FIGURE 14.2
Economic Flows of Developing
Countries: The Hollow Economy

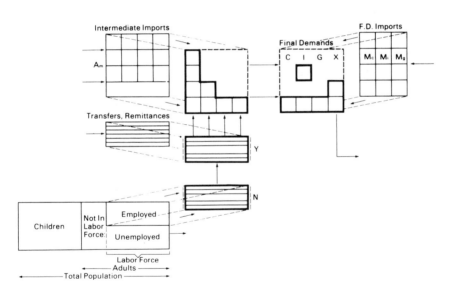

FIGURE 14.3
The Complete Economy:
The Hollow Economy and Its Backup

ed investment, imported raw materials, and imported spare parts (figure 14.3). These are the third dimension. Even the employed labor force, as we have seen, is but a fraction of the total adult population.

All economies are to some extent hollow, in that each region produces only a fraction of its actual needs. Every section of a single nation necessarily specializes in certain services or commodities. The inclusion of foreign states within a larger economic entity annexes the peripheral area, overwhelming its economic power without a concomitant sharing of its political power. This is one of the essential differences between, say, a tourist-dependent county in New Hampshire and a small island in the Caribbean whose economy, in contrast to its nominal political status, may be said to be dissociated.

Income Distribution in the Dissociated Economy

In chapter 2, I explained why it is necessary to close an economy to imports in order to make operational the necessary circuits within the economy. We discovered that the lower-class bundle of consumption leads to higher national income and lower employment, while the upper-class bundle generates less income but more employment. This was the mechanical, experimental result.

In developing countries, two trends have been observed regarding the growth of incomes of the different social classes.[2] The rich become the superrich and the poor and middle classes become either richer or poorer. But even the miserable are buying more imported things, from instant infant formula to transistor radios. Thus, either condition of the poor—whether they become poorer or richer—generates demand for foreign, not local, labor to satisfy even feeble consumption needs.

Meanwhile, the upper class grows richer, for that is the process of economic development, and they buy, as we have measured, not only more things but more services. Since the labor market in services is less constrained by the limits of machines and international unions, the rich are able to purchase more services: maids, chauffeurs, beauticians, domestic help, gardeners, guards, doctors, nurses, tennis coaches, and so on. They explore all the nuances of consumption, the subtleties of modern living. They also invest their fortune or they collaborate with the foreign investor.

But "thing" consumption does not absorb the labor sloughed off by the decline in the traditional sector and service consumption does not absorb enough. Why? If the upper class is conscious of its leadership role in a democracy, it abjures the colonial image of a retinue of servants. Rather, it consumes conspicuous "things," like jeeps and autos and clothes, and labor-saving "things," like washing machines and synthetic fibers, vacuum cleaners and power lawn mowers. Air conditioners require electric power and constant imports of fuel to sustain the "cool" life-style.[3] If a regime were to redistribute income from the rich to the poor, then the rich would employ still fewer people. The poor would take their increased money and buy things, inevitably imported. So it is that a pattern of unequal income distribution creates an economic force against egalitarian change at the same time that it breeds a politically explosive situation.

The point here is that the production and consumption link does not draw the economy together but rather renders it dissociated. This is an empirical point found for a particular economy, the Puerto Rican model. It is not necessarily an economic law for all developing countries, and other societies may find it not to be the case. However, two recent and comprehensive studies of India and South Korea tend to confirm the findings of the Puerto Rican model.[4]

Alternatives within the Same Paradigm

The process whereby world commodities invade the local market and replace domestic goods or services may be described as the importation of substitutes,[5] which results in a hollow economy. Exporting primary minerals or specialty crops and related products enables a country to continue to import substitutes but with the aim of filling in the hollow economy. The opposite path is to build local industries in order to displace imports.[6] To pursue this path, many national industries must be created for each national product. The national automobile requires national steel, rubber, glass, and tire factories. National steel requires national coal or charcoal, iron ore, and limestone, and so on; for each new product, a new industrial network. But the end result of either path is the same: continued massive unemployment, since the new industries still employ but a fraction of the adult population; and continued dependence on some imported resource, like oil or coal, since the country cannot reformulate the technology.

These two opposite paths, the substitution of imports and the promotion of exports, are locked in a continual, competing, and dynamic conflict. When inputs are substituted—clothing, for example—a protective tariff is erected, and national production responds by reclaiming the market with its own production. Then a new style of imported clothing, say, blue jeans, reinvades the market and the process begins anew. In the export-promoting economy, sugarcane may be exported, and this industry gives rise to rum and industrial alcohol, then bottles, paper, cardboard, printing, fertilizer, and machinery repair. When cane fails, all of the connected industries also falter, and the country must undertake to build new exports with new linkages, like citrus fruit or microcomputers.[7] But neither of these ways of creating whole networks of technologies to fill in the hollow economy results in fully employing the adult population or in getting a greater share of income to the majority (figure 14.4).

There is a third path, and that is to redistribute income directly from the top to the bottom and alter the entire wage/employment relationship. That is, rather than looking to chains of industries to employ people, effect the income and employment relationship directly. This spells revolution, however, a solution blunted as a viable alternative in many countries at present.[8]

This leaves only one alternative, a change in consumption patterns, establishing a national life-style that maximizes local production and employment. But such an

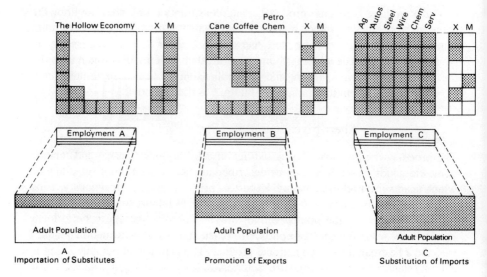

FIGURE 14.4
Alternative Input-Output Patterns

alternative is increasingly unlikely; the trend in consumption is toward more things and services that require payments abroad—ice cream machines, factory-made designer jeans (even for the once custom-tailored upper classes), household appliances, vehicles, electronics, stereos, computers, and foreign travel. All these create few linkages, employ few people, and send local earnings abroad. Modern consumption in the open capitalist economy, in short, has become a subversive activity.

IV

The Historical Setting

CHAPTER 15

History and Counterhistory

IF THE labor-surplus model does not work, then what does? And where do we find it? Such a challenge, taken seriously, would send us around the world searching for another real economy to study in depth. Perhaps to North Korea, Albania, or Cuba, among the small, relatively closed, socialist economies; or to China, a large, densely populated giant. Or perhaps we could compare in greater detail other successful Western-style "miracle" economies, South Korea, Brazil, and Taiwan, all likewise known for their repressive domestic treatment of labor.[1]

Such a question begs the point, for the critique of the labor-surplus model made in this book comes from two angles. The first is empirical, namely, from the experience and the data specific to Puerto Rico. Similar data for Hong Kong, Peru, Brazil, Pakistan, Ecuador, Sri Lanka, South Korea, and India also tend to support the findings of the Puerto Rican model, although they too are partial and experimental.[2] Their authors are not prepared to recommend that these countries implement their computer findings. My second angle of criticism is theoretical, for an alternative paradigm must answer those points and give due consideration to the situations and structures omitted in the labor-surplus model.

It is the temptation of every social scientist to offer an alternative vision of the future, a new model or method toward economic redemption. Sometimes the model becomes an operating blueprint, a guide to actual policy. It may also become, as in the case of the labor-surplus model, an idealized goal that obscures the fundamental issues. In formulating alternative courses of action for the Puerto Rican economy, two basic principles must be constantly applied.

First, before departing from the present path to some alternative future path, we must be guided by how we got here, the historical legacy and fallacies, the real and imagined material base, the human resources and their formation. Just as the statistical model was calibrated before it could achieve predictive force, so must a comprehensive model step backward before leaping forward. This is a most controversial endeavor, since correct interpretation of history requires both detailed analysis and abstraction, each of which is constantly being revised by scholars.

The second principle is the acceptance of the economic and policy record of the past, free of the recrimination and vindictiveness characteristic of insular debate.

Policies once thought to be correct may have led to undesirable consequences. A cool evaluation of both the negative and positive effects will prepare us for the challenge of remedying the historical situation. Rigid adherence to or rejection of economic policies associated with certain political positions reduces flexibility in dealing with present dilemmas. No idea is the patented property of a political party. Nor does recrimination and countercharge clarify rational policy.

America's Colonial Legacy

The economic development of Puerto Rico was guided by a policy of inviting private capital to locate factories on the island and of providing public infrastructure—roads, port facilities, electric power, and factory buildings—to support private industry. A powerful magnet in the invitation was the exemption from the U.S. income tax. Thirty years of these investments has resulted in accelerated capital formation, a skilled labor force, the decline of agricultural output, and a pattern of overall industrial production strikingly similar to that of the United States. In these achievements, Puerto Rico is ahead of similar small, open dependent economies. However, Puerto Rico finds itself with more than a majority of its residents supported by food stamps and another considerable share of its people living as emigrants and supported by welfare in the United States. The highest level of the Puerto Rican model bears a striking similarity to Alain de Janvry's observation of the international food programs.[3]

In the Puerto Rican case, the historical point of departure is crucial. The industrialization program came after several impasses at transforming agriculture, and the nature of that struggle and the reasons for abandoning that transformation are still unclear to this day.

Historical Legacy and Fallacies

Puerto Rico before industrialization was an agricultural country characterized by complicated relations between the rural proletarian sector (Mintz's factory in the field, as he called the sugar mill) and the rural self-employed sector, in which peasants raised food and cash crops on their own land.[4] Even in the interior mountain areas, where the small, independent farmer was still dominant, a cash economy remained from the era of the coffee plantations.[5] The coastal sugar economy of the 1900s, which followed the collapse of the interior coffee plantations in the late 1800s, took on the same labor force as the coffee plantations.

The United States in 1898 had come into possession of a colony in disarray from Spanish mercantilism, and its transition into the American economic sphere accelerated the crises in its traditional sectors. The transfer of allegiance from Madrid to Washington brought a new currency and a new tax system, a substantial devaluation of the existing money supply, and the subsequent transfer of immense tracts of land to U.S. sugar companies. The cheapening of all its real and cash assets relative to the United States and the need by the colonial landowning classes for the new currency encouraged rapid sale of what seemed like an obsolete asset—land.[6] With the acquisition of the estates by the absentee corporations came Puerto Rico's first real industrialization—the modern sugar economy.

The transformation from a coffee/tobacco/peasant economy to a sugar economy extended the proletarian work relations into every corner of the island, for unlike transformations of other Caribbean islands, the sugar economy of Puerto Rico could draw for its labor only upon mountain peasants, who were surrounded by the coastal sugar lands. Relative latecomers to industrial sugar cultivation, the sugar companies of Puerto Rico could not import African slaves, Indian indentured servants, or Chinese coolies, as other Caribbean sugar economies had in earlier centuries. Puerto Rico forged its own native population into its wage labor force.[7] The unity of the proletarian labor force became evident as the international sugar crises of the 1920s and then the Great Depression shook the industry and disrupted national and international markets.[8]

President Franklin Roosevelt's appointment of Rexford Tugwell as the colonial governor of Puerto Rico in 1941 brought the New Deal to the Caribbean.[9] The Tugwell era is generally credited with institutional and administrative changes and, in Tugwell's eyes, laid the groundwork for public enterprises in lieu of private investment, which he thought would not be attracted to the island. The numerous public authorities formed in this period were later to provide the infrastructure needed for another style of development.[10] Through patronage, Tugwell also facilitated the consolidation of power in a new political party, which won its allegiance ironically from the peasantry and from rural workers, a peasantry whose destruction it was to oversee.

With the promise of bread, land, and liberty, the reformist Popular Democratic Party (*Partido Popular Democrático*) did break the power of the large sugar companies through the partial enforcement of a federal act prohibiting holdings in excess of five hundred acres in the colony.[11] The Land Law established an alternative to the large expatriate sugar combine, the "proportional profit farm," in an effort to maintain the efficiency of large-scale production. To modernize and democratize agriculture, the institutional paraphernalia of American farming—extension service, experimental farms, the land grant college—were strengthened. After all, Tugwell had been undersecretary of agriculture in the early New Deal days. This done, however, the *Populares* left agriculture to itself, and after Tugwell departed from the scene, the state-owned cement, bottle, and paper factories and a hotel were sold off, ridding the insular government of any association with "socialist" intervention.

The original Tugwell vision, perhaps once shared by the local populist reformers, linked industry to agriculture, giving the promise of survival to the rural work force. The agricultural program was also logical in terms of utilizing land, rainfall, and climate. The populist agricultural-industrial program drafted in 1950 by Harvey Perloff anticipated by twenty years the integrated rural development of the

Third World, and the technical program drafted by Nathan Koenig in 1953 showed in convincing detail how the farm base could be improved to achieve considerable agricultural self-sufficiency.[12] Both studies remained, however, scholarly ideological showpieces, historical scenarios of what might have been.

Puerto Rico, even in its land reform, led the Latin American nations. Luis Muñoz Marín ranked with the great populist reformers of the continent—Rómulo Betancourt of Venezuela and José "Don Pepe" Figuera of Costa Rica[13]—and his chief economic architect, Teodoro Moscoso, became John F. Kennedy's economic overseer for the Alliance for Progress. The Puerto Rico model was to be writ large for Latin America. Indeed, all this was still consistent with the vision that Tugwell had expressed early in his tenure as governor, namely, that the land question had to be solved if social peace was to be achieved and if America was to have firm allies in the Caribbean.[14]

The model of integrated agricultural development was abandoned in Puerto Rico with little fanfare and, with it, the rural work force. Why was agriculture written off? The execution of the program encountered ideological obstacles: heavy government participation in production—running factories and farms— was not viewed favorably in Washington in the cold war climate, or so the Populares believed. The newly elected Puerto Rican reformers held power vacated by the colonial governor, deriving their mandate from periodic mass elections and from the federal treasury. These leaders had to show something for their tenure; they were not particularly interested in becoming economic czars of state enterprises or the managers of public corporations facing strident unions. The indigenous style of management in retrospect seems to be that of a colonial patrón, who also mediates the exploitation process—in this case, between the labor force and foreign government and capital. The Tugwell model of state-owned factories was rejected in favor of a return to the familar colonial plantation model of the nineteenth and early twentieth centuries, in which the foreigner owns and operates the factory while the local elite oversees the workers and overlooks the foreigner. The true genius of Puerto Rico in the 1950s and 1960s was to extend this model from agriculture into industry in the face of all the conventional wisdoms of the times.

At least three major problems unfolded from industrialization. First, the programs did not employ enough people. Second, they did not employ the former farm workers and farmers. Third, there was no necessary connection between production in the new factories and the needs of the local people. The former farmers emigrated to the cities of the U.S. Northeast, where they might earn higher wages. And more outside capital emigrated into Puerto Rico prompted by the lure of tax-exempt profits and low wage costs. Both of these flows were to set up conditions for later remittances. The emigrants would send some of their earnings to Puerto Rico, and the corporations would remit their profits back to the United States. But the heavy outflow of profits, which has proved to be of such importance in the balance of payments of other Third World countries, is not a real factor

in the colonial trade of Puerto Rico, since the island's money supply is treated as an
appendage to the Federal Reserve system. Only the positive employment effects of
capital, not its profits, were the object of the Puerto Rican strategy.

In conclusion, the motivating force, which also set the limits for Puerto Rican
development, was, as Tugwell so clearly described it in his early years as governor, the concern for national security—or how to keep the island loyal to America.
Economic development meant providing a viable livelihood and avoiding the
instability that was afflicting the British islands with the collapse of the sugar
market. Economic development was to undermine the call of worker movements
for political independence and their search for an alternative economic model.

This strategy has proved successful. Material prosperity, coupled with repression and intimidation, have blunted the demand for independence. A decline in
living standards is threatened if the ties with the colonial power are severed.
Bergad suggests that the short-lived rebellion in Lares, which proclaimed the
Republic of Puerto Rico in 1868, was precipitated by the decline in fortunes of
the coffee elites in the mountains.[15] In 1942, Tugwell was more concerned with the
attraction that Pedro Albizu Campos' independence movement held for the unemployed sugar worker. In wartime, fascism was linked to nationalism and independence, which were treated as subversive; in the postwar period, communism is
periodically linked to nationalism and independence. The American approach to
colonial problems is to build the economy in order to undermine the opposition's
material program and, simultaneously, to utilize the apparatus of the state to
obstruct the opposition's political activities.[16] All during this process, the old
elites have retained their position in Puerto Rico. The political dynasties that
served the Spanish in the nineteenth century as *autonomists* or *annexationists*
(independence being underground) have survived to serve the Americans in the
twentieth century as commonwealthers or statehooders (independence still being
politely underground).[17]

Three points emerge from this historical summary. First, the industrialization of
the fifties was an extraordinary achievement, vis-à-vis the legacies of poverty,
boom and bust cycles, administrative mismanagement, corruption, and irrespon-
sibility so characteristic of the colonial period. The attempts in the Tugwell era to
recreate a viable economy formed the institutional basis for turning power over to
the colonial elites. The real economic achievement was to tie the island more
closely to the economic expansion of U.S. capital and to draw upon the "surplus"
labor from the mountains and fields, dissociating the labor force as well.

Second, the Puerto Rican economy had undergone a continual proletarianization, first with coffee and tobacco in the nineteenth century, next with sugarcane in
the early twentieth century, and then manufacturing since the 1950s. Puerto Rico
was never as complete a sugar island as Barbados or Cuba, for even at mid-
twentieth century, Puerto Rico retained a large reserve sector, which mixed wage
work and piece work when industry required it and which promoted home food
production in times of international collapse or war.

Third, the importance of each crop in the economic base must be analyzed separately in the formation of social classes and their interests and actions. The character of the coffee culture in the mountains was quite different from the sugarcane culture on the coast. The subsequent rise of the independence movement impressed upon Tugwell and his local allies the urgency of remaking the economic base to undermine political opposition, a uniquely colonial American approach to discontent and envy in the Third World, an approach that also plays upon the humanitarian drives and doubts aroused in the exercise of imperial power. This has led to the formation of an economy whose material base is insufficient and where the needs of local consumption meet with no corresponding production, a somewhat embarrassing finale for thirty years of uninterrupted economic growth.

Historical Dissociation over Time and Space

The historical development of an economy is often viewed in terms of its place in the international division of labor: Puerto Rico produces coffee; the United States produces wheat. Country A provides labor; country B provides capital.

These functional roles may be clearer if we consider for a moment the process by which one commodity becomes another. Bread and beer are sold to workers and farmers, who in turn produce more bread and beer. Bread sold in San Juan may be made from wheat from Nebraska and sugar from the Philippines; beer drunk in San Juan is brewed in Milwaukee and sold in cans made from Jamaican bauxite. This is the production of commodities by means of commodities, in which humans are the medium and profit is the motivating force.[18] Economic development is merely the dispersion of these chains of commodity conversions all over the world, into every nook and cranny of social existence, conversions seeking opportunities for profit derived from cheaper labor or materials, tax exemptions, transport advantages, or any other element that enters into the circuit. What appears as the disconnectedness of an island economy is actually the increased interconnectedness with the outside economy. Only when those connections fail, as occurs periodically, does the geographical unit appear in its dismembered, orphaned status.

An alternative view of the economy takes people as the starting point and commodities as the intermediaries, an age-old story of the reproduction of people by means of people. Here, brewers and bakers produce beer and bread, which in turn sustain brewers and bakers (see figure 15.1). The goal is to provide for the needs of human beings. Just as in the cycle of commodities–people–commodities, this cycle of people–commodities–people spreads across geographical boundaries. However, it may be the labor force itself that becomes dispersed or dissociated, one sister working in the Consolidated Cigar factory in Cayey and one brother as a migrant in Consolidated Cigar's tobacco fields of the Connecticut Valley. Or the same person may work in different places in different seasons of the year or in different seasons of his or her life.

The point is simply that only with the exchange of labor for a wage and the exchange of that wage for a desired object can profit possibly be realized and

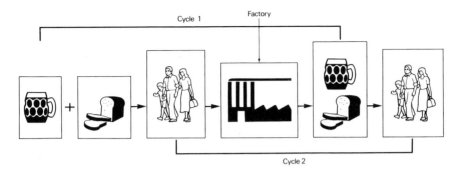

FIGURE 15.1
Two Views of the Material Force-Flows: Cycle 1—Production of Commodities by
Means of Commodities; Cycle 2—Reproduction of People by Means of People

carried off to other sectors or lands. In the closed, self-sufficient peasant economy, in which a family grows 60 percent of its own food, builds 80 percent of its own house from local materials, and cooks with charcoal made from its own forest, there is simply less opportunity for the merchant trader or manufacturer to get into the chain of events and, correspondingly, less need for the peasant to exchange his time for cash. Modern economic development, especially in the interior of Puerto Rico, has meant the replacement of all the simpler exchange relations by cash relations and the immediate integration into the world cash network. A failure in any part of that network—say, of the world sugar market—brings on a crisis in the local economy. Economic development has meant the geographical dispersion of the pieces of the circuitry: a labor force spread out from Maine to the Tropic of Cancer and commodity specialization tying Humacao to Hong Kong. The latest attempt in the Puerto Rican chronology to fix the broken chain is to offer food stamp grants.[19]

In summary, the dispersion or dissociation of the economy has resulted in a three dimensional disarray. First, the home labor force is spread over space outside the island (the Puerto Rican diaspora). Second, the production of things to satisfy human needs is spread over the globe (the international market). Third, the circuitry has become partial and incomplete (specialization and the international division of labor). Periodically, politicians mistake the island's high degree of interdependence for integration with the United States. The economic crises jolt the small unit out of its fantasized security and into recognizing itself as a dissociated economy, still in search of a viable political economy.

Counterhistory

Sometimes the statistical tools of modern economics shed light on the historical questions raised here. The quantification of parts of the detailed microcircuits noted in earlier chapters may be of use in refining the analysis of the broad cycles

PHOTOGRAPH 15.1
Looking into the industrial zone of the Cayey Valley. In the background, the tall smokestack marks the Consolidated Cigar Corporation, one of the world's largest cigar factories, which processes imported tobacco from North and South America.

PHOTOGRAPH 15.2
A nutmeg-sorting center in Grenada.

and their dispersion during the recent decade. The technical economist asks, "Which particular circuit failed? By how much? What would have happened if . . . ?" Such counterhistorical fantasies have no realistic answers, for history, unlike tossing coins, is not statistically repetitive. Nevertheless, we shall venture to ask such questions by returning for a moment to the accounting model and examining critically each major segment of the Puerto Rican economy in historical perspective, another exercise of a might-have-been scenario.

In the economic model developed in chapters 3 through 5, three black boxes are linked. One box contains the circuitry of final demand. The second contains the circuits of technology (input-output), and the third, the circuits of employment and income distribution. Each black box was calibrated for each of two different years. The earlier year, 1953, corresponds to the beginning of the industrialization process, and the later year, 1963, corresponds to its midpoint. I shall substitute each of the boxes as measured in the later year into the model for the earlier year and note by how much the employment and income distribution would have changed had only that particular element been modernized. By successively transplanting the later for the earlier box, we measure the relative impact on the whole economy of modernizing that particular organ. This is, in a sense, a crude empirical way of uncovering the true functions of the dismembered organs.

The three boxes and their successive replacements are sketched in figure 15.2. The box of final demand includes consumption, investment, government, and exports. The box of input-output corresponds to technology. And the employment box incorporates the work rules and occupational needs of each industry. By substituting the 1963 boxes for 1953 boxes, we can ask, What would have happened if demand had not grown but new technology and new work rules had been introduced anyway? This is the case of the stagnant modernizer. When we put the actual 1953 final demand box with the 1963 input-output and employment boxes, only 412 thousand people would have been employed, and the distribution of income would have been less equal, as indicated by the Gini coefficient of .480. This is the full measure of the potential disaster faced by an economy that modernizes but fails to grow.

However, if the economy could have maintained its old technology and old work rules to meet the new demands of 1963, then a total of 1,064 thousand workers would have been needed. This is called the expanding frozen-plantation economy and represents the mirage-like modern economy to those at the beginning of the process. They see only the success of thing production at the top of the mountain but not the changes they will go through to get there.

If input-output alone had changed but not the labor rules (due, say, to a strong union or labor tradition), then the expanding closed-shop economy indicates that only 856 thousand workers would have been needed. This is still more than the 1953 actual economy, and the distribution of income would have been much more equal (.363). With both technology and work rules modernized, (the actual 1963 economy), 606 thousand workers were employed and income was less equally distributed than the 1953 starting point (.471).

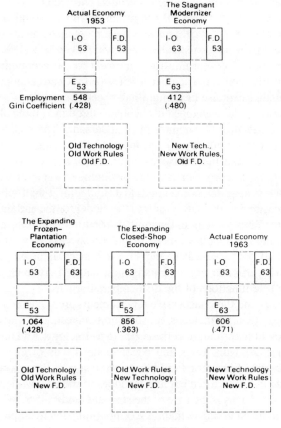

FIGURE 15.2
Counterhistorical Retrospectives, 1953 and 1963. I-O indicates the input-output
technology and 53 and 63 indicate the relevant year; FD indicates the level of
final demand; E indicates the employment structure of work rules.

We learn from this exercise, first, that final demand alone is a powerful loco-
motive, either moving forward toward greater employment or backward toward
stagnation. Second, modernizing technology or work relations brings about a
diminution of the number of jobs required relative to those expected from an
expanded, traditional economy.

There is no partial solution to this problem. Therefore, there is no partial cause
for its failure. The changing employment or income distribution cannot in reality
be broken down, as I have done, saying "this much was caused by technology and
this much by new work relations." An economy to produce automobiles for local
consumption or new levels of sugarcane for export must take the new technologies

and the new occupational configurations required by those industries. An auto assembly line is built precisely by utilizing the newer technology, which is by its very design labor saving. The sugar plantations are able to expand only by introducing modern mills and field machinery, not in replicating antiquated techniques. The pieces we have examined individually come as a unit; they are part of the same package. The paradigm of the accounting framework can be taken apart in its segments, but is there no other way of putting it back together again?

CHAPTER 16

Crops versus Coupons: Puerto Rican Agriculture, Record of the Descent

ONE IMPORTANT piece has eluded the analyst of the Puerto Rican puzzle: what has become of agriculture? How could such an important sector of economic life disappear so completely so quickly? Today, the island looks like an uncultivated garden. How did it become this way?

We have noted that the economic path that Puerto Rico has followed associates agrarian life with traditional, or "backward," societies. The key to growth, it was thought, was to transform the rural, backward peasantry into a modern, urban proletariat. The presumption was, of course, that agriculture must decline and its workers must be retrained to find employment elsewhere. Food could be imported and manufactured goods exported. Puerto Rico, it was thought, would thus become a well-ordered society of factory workers, a little England, a New World Belgium.[1]

The reality has proved quite the contrary. Puerto Rico could not, in thirty years, attract and hold sufficient industry solely on the basis of granting exemption from U.S. income taxes. Agriculture did not simply pass away; its workers did not melt into the cities. Agriculture was destroyed by a series of painful policies unfavorable to its existence, and the jobs created in industry were but a fraction of those being destroyed in agriculture. This imbalance between job creation and job destruction lies at the root of the continuing massive unemployment.

There are two important considerations to be kept in mind at the outset. First, the decline of Puerto Rican agriculture was part of the same process that built Puerto Rican industry, although the relationship between the two is not so clearly understood. The introduction of the food stamp program into Puerto Rico hastened agriculture's final demise. Second, and somewhat contradictory, is that agriculture and rural life in Puerto Rico may not have irrevocably vanished.

The conventional view is that Puerto Rico is a highly urbanized society, with San Juan as the center surrounded by scenic but depopulated mountains. The truth is quite otherwise. The 1980 census indicates that 42.6 percent of the population still live in rural zones despite the decline of agriculture and the apparent absence of economic activity.[2]

Land Abandonment

Between 1950 and 1974, the number of farms in Puerto Rico declined from over 53 thousand to less than 30 thousand (table 16.1). The total area farmed fell from 1.8 to 1.3 million *cuerdas,* and the size of the average farm increased from 35 to 43 *cuerdas.* (A *cuerda* is .9712 of an acre.) Cultivated farmland, as opposed to grazing, forest, and fallow lands, also declined. The number of farms that cultivated crops fell drastically between 1959 and 1974, the cultivated area fell from 724 to 353 thousand *cuerdas,* and the average size of the cultivated plot declined from 17 to 15 *cuerdas.* The typical farm that emerges from this aggregate data is one of increasing size but with a reduced area under cultivation.

The decline in the relative importance of farming on the island is highlighted in the comparison of total land use in Puerto Rico. In 1950, 82 percent of the entire island was covered with farms; by 1974, this fell to 56 percent. Of this declining farmland, a further reduced share was cultivated. In 1959, when three-quarters of Puerto Rico's surface consisted of farms, nearly half of that farmland was cultivated. By 1974, when farms covered a little over half the island, only a quarter of it was cultivated. In short, one-third of the total land area of Puerto Rico was cultivated in 1959 (the first year for which these data were available), and this fell to one-sixth of the total land area by 1974. Indeed, the rural landscape of Puerto Rico was changing quickly, as farmland, and cropland in particular, was being abandoned.

From 1974 to 1978, certain general trends continued at an accelerated pace once food stamps were introduced. Land held in farms fell 14 percent, compared to the 6 percent decline that characterized the preceding five year period. Cultivated cropland fell 20 percent, compared to the 3 percent decline between the previous censuses. By 1978, 48 percent of all Puerto Rico remained in farms, and of that farmland, only slightly more than a quarter was cultivated. By 1978, in short, only 13 percent of all Puerto Rican land remained in cultivation. The general downward trend in all farm area and cultivated cropland is indicated in figure 16.1. Both curves fall most dramatically from 1964 to 1969 and again from 1974 to 1978. Part of the land abandonment is reflected in the erratic behavior of the value of farm crops. Value of crops rose from $83 million to $153 million from 1969 to 1974 and then declined to $95 million in 1978.

The aggregate figures on farm units for Puerto Rico indicate a trend toward fewer and bigger farms until 1974, but this trend was reversed by 1978. Were the large farms getting larger while the small farms became more numerous?

The Rise of the Minifarm

Data on the size distribution of farms suggest a complicated spectrum of farms and their changes. First, we note a dramatic increase in the number of farms of less than three *cuerdas.* In 1974, these minifarms averaged one and a half *cuerdas,*

TABLE 16.1
Farm Characteristics of Puerto Rico, Selected Years, 1940–78

Characteristic	1940	1950	1959	1964	1969	1974	1978
All farms							
Number	—	53,515	45,792	44,859	32,687	29,650	31,837
Area (thousand cuerdas)[a]	—	1,845	1,683	1,641	1,355	1,260	1,084
Average size (cuerdas)	—	34.5	36.7	36.6	40.8	42.5	34.1
Cultivated farms							
Number	—	—	42,666	39,238	25,662	23,000	26,726
Area (thousand cuerdas)[a]	—	—	724.2	585.4	362.6	352.7	283.9
Average size (cuerdas)	—	—	17.0	14.9	14.1	15.3	10.6
Farmland (% of all land)[b]	—	81.8	74.6	72.8	59.2	55.9	48.1
Cultivated land (% of farmland)	—	—	43.0	35.7	26.8	28.0	26.2
Cultivated land (% of all land)	—	—	32.1	26.0	16.1	15.6	12.6
Value of crops ($ million)	—	—	—	14.1	83.1	153.3	95.4
Minifarms (less than 3 cuerdas)							
Average size (cuerdas)	1.8	—	—	—	1.4	1.5	1.2
Number (% of total)	2.2	c	c	c	8.9	9.4	20.3
Land (% of total)	0.1	c	c	c	0.3	0.3	0.7
Small farms (3–9 cuerdas)							
Average size (cuerdas)	5.1	5.1	5.0	5.1	5.1	5.3	5.2
Number (% of total)	50.7	52.3[d]	50.2[d]	50.5[d]	43.8	38.9	36.9
Land (% of total)	7.6	7.8[d]	6.9[d]	7.1[d]	5.5	4.9	5.7
Medium farms (10–49 cuerdas)							
Average size (cuerdas)	20.7	21.2	20.9	20.8	20.7	21.2	20.6
Number (% of total)	35.7	35.9	38.1	38.2	35.5	38.4	31.8
Land (% of total)	21.7	22.1	21.6	21.8	17.9	19.1	19.3
Large farms (50 or more cuerdas)							
Average size (cuerdas)	211.6	205.2	223.5	231.3	265.9	240.9	231.7
Number (% of total)	11.4	11.8	11.7	11.3	11.6	13.3	11.0
Land (% of total)	70.6	70.1	71.6	71.1	76.2	75.7	74.3

Sources: U.S. Census Bureau, Census of Agriculture, 1964; 1974; 1978: vol. 1, Statistics for Puerto Rico and Municipios.
[a]A cuerda is .9712 acre. [b]Total land area is about 2,255 thousand cuerdas. [c]Included in small farms. [d]Includes minifarms.

130

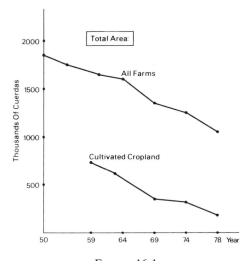

FIGURE 16.1
Farm Area and Cultivated
Cropland, 1950–78

accounted for 9 percent of the farms, and occupied 0.3 percent of all farmland. By 1978, their average size had fallen, their number had increased, and they accounted for 0.7 percent of all farmland. These data record the formation of a new class of farm, the nonfarming rural home, producing virtually nothing! The point here is two-fold. First, the growth of the minifarm is a postwar phenomena, as the census notes that this size of farm accounted for only 2.2 percent of all farms and occupied 0.1 percent of farmland in 1940. Second, the formation of minifarms became greatly accelerated between 1974 and 1978.

The small farm (about 5 *cuerdas*) accounted for half of all farms in 1940 and occupied 8 percent of the land. By 1978, the prevalence of the small farm declined to a third of all farms and occupied 6 percent of the land. The medium farm (21 *cuerdas*) until 1974 accounted for over a third of the farms and occupied about 20 percent of the land. By 1978, their share fell to less than a third of the farms and occupied less land.

The large farms grew in size from an average of 205 *cuerdas* in 1950 to 266 *cuerdas* in 1969 and then declined to 232 *cuerdas* by 1978. Throughout the entire period, the share of these giants remained relatively constant. Only in the last data year in the table, 1978, did the share of these large farms dip slightly, accounting for 11 percent of the farms, but still occupying nearly three-quarters of the land.

At whose expense, then, has the minifarm been formed? Were they cut from the large, medium, or small farm? The census data give no clues as to the process of consolidation and fragmentation. The increase in the land of the minifarm (0.4 percent of the farmland between 1974 and 1978) could have been drawn from any of the other size categories. The distributions reveal a relatively stable picture of landholdings during the forty years, with the exception of the rise of the minifarm and reduction in the number of the small farms. The medium and large farms maintained the same hold on Puerto Rico's farmland, accounting for 47 percent of the farms and 92 percent of the land in 1940 and 43 percent of the farms and 94 percent of the land in 1978.

The reduced number of total farms between 1950 and 1974 was the result of the destruction of the small farmer and farm laborer, who emigrated to the cities or to the United States. In the 1974–78 period, the minifarms (cut from the large plantation and from a sequential rearrangement of the existing farms) house the remnant of the agricultural population, whose continued rural survival is made possible only through the food stamp subsidy.

The Decline of Agricultural Production

The discussion of agriculture has thus far focused on the sources—farms and farmland—devoted to production. But is it not possible that improved technology has permitted increased production on less land? As we turn to the record of the actual performance of the crops and harvests of Puerto Rican agriculture, it must be remembered that the arrangements that characterize this sector are not strictly comparable to the arrangements between the worker and employer in other industries.[3] Only in one part of agriculture are workers paid a wage. On the small family farm, the workers, called *jíbaros,* raise their own crop, and only after the harvest is completed and the product successfully marketed can the farmers realize how much their labor was worth. On other family farms, homegrown food supplements the cash earned from work on the larger farm or plantation and enables the family to eat during the seasons when no wage work is available.

Subsistence farming is certainly a misnomer for either the arrangement in which farmers sell their product in the market or consume it themselves. The farm that produces for itself may be called more appropriately self-sufficiency farming, similar to the traditional family farm in the United States, and the farm that also sells on the market may be termed supplemental farming. Both farms provide workers some measure of independence from the national and world markets, insulating and protecting them from changes in the fortunes of the giant growers.

These farms are the remnant of a noncapitalist agricultural economy, which was reduced and appended to the expanding capitalist sector in response to that sector's need for cheap seasonal labor. The abandoned farms produced the labor to convert the coastal grazing lands into profitable sugar plantations. When the capitalist sector collapsed during economic crisis or war, the small family farm sector expanded to reabsorb the workers. As modern industry displaced sugar as the chief wage-provider, the noncapitalist sector was never effectively destroyed. In short, the widespread distribution of small family holdings, the year-long growing season, and the wide swings of the capitalist sector first in plantation agriculture and then in manufacturing, contributed to the survival of these family self-sufficiency arrangements.

Crops and Farm Types

As both capitalist and noncapitalist farming are carried on side by side, and even on the same farm, specific crops may prove a helpful surrogate for identifying the different arrangements. Sugarcane, for example, being the classic plantation cash crop, is grown on large corporate units, requiring large quantities of specialized labor, especially during harvest season. But cane has also been grown by *colono* farmers on their own land, carted to the company mill, and sold according to sugar content and weight.[4] Cane farms thus range from the classic thousand-acre giants on the coastal lands to small plots, the average farm covering but thirty *cuerdas* in 1949 and seventy-four *cuerdas* in 1978.

Coffee and tobacco, the two other principal cash crops, are grown on much smaller farms. Coffee culture, widespread in the western mountains, is grown on an average eight-*cuerda* plot, while tobacco is traditionally raised in the eastern hills on an average two-*cuerda* plot.[5] While both coffee and tobacco require seasonal labor, that is, labor hired at a piece rate or an hourly wage, ownership of these farms generally is held by a farm family rather than an absentee corporation. It is in the marketing and processing stages that the large commercial houses, exporters, and manufacturer's agents enter, as buyers and monopolizers of the small farmers' produce.

While the rough geographic specialization of coffee in the west, tobacco in the east, and cane on the coast has always been associated with the three major cash crops, the cultivation of tropical food crops for home consumption, exchange, or local cash sale has spread throughout the island. These traditional foods—fruits, vegetables, and roots—have until recently supplied the basic food needs of the rural family. On the coast, where the lands were devoured by the plantation, foods were not cultivated, and imported foods were the staples. At first these were dried codfish, beans, and polished rice. More recently, temperate-climate foods, such as wheat, dairy products, and grain-fattened meats, have displaced these.[6]

The point is that cash crops and indigenous food crops once enabled the rural family to survive. Cash crops allowed the farm family to purchase necessities other than food; a decline in the cash crop, a fall in the rural wage, or a disruption of shipping or harvest could be weathered by increased reliance on homegrown foods. The cash sector has been affected in recent years by the closing of the cane plantation and by the decline in prices for cash crops, tobacco for example. The homegrown sector has been affected by the "voluntary" absence of the farmer migrating to the United States and also by the rising price of purchased materials, such as fertilizer and sprays.

The Empirical Record

The division of Puerto Rican agriculture into two segments, the three main cash crops and the minor food crops (*frutas menores*), is one rough way of distinguishing the market, or purely capitalist sector, from the noncapitalist, or self-sufficiency, sector. In table 16.2, we can examine the historical record of the number, land, and harvests of both the major and minor crops.

The decline in the number of sugar and tobacco farms from 1949 to 1978 indicates the almost total dismantling of the coastal plantations and the tobacco fields in the eastern mountains. The number of coffee farms has also declined drastically. The land harvested in cane fell by less than the fall in number of farms, indicating the conglomeration of sugar lands into larger and larger units. However, land planted in coffee was cut in half, while barely two thousand *cuerdas* remain in tobacco cultivation. About two million tons of cane and two million pounds of tobacco were harvested in 1978, mere fractions of their former levels. The coffee harvest, by contrast, has been sustained due to the introduction of new varieties and techniques of cultivation, although with wide fluctuations.

The minor crops—fruits, vegetables, and roots—declined from 1949 to 1969 in number of farms, but then began to rise. The land dedicated to the cultivation of these food crops also declined from 1949 to 1969 and then, for most of them, began to recover. From 1974 to 1978, the land dedicated to some of these crops (taniers, corn, and dasheen) declined or remained stable, while land planted in the others increased.

The harvest of these food crops, especially in the most recent years, presents a totally different picture. The highly variable banana harvest fell 78 percent between 1974 and 1978, coconuts 68 percent, oranges and taniers 57 percent, plantains 54 percent, dasheen 38 percent, cassava 31 percent, corn 21 percent, and sweet potato 16 percent. Increases are recorded in the harvest of only two food crops: pidgeon peas 61 percent and yams 5 percent.

We are here viewing three trends. First is the unqualified, quarter-century decline of the three major cash crops—sugarcane, coffee, and tobacco (figure 16.2). Second is the decline for these minor food crops in number of farms, area under cultivation, and quantity of harvest from 1949 to 1974 (figure 16.3). Third is the marked increase between 1974 and 1978 in the number of farms producing minor crops (table 16.2) together with the drastic decline in the harvests recorded in 1978 (table 16.2 and figure 16.3).

What lies at the root of this long-term decline of agriculture? How can we explain the contradictory observation of the last census, that is, the increase in number of farms and the dramatic decline in the quantity of the harvested crops?

The reasons for the general decline in agriculture during the past decades are both complicated and simple. The complicated reasons lie in the analysis of a whole series of programs, experiments, subsidies, "improvements," speculations, and reforms that have affected agriculture.[7] Much of the criticism leveled at

TABLE 16.2
Farms, Land, and Harvests of Puerto Rico, Selected Years, 1949–78

Characteristic and Year	Major Crops							Minor Crops						
	Sugar Cane[a] Caña	Coffee[b] Café	Tobacco[c] Tabaco	Banana[d] Guineo	Orange[e] China	Plantain[d] Plátano	Coconut[e] Coco	Tanier[b] Yautía	Pidgeon Pea[b] Gandule	Yam[b] Ñame	Sweet Potato[b] Batata	Dasheen[b] Malanga	Corn[b] Maíz	Cassava[b] Yuca
Number of farms (thousands)														
1949	11.2	24.7	14.9	31.8	23.9	16.8	16.5	21.0	23.7	12.5	25.6	12.5	24.3	8.1
1959	9.8	23.0	8.3	22.4	18.9	13.8	9.2	11.0	10.5	6.5	9.0	5.4	8.4	2.3
1964	7.3	21.6	7.9	20.4	25.8	11.9	12.3	8.5	8.5	4.5	5.8	3.8	3.4	2.0
1969	3.7	14.1	12.1	6.4	3.1	6.3	—	5.8	3.9	3.1	2.5	—	—	—
1974	1.9	12.9	0.9	10.5	7.8	7.8	—	5.5	4.3	2.7	2.4	2.0	2.2	1.7
1978	1.4	11.1	0.6	17.2	14.7	13.8	8.1	6.0	5.4	4.1	2.9	2.7	2.5	2.4
Land cultivated (thousand cuerdas)														
1949	344	176	27	44.2	—	15.1	—	14.7	20.4	6.1	23.8	7.8	39.5	3.7
1959	320	183	17	34.4	—	15.9	—	8.7	11.6	4.3	8.0	3.5	16.1	1.3
1964	276	178	19	28.5	24.5	13.5	7.1	9.0	10.0	3.4	5.3	2.2	5.2	0.9
1969	180	125	4	14.1	16.2	8.3	—	5.2	6.2	2.2	3.0	—	—	—
1974	128	115	2	32.3	16.7	13.3	—	5.6	7.9	2.2	2.0	1.6	2.9	1.1
1978	105	83	2	—	—	—	—	4.2	8.5	2.8	2.2	1.6	2.5	1.3
Amount harvested														
1949	10,699	257	22.3	—	1,789	100	255	241	69	324	325	163	231	48
1959	10,155	290	19.4	—	1,594	—	234	188	76	159	160	97	128	24
1964	9,418	332	22.7	1,037	2,187	184	122	257	87	139	129	66	44	22
1969	5,894	175	4.8	332	1,338	95	68	138	40	85	48	—	—	—
1974	3,858	231	3.5	1,039	1,117	165	47	168	57	93	56	58	24	36
1978	2,297	183	2.3	229	481	76	15	73	92	98	47	36	19	25

Sources: See table 16.1. [a]Harvest measured in thousand tons. [b]Harvest measured in million pounds. [c]Harvest measured in thousand hundredweight. [d]Harvest measured in hundred thousands. [e]Harvest measured in millions.

135

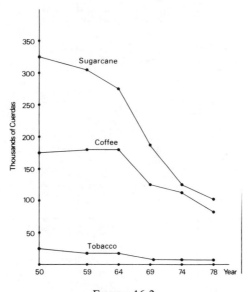

FIGURE 16.2
Three Major Crops, Area Cultivated

the agricultural sector by Nathan Koenig in 1953 is still valid today, but remedial programs on a massive scale have never been adopted or even considered.[8]

The decline of Puerto Rican agriculture is, on the one hand, simple to understand: apart from occasional rhetoric, the commonwealth was never committed to sustaining or modernizing the farm sector. Its land policy, which in the early 1940s had promised to enforce the five-hundred-acre limitation and break up the large, absentee plantations, had become anachronistic by the late 1950s. It is somewhat ironic that policies enacted or neglected by the political party, whose slogan was "bread, land, and liberty," resulted in massive land abandonment and the destruction of agriculture.

The particulars of the decline in farming can be traced to a litany of causes: rising cost of labor, low farm price of product, absence of mechanization, the backwardness of the farmer, monopoly by buyers, absence of quality control, poor marketing, and ineffective land reform, to mention a few. There are, of course, programs to "resolve" these obstacles. The decline in farming in the United States is replete with programs that ended up favoring large commercial enterprises at the expense of the family farm.[9] The decline of farming in the Third World is also replete with programs and reforms that attempted to solve the land problem, provide the benefits of the green revolution, and arrest the outflow of peasants to the cities.[10] A Puerto Rico dominated by a truly farmer-oriented regime might have persevered in those policies that would result in higher productivity. Mecha-

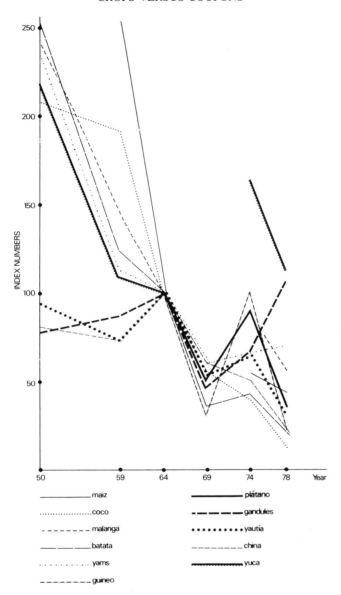

FIGURE 16.3
Minor Crops, 1950–78 (1964 = 100)

nization in cane could have been promoted.[11] The policies to promote small machines and labor intensive agriculture could have aided the small, mountain food grower. Modern science applied to agriculture and spread by extension services to the small farmers could have improved the crops and practices of the food grower.

But there is no point in subjecting the reader to this type of retrospective. The glaring historical fact remains that it was the dismantling of the plantation sector and, with it, the small-farm food grower that led to the great exodus of the Puerto Rican people in the fifties and sixties, to the continuing high rates of unemployment in the seventies, and currently to the dependence on federal subsidies. Nor does Puerto Rico's current political status provide the explanation for its destitute agriculture. The Caribbean is replete with island nations that have neglected local agriculture and relied on imported foods.

Agricultural demise continues in Puerto Rico despite the size of the rural population. The number of farms increased between 1974 and 1978, while the number of hired farm workers fell (table 16.3). The number of farms participating in government programs fell, and the number of farms whose principal income originated outside farming rose. By 1978, two-thirds of all farms received less than a quarter of their income from farming, while three-quarters received half or less from farming. We must conclude that little farming is done on farms, and fewer and fewer farms derive any notable income from their land.

In short, farming had by 1978 become a sideline, a minor field of endeavor, a residential category. Even the livestock industry, whose sales rose by 36 percent from 1974 to 1978, involves little farming. The increase in purchased inputs, such

TABLE 16.3
Farm Characteristics of Puerto Rico, 1974 and 1978

Characteristic	1974	1978	Percent change 1974–78
Number of farms	29,650	31,837	7.4
Number of hired farm workers	81,112	65,029	−19.8
Farms participating in government programs	6,733	4,641	−31.1
Farms with nonfarm income as principal source			
Number	17,528	22,375	27.7
Percent	60.2	71.3	11.1
Percent of farms with less than 25% of income from farming	50	65	30
Percent of farms with 50% or less income from farming	68	77	16
Value of sales from livestock ($ million)	137.6	186.7	35.7
Purchased inputs ($ million)	76.2	119.2	56.5
Net value created ($ million)	61.4	67.5	9.9

Sources: U.S. Census Bureau, *Census of Agriculture 1974; 1978.*

as imported feed grains, chemicals, and breeder stock accounted for much of the increased output. The net value created rose by only 10 percent and did not absorb the labor power released by the abandonment of the food and cash crops. Today, cattle graze where corn and beans, coffee and cane were cultivated ten years ago.

How is it that a continued decline in farming and the lack of employment opportunity have not stimulated a vast migration out of the countryside, as they had in the earlier decades? The answer, of course, is that the failure of export cash crops and of local food production has been replaced by food stamps and welfare payments, which have allowed the people to stay on the land. Needed cash is raised by occasional emigration, black marketeering, the drug trade, and the subdivision of family farms. The last mentioned has given rise to the increase in minifarms in the 1978 census. Imported food has displaced local foods and the supermarket has replaced the local market and informal exchange among families.

The dependency of the island is now complete. Industrialization strategy has cut both ways: backward into the land, where food production has been virtually eradicated; and forward out from the land, from whence the people and industrial products are sent in exchange for federal money and raw materials. Thirty years of antiagrarian policy have ruined the countryside; food stamps are merely the coup de grace. Seasonal workers, the residual of a rural labor force, with food stamps, demand higher wages for their casual labor—or let the harvest rot on the trees or in the earth. *Their* food can be purchased with coupons in the local supermarket.

Food stamps, by guaranteeing a minimum standard of living, have the effect of raising the price of local labor to the grower. Monopoly of the other inputs needed for agriculture—implements, fertilizer, chemicals, and feed grains—together with poor marketing, transportation, and excessive waste, also contribute to the high production cost of Puerto Rican agriculture. Expensive, locally produced foods must then compete with imported foods, themselves highly subsidized exports of the most advanced marketing and agribusiness technique in the world. Local foods come face to face in the market with imported eggs and poultry, meat and temperate-climate fruits, grains, and white potatoes. Even tropical staples not produced in the United States, such as plantains, bananas, and root crops, are brought in cheaper from the low-wage islands in the Caribbean and from corporate plantations in Central America.

What keeps the local Puerto Rican farmer from benefitting from the high supermarket price for vegetables like tomatoes, eggplant, green peppers, and corn that he too can produce? The price charged the consumer in the supermarket is separated from the price the farmer is paid by a series of markups and intermediaries. Moreover, the supermarket as capitalist enterprise earns profits only when large masses of tidy, prepackaged, and processed foods pass through its checkout counters. The profitable enterprise cuts its costs by importing large quantities of standardized produce—onions, potatoes, rice, fruits—readily accessible from the U.S. supplier. The supermarket operation, at least as it is presently carried out by the Grand Union and Pueblo chains, is not an agency for the selection, sorting, grading, and promotion of indigenous foods. It is not a marketing board for the local farmer.

The irony, of course, is that it is American agriculture, which hires the Puerto Rican migrant to pick and package tomatoes in New Jersey, that has driven Puerto Rico's tomato farms out of business. It is American agriculture, which hires the Puerto Rican migrant to harvest oranges in Florida, that has driven local *chinas* from the shelves to the street corners of San Juan.

To summarize, food stamp payments have raised the effective cash wage of labor. They have put the demand for food on a cash basis and have allowed international suppliers to capture this cash demand. This cash welfare program has completed the task of the American occupation of Puerto Rico: to weed out even the most remote of the *jíbaros* (mountain farmers), sever their connection with the land, and substitute instead cash relations. All this has worked to the benefit of the local Puerto Rican business interests and their American suppliers, the banks and transporters, importers and dockworkers, and to the detriment of the Puerto Rican farmers, who have lost their livelihood. The American taxpayer pays for the entire transaction.

V

The Future

CHAPTER 17

Conclusion: Toward a New Political Economy

Summary of the Puerto Rican Model

THE ECONOMIC model of Puerto Rico, described in the opening chapters of this book and calibrated with data from the 1950s through 1970, proved to be an exceptionally accurate forecaster of the economic situation in 1980. The model's predictions for the key variables of employment and income distribution, calculated a full ten years earlier, missed their mark by less than 1 percent. Even the predictions of income and consumption proved to be relatively accurate for the decade.

The near-perfect success of these predictions should give the reader some confidence that the innovative features of this model may be of some importance in analyzing an open, dependent economy. The model is simply an augmented input-output system based on very traditional techniques used in interindustry analysis. The innovation here, however, was to extend the model to include details of the size distributions of income generated to families by each sector and also to extend the consumption accounts to include the particular purchases by income classes. External investment, government transfers, and foreign demand for its exports, then, determine the general growth of Puerto Rico, but the workings of the internal economy determine how and how much of this external final demand is retained and how much leaks out again via imports. A particular advantage of the input-output techniques employed here is that we can observe the direct and indirect flows at each point through all the detailed circuits—the consumption of different social classes, the roundaboutness of the production technology with all its indirect requirements, and the generation of incomes to the full range of families, rich and poor.

The second innovation was the portrayal of various classic scenarios of alternative growth paths. When the results of an import substitution strategy were compared to an export promotion strategy, it became obvious that the economy first had to be closed before the benefits of expanding exports could be fully realized. These intricate calculations demonstrated the difficulties that a small, open economy encounters when it seeks to expand exports without first restricting its own imports. Such an economy finds itself on a perpetual treadmill. The constant danger of losing its export industry to other regions implies that these promoted enclaves, in the absence of import substitution, do not connect fully with other branches of the economy. Elsewhere, I have also shown that these enclaves have, in fact, reached out and created linkages with many other sectors even in the absence of special tariff protection.[1] But the pure form of the model demonstrates the full need for hastening and encouraging the process of selective import substitution.

The workings of the model also demonstrated a peculiar contradiction between growth and equity in formulating different scenarios: faster growth resulted from more intensive production of basic wage goods, while greater employment was generated by the production of goods typically consumed by the upper classes. These findings might be interpreted in two ways. First, a society that seeks to redistribute income and replicate a bundle of "superior" goods and services for the masses should expect to encounter handicaps in the growth process due to the direct and indirect effects of technology and employment. Second, an unequal society, in which the upper classes already command such purchasing power, carries with it a strong employment stabilizer due to the labor intensity implicit in producing and delivering the services they require. The initial movements away from such inequality, then, may create hardship not only for those whose income is being redistributed, but also for those whose livelihoods depend on the demands of the affected classes. Thus, by analyzing production, income distribution, and consumption, all connected to each other, the model has been able to play through the effects on each segment of the population and industry. This model differs from conventional models, which begin first with capital formation, population, natural resources, and the like, or are based on more complicated time-series relationships between variables, which may not be in the proper control of a small, dependent economy.

The major shortcoming of the model presented here is that, for all its predictive power, it does not tell us what to do. The obvious solution, for any developing country attached to an industrial nation, will be achieved with a universal, stable, and equitable world economy—or at least Western economy. Having been stripped of its insular character and opened into the United States and hence the world market in so many ways, the Puerto Rican economy could be stabilized only, it may be thought, if the U.S. economy itself were stabilized. But the U.S. economy cannot be purged of its cyclical nature, and the booms and recessions built into the West play havoc with Puerto Rico's fragile dependent shell.[2]

Restoring Consumption to the Economy

Putting consumption back into economic planning explicitly and dealing in a forthright manner with the needs of different social classes can lead to a reassociation and a reintegration of the local economy. This too is counter to all historical trends, for currently consumption is the sole domain of marketing agencies, for whom anything sold is a "good," simply because it means markup, turnover, and profit. Putting consumption knowledge back into the picture is not a reactionary solution. It is not a return to the plantation or to backward living, malnutrition and hunger, isolation and illiteracy, which is the way advocates of high consumption picture any other than the current state of affairs. Rather, it is present consumption, with its addiction to overeating and television, that creates functional illiterates. Consumption knowledge means simply better management of consumer needs, simplifying them, and satisfying them as much as possible with local products and services.

The alternative path is to keep the best of the present world and to change directions. The links within Puerto Rico are already built; the physical infrastructure and the electrical networks within the island are all intact and relatively new. The population is well informed and disciplined and shares a history of experiences and work. The society, in spite of its differences, is integrated geographically, racially, and socially. And there are supermarkets in almost every village.

Agriculture as a Missing Piece

I have argued that Puerto Rico's agricultural sector is actually a composite quite different from other industries, and that it alone was responsible for the retention of large numbers of workers, some of whom became available as wage workers in manufacturing and services. However, the collapse of agriculture—both plantations and small family farms—released far more workers into the labor market than was foreseen. Some of these retired out of the work force, some migrated from their homeland. The industrialization program, for all its great success, was unable to absorb all the labor thrown off by the rural sectors. This is not a unique process to Puerto Rico; virtually every Third World country is passing through a similar process, its rural work force streaming toward its cities or toward the cities of some associated metropolitan power.

The political economy of Puerto Rico, however, has been changed by a major redistribution to the bottom 60 percent of the population through the extension of U.S. food stamp programs to its territory. This is, in fact, the very scenario worked out previously in our computer model, except that in the food stamp program there has been no need to reduce the incomes of the upper classes to give to the lower classes. This also is a scenario being played out in Third World countries, on a somewhat smaller scale, through the international food aid programs. In the Puerto Rican case, the computer model set out what might be expected in the absence of local production to satisfy demand: an increase in imports, some first-round increases in service employment, and the continued decline of local agriculture.

In one sense, then, Puerto Rico has already woven through the three classical alternatives that have been pursued by developing countries in the postwar period. It has pushed export promotion in industry through most of the major sectors. It has entertained the idea of import substitution within its own political context.[3]

And finally, it has achieved major redistribution of income to its lower classes at no financial cost to its own elites. It may be no surprise, then, that open unemployment of nearly 25 percent persists as industry keeps growing.[4]

Toward Agricultural Self-sufficiency

On March 16, 1981, an economics professor from Iowa State University, recently returned from an apprenticeship in the interior mountains of Puerto Rico, presented testimony to the U.S. Senate Committee on Agriculture, Nutrition, and Forestry, suggesting that the billion-dollar food stamp subsidy to Puerto Rico, however necessary for its people's survival, was, in fact detrimental to their economic welfare because it encouraged a growing reliance on the subsidy. He recommended instead that a share of the subsidy be used for an emergency study of the possibility of a food self-sufficiency program.[5] The professor cited the technical agricultural programs drafted by the team headed by Nathan Koenig, written nearly thirty years earlier. "It is on the farms that the island's basic economic problems must be met and dealt with . . . diversifying and increasing production for local needs while at the same time maximizing economic production for export. This Study shows that the proposed attainable production pattern would yield enough food to meet the requirements of a low-cost adequate diet for a population of 3,000,000 and permit some reduction from the high volume of food imports. . . . Once achieved, it would enable Puerto Rico to become much less dependent on food imports."[6]

A debate between the governor of Puerto Rico and the professor, which occurred in the Helms' Committee in the form of sequential and conflicting testimony, opened the national debate on the U.S. food stamp program and a new era in the debate on Puerto Rican agriculture. Until that time, the accepted position was that the island was basically poor but growing and that the food stamp subsidy was, as in the United States, necessary to support the very poorest who could not possibly subsist without aid. Once the collapse of the island's plantation and subsistence agriculture was brought into the public light, the debate in Puerto Rico and in the U.S. Senate took on new proportions, namely, that a billion-dollar food program might also be used to promote local agriculture and reduce the continued reliance on congressional funding. As a result, an amendment was written into the federal legislation authorizing the food stamp appropriation for Puerto Rico, allowing a "small proportion" (the amount was not specified) of the funds to be used for the promotion and cultivation of local foods.[7] The disposition of that money and its ultimate use now fueled the debate on the rural sector.

The food self-sufficiency program outlined in 1981 in the congressional testimony flew in the face of ongoing tendencies and contradicted the conventional wisdom, namely, that Puerto Rican agriculture could never be competitive or productive, even for the most basic tropical food crops. This conventional wisdom, which served as the rationalization for continuing food aid, was also contradicted by technical studies, which as late as 1970 demonstrated quite the reverse; namely, that Puerto Rico was already competitive in the export of certain premium crops and could supply, as well, a greater share of its own consumption needs.[8]

In retrospect, the food self-sufficiency program proposed in the congressional testimony probably could be realized only under emergency pressures of war and isolation. But the debate on the elements of such an agricultural reconstruction program helped to break the impasse that had been reached on alternatives for the island. The uncultivated cane lands could be converted into citrus or vegetable cooperatives. The first-class highway system, which had already been built, could facilitate the movement of the labor force from the city as day laborers. And greenbelts of cooperative farms, instead of abandoned farmlands, could be promoted to surround the metropolitan areas. The thirty thousand mountain farms, protected by price guaranties, could utilize drip irrigation and small mechanized implements. Produce for local markets could be graded and quality maintained through local marketing boards, and supermarkets, which now measure their profits by rapid turnover of homogeneous imports, might then stock local foods. Farmers' markets, to promote direct marketing from farmer to consumer, could be encouraged by means of legislation.

Other suggested agricultural improvements included the dredging of the inland reservoirs, restocking them with fish, and using their surplus waters for mountain irrigation. Contour plowing and terracing could be promoted to halt the erosion of the countryside, the result of haphazard road construction and intensive grazing. A national nutrition campaign could shift the strong demand for imported foods back to indigenous foods, emphasizing the nutritional advantages of the native diet.

The government of Puerto Rico was urged to halt the fragmentation of and speculation in farmland and reduce the importing of tropical foods from other Caribbean islands. An ombudsman for agriculture could be appointed—a Puerto Rican trained in both modern and traditional techniques of tropical agriculture. By redirecting its energy toward self-sufficiency, Puerto Rico might no longer have to rely on emigration as the solution to the underemployed population.

To accomplish this, the Puerto Rican government was urged to undertake a crash program to update and revise the old studies and find out what the small farmer needed. At the same time, it was proposed that the commonwealth declare a temporary emergency tax of 5 percent on the net income of tax-exempt industry in Puerto Rico, which would generate $170 million a year and compensate for any cuts in the food aid programs. The advantage of such a temporary emergency tax, to be paid directly to the commonwealth in lieu of federal income tax, is simply that the money could be used directly in the agricultural reconstruction program without intervention from the federal bureaucracy. The restoration of a tropical agriculture in Puerto Rico could be firmly financed.

Five years was the suggested time frame to undertake this crash agricultural program. The first step was to update the technical studies, say, in six months, and

PHOTOGRAPH 17.1
Neighbors join in spontaneously to prepare soil, for *batata* planting on a small farm
in rural Humacao, Puerto Rico.

PHOTOGRAPH 17.2
A small tractor in northern China. Such
inexpensive small tractors could be helpful in
preparing soil on steeply sloped lands.

then to begin intensive planting, installation of irrigation tubing, construction, terracing, contouring, the preparation of seedlings, cleaning and restocking the inland lakes, and outfitting new fishing fleets. In the second through fourth years, federal food stamps and grants could be phased out.

The food self-sufficiency model suggests what could be done both technically and legally. Irrespective of its economics, the debate over the proposal opened up an alternative political direction.

Toward an Agroindustrial Economy

By the fall of 1983, agriculture had become a full-blown political issue. In search of a new agricultural policy, the commonwealth late in 1983 contracted an Israeli engineering company to draft an emergency program in six months time toward the building of a modern agriculture. This report, nearly one thousand pages of technical analysis, updates the 1953 Koenig report and follows a narrower methodology.[9] Working with soil and water resources, the 1984 Tahal report begins with the historical prices, both international and local, for the full range of agricultural products. The report then examines the production costs for each crop in each region and develops a comprehensive agricultural program based on the best available technologies.

Several important features emerge from the study. First, even if the total program were implemented, only 41 thousand new jobs would be created during the first five years as a result of the nearly five-hundred million dollars required investment and credit. The techniques to be introduced would be among the most advanced available, with heavy reliance on mechanical and chemical inputs. In areas such as dairying, in which Puerto Rico already has achieved near self-sufficiency, the report recommends organizational and institutional changes in order to achieve higher yields with no further acquisition of livestock.

Second, the report does see realistic opportunities in producing food for local use as well as export. Exotic fruits, such as citrus, mango, and pineapple, could capture places in the U.S. winter market, while poultry, eggs, dairy, pork, and local root crops, vegetables, and fruits, could, under conditions of modern technology, compete successfully both with equally efficient U.S. imports and with the low-wage products coming from the Caribbean and Latin America.

Third, although agriculture has always been a political issue, the technology that could be adapted to Puerto Rico might take a longer commitment than the four-year terms of the political calendar. This means that either several administrations must become associated with an agrarian program, or agriculture must be entirely removed from the current political context and put into a different arena, perhaps under federal jurisdiction or international business. Since neither of these developments is likely, the fate of agriculture still rests with each administration, and the strategic program, in the words of its project coordinator, remains in its essence a political document.

PHOTOGRAPH 17.3
Looking into an uncultivated valley in the
mountains south of Arecibo, Puerto Rico.

PHOTOGRAPH 17.4
A terraced canyon in Tachai commune,
north China, with a stream channeled in a
tunnel beneath the cropland.

Toward a New Political Economy for Puerto Rico

The time has come to put away the political stereotypes and make peace with the past. The Puerto Rican situation is simply that food stamps and other transfers from abroad support a majority of the population. Manufacturing, Puerto Rico's great industrial strength, is based on a tax gimmick that is also subject to revision. Much of the economic survival of Puerto Rico is due to pecuniary advantages, to fiscal or international bookkeeping rules that, if changed, can bring on more hardship.[10] Because Puerto Rico has no direct political representation in the U.S. Congress, it must rely essentially on the goodwill and discretion of the elected representatives of another people. Ironically, the tax exemption had been granted Puerto Rico because of its absence of congressional representation in the first place. Today, however, Puerto Rico relies on continuation of the tax holiday and, therefore, on continuation of its *non*representation in Congress. As a state, Puerto Rico would be included in many federal programs, but it would lose the tax exemption. As a commonwealth, it retains the exemption but is limited in many federal programs. As profound an issue as its political status has been reduced to a cost-benefit calculation.

In Latin America, the threat of national bankruptcy jeopardizes both the borrowing and the lending country. The borrower faces the prospect of having its credits for its supply of imports cut off. The lender also fears a widespread collapse of confidence and possibly of its global operations if but one major debtor is allowed to fail and others follow.[11] Puerto Rico and the United States, too, are subject to their own pernicious game of mutual ransom. If the transfers, food subsidies, and tax holidays are not forthcoming from the Congress, the Puerto Rican citizen can simply leave his land and obtain all the benefits of the American welfare system. Therefore, the transfers actually keep Puerto Ricans at home, not in the cities of the United States, and, as the system operates, without work. Some of the billions of federal dollars spent in Puerto Rico may have led to growth: jobs, government services, and federal and municipal buildings and infrastructure. Food stamps, perhaps the most pernicious of all transfers, I have argued, affect the wage structure, spending patterns, and attitudes. They are direct payments for poverty, and have led to countergrowth in the open, island economy.

On the basis of this economic and historical analysis, agriculture appears not only neglected but as a crucial missing piece of Puerto Rico's economy, which in its decline continues to release labor. Economic policy clearly must be focused on remedying this fragment and, in doing so, remaking the economy.

Several positions are possible. The first is toward food self-sufficiency, a somewhat romantic notion, a technical possibility that flies in the face of all political and economic tendencies. The second is a major state-promoted agroindustrial sector, which would allow Puerto Rico to export premium fruits and vegetables and promote local food crops. The third alternative is to build agriculture in much the same way that industry was promoted: to lease the land to agribusiness corporations, give them tax exemption, and encourage them to import capital, technique, and skilled personnel; in short, to bring Operation Bootstrap into agriculture. But agriculture is not altogether like the other industries. The political constraints are more complicated due to the historical controversy over farmland and farm labor, the uncertainty inherent in cultivation, and the need for longer term investments in developing land and technology for new crops.

It is time now to redress the historical neglect and to reconstruct agriculture by drawing on all three positions.[12] It may not be necessary to integrate a new agriculture into the economy. The first task would be to produce for the local U.S. or world market, which itself would obliterate the conventional stereotype that a high-wage, tropical agriculture simply cannot compete with low-wage economies of comparable climate. This, however, can be done only by employing as few people in the process as possible. In this case, the agribusiness sector becomes but another enclave, exporting its premium products and profits, importing its raw materials, and using local energy, water, soils, and some labor. The point here is simply that this task can be done immediately. The product-oriented Tahal Report takes the latest world technology and market information available and provides a strategic program for all branches of Puerto Rico's agriculture by season, price, and region. This package of technology and marketing, if implemented, is designed to make a competitive agriculture, but it cannot solve Puerto Rico's unemployment problem.

Many arguments made earlier in this book point to the hollowness of the economy. Like many nations on the periphery of large, industrial countries, Puerto Rico does not produce what it consumes. Nor does it consume what it produces. One way of reconnecting a people to its economy is through what it eats, by connecting its stomach to its hands through its head.

Food, the anthropologist tells us, holds a people together. The Puerto Rican people have become alienated from its native foods and alienated from its land. The Puerto Rican resident is constantly faced with an invasion of totally new temperate-climate products, well-advertised, packaged, available in the local chain supermarkets, and underwritten by food stamps. The Puerto Rican emigrant also returns home having acquired the tastes of the North American diet. The traditional foods are considered old-fashioned and nutritionally inferior. Yet it is known that Caribbean cuisine can produce a superior-tasting and nutritionally-balanced diet.[13] Reference to a local diet in Puerto Rico sometimes evokes memories of the 1930s and the starvation days of the early food programs. Images of that period, if taken seriously, merely keep a people from moving ahead into a new era.

Two further points are important here. First, new technologies are now available for using tropical products, for growing and utilizing plants, and for selecting improved animal stock and seed varieties. Second, a new science of nutrition based on tropical foods is also available. Puerto Rico need not specialize solely in exotic fruits for the winter market of North America and Europe or in basic export staples. Currently, economics demands that the hotel industry serve a uniform imported diet. This all can be changed with a scientific and tasteful Caribbean cuisine, supplied with local grains, legumes, nuts, fruits, vegetables, fish, and dairy products. Style setters and political leaders, however, who have taken their culinary cues from the metropolis, must also alter their diets and savor the local foods. In short, *calabaza* and *malanga* must make it to the governor's table and to the gourmet menu of the Caribe Hilton.

The economics of such a campaign is very straightforward. Every orange tree planted and every fruit picked, sold, and eaten in Puerto Rico generates an economic, as well as psychosocial, multiplier. The dollars diverted to the *china* from Florida oranges and to the *batata* from the Maine potato pay Puerto Rican salaries and rent. If the orange workers and landowners, too, eat locally grown food, their dollars lift the economy that much higher. This is the application of the true Puerto Rico model, closing its economy and linking its people to their own production.

Where and how is all this to be done? In the recent agricultural studies, one major factor has been overlooked: the human potential of the interior and the survival of the family on the minifarm in the mountains, remotely connected with the migrants on the American mainland. The mountain population retains title to its homestead. Nearly half of Puerto Ricans still live in rural communities.[14] The Tahal Report ignores totally the productive possibility of these peoples; it regards the minifarm as anachronistic and inefficient. Yet, it is precisely this quasi-retired proletariat who can best utilize adapted forms of the new water-saving techniques, intensive cultivation, and chemical inputs, and who can, by working their own land, circumvent the minimum wage.[15]

To disseminate technique and credit, bringing the minifarm into the productive sphere, would require a complete reorientation of the Department of Agriculture in order to deal ably with large numbers of farms, not just large farms, as is the current practice. Just as the Israelis have pioneered in water-saving, mechanized technologies on flat land, Puerto Rico could likewise acquire and develop the latest technology to assist in cultivating the steeper slopes, borrowing techniques from Taiwan, for example. The newly founded Universidad de la Montaña in Utuado could be expanded as a key research and extension center. And all the knowledge of traditional mountain agriculture, with its complex interplay of root crops, vines, bushes, and fruit-bearing shade trees, can be systematized and reemployed.

In a new economy, the government could guarantee high prices to the farmer and fix low prices for the consumer, absorbing the difference through the food stamp budget, which now underwrites only high prices to the consumer and low prices to the producer. Since Puerto Rico does not control its own tariffs, zealous health officials would have to meticulously inspect imported foodstuffs for contagious plant diseases. After all, the small mountain producer in Puerto Rico must be given some protection. A new political economy for Puerto Rico would depend on the consciousness of the leaders, the politicians, who are the real educators of the people. In the colonial hot box of Puerto Rico, to attempt to rechannel food stamps or the current subsidy arrangements may prove politically unrewarding.[16] And it must be done.

Toward a Consciousness of Popular Economy

The same thinking that must promote the link of food with agriculture must also be applied to the other enclaves. At present, the branch plant located in Puerto Rico is an almost pure enclave from the consumer's point of view. Johnson and Johnson may produce bandages efficiently in a large-scale operation, exporting in bulk to the continental market, but bandages for the local market are reimported through normal wholesale channels. This is the simple economics of the enclave and can be changed. Tax incentives can be tailored to encourage the local firm to purchase a larger share of its materials from other branch plants in Puerto Rico and also to sell a fraction of its exported product locally. Ironically, one impediment to increased local sale is the consumers' own sophistication and preferences for variety and quality, which are satisfied by imports from the global market. Even to the buyer consciously seeking local products, the anonymity of the standard package disguises the true origin of its contents.

Again, two attacks are needed. First, the consumer must be made aware of what is local and what is imported. Puerto Rico is a small society with a large number of factories, a limited number of which produce for local needs. Any connection between consumer product and factory can be well publicized. Second, consumer demand for manufactured goods must be simplified. This again flies in the face of the last twenty-five years of marketing in Puerto Rico, in which the needs of the population have been successfully differentiated and segmented by a wide array of models. In the United States, this differentiation has been an instrument of competition among firms, and efficient production of many varieties can be carried on in a large market. Small-scale production, however, may be efficient only for a limited, basic model. In this case, the desired variety may be affected directly by the purchaser by the addition of accessories, engraving or embroidery, additions, for example, to the basic-model sewing machine, bicycle, or T-shirt. Again, it is the consumer who must realize that the real price for sophistication is paid in severing the connection with his and her own people. Every purchase of locally made products—food, furniture, simple appliances—is an act that reconnects the productive system, a method by which a people is reunited.

All economic policy must be redirected to this goal: in agriculture, manufacturing, trade, services, in businesses of all sorts. Every possible production link, beginning with food, must be seized upon. How is each item produced? Where? What is the substitute in tropical production? How can people satisfy this need without importing that product or service?

The same attitude must be applied to the improvement of services, which make urban life in Puerto Rico a caricature of that in North American cities. The transport problem also must be addressed. Congestion in physical space is a mirror of immobility in intellectual and spiritual space. After years of supersized cars on a mini-island, small cars are now in fashion, but the majority of autos are still hybridized gas guzzlers. The bus system and *públicos,* or collective taxis, are all

PHOTOGRAPH 17.5
San Juan at rush hour becomes a giant *tapón*, a Gordian knot–like traffic jam.

PHOTOGRAPH 17.6
A quiet harbor near Cabo Rojo, on Puerto Rico's western coast.

inadequate and slow moving; they too fail to meet the needs of the people. San Juan is notorious for its *tapones,* Gordian-knot traffic jams, the internecine dance of the rush hour and symbol of the motionless burning of resources. The time lost in getting home from work is compensated for by a TV dinner, testimony to the inverted quality of life in the Caribbean colony.

That agriculture should have hitherto failed in Puerto Rico, reflecting historical trends, a lack of will, or the application of faulty technique, may be consistent with the unconscious goal of the colonial political system. The undermining of the economic base and the subsequent reliance on federal funds to feed the majority sustains a false economic prosperity. It reaffirms to Puerto Ricans their ultimate dependence on the United States.

None of this is unknown in Puerto Rico. With the deepening economic crisis in the early eighties, the debate on new directions for the society is being carried on with increased clarity and vigor.[17] However, the political debate revolves not around these issues but around the status of the island: statehood, independence, or continued commonwealth. Yet as a bankrupt, dismembered economy heavily dependent on welfare, Puerto Rico has in reality no present choice.[18] A people without a livelihood, Puerto Rico is a hollow economy, a residential configuration that keeps its latent labor force at some strategic distance from the industrial heartland. Modernizing agriculture, producing local foods for a Caribbean cuisine, and orienting industry and services to local needs can prove as successful as the earlier efforts at industrialization and tourism, which, in their day, defied the conventional wisdom.

In the past, consultants have concluded that there has been a failure of will, that no serious interest exists by the Puerto Rican leadership to solve the economic or the agrarian problem.[19] Others claim that the U.S. Congress has failed to exercise responsibly its ultimate power over the commonwealth. The economist, practitioner of the dismal science, recommends heavier doses of a standard medicine, new devices and old ones, biting the bullet (and there are plenty of these in Puerto Rican history), plus a perpetual dole.[20]

The economic facts are simply that Puerto Rico has human energy and creativity, resources, land, rain, and access to technology. It has the experience to build in a fresh direction. How to get it all moving? A people cannot be expected to vote to exchange their material livelihoods, incomes, and hopes, for a six-day workweek and more political independence. But market and business cycles have their own logic, as congressional cuts, market failures, withdrawn investments, and remitted profits continue to drain the colony of its wealth. They all exercise a will independent of elections.

Many political and intellectual leaders analyze Puerto Rico's problems imaginatively and correctly, but there is little personal or public reward to encourage them to do what must be done: first, channel food money into producing food; second, manipulate the tax incentives and the tollgate tax to encourage companies to produce things that the local people need; third, set styles of consuming in all the social classes that conspicuously display what is or can be produced on the island:

local foods, clothing, house furnishings, and services. In short, the task is to reintegrate the economic structure with people's lives and, in doing so, to guarantee their livelihoods.

Puerto Rico has, it thinks, a trump card on the metropole. If Congress cuts funds for the island programs or lowers the ceilings on its entitlements, Puerto Ricans, citizens of both worlds, can emigrate on a mass scale to the already overburdened U.S. cities.[21] Since the total economic cost of support in either location is not clear, it may be cheaper for the United States to continue to support Puerto Rico in its current style. To continue this countergrowth, of course, is not in the interest of either the American or Puerto Rican people. The American people need strong allies in the Third World, especially in the Caribbean, not more dependent nations whose very livelihoods have been undermined through the generosity of the metropole. Nor do the Puerto Rican people benefit from their deepening dependence. They achieve material prosperity based on the accumulation of things and debts, but the welfare of an entire people has come to rely on the largesse of the U.S. Congress.

A new political economy for Puerto Rico must be based on the alliance of all her citizens, both inside and outside the island. From the migrant camps from Maine to Florida, the slums of eastern cities, and even the more respectable neighborhoods where the successful emigrant has settled, a people can return to claim their homeland and rebuild the dismembered economy, ushering in a new era.

Epilogue

As the United States and Puerto Rico enter the latter half of the 1980s, a new urgency overtakes the island economy. Newly reported trends testify to a situation that cries out for prompt action—and underscores the need for the novel approach in political economy advocated in this book.

From 1981 to 1984 the unemployment rate has held steadily above 21%. This means that, together with the lowest participation rates in the postwar period, fully two-thirds of adults continue without work.[22] Between 1982 and 1984, 110,000 families, or one-fifth of the total, were cut from the food stamp program, now labeled nutrition assistance, making the subsidy less successful as a rescue operation.[23] The situation in the countryside continues to deteriorate. Between 1978 and 1982 the sugarcane harvest fell by a third; tobacco growing virtually disappeared; and most all the basic food crops continued their precipitous decline.[24] As the economic base erodes, the euphemistic escape valve—outmigration—opens on a scale unprecedented since the 1950s. From 1982 to 1984, 115,400 people left Puerto Rico, more than in any recent three-year period.[25] The irregular net outflow of the past decade may now become large-scale depopulation. However, in the United States, the Puerto Rican man also faces an unemployment rate of 21%, and his family income amounts to barely one-half the level of the general population.[26] The migrant jumps from a failing island economy into the least advantaged strata within the United States!

To compound the uncertainty, the U.S. Treasury Department continues its attack on the Puerto Rico tax exemption, arguing that the program has been abused. As an alternative, it seeks to link a tax credit to the creation of new jobs. Puerto Rico's counterproposal would tie the existing tax exemption to the Caribbean Basin Initiative by encouraging new branch plants to divide their operations between Puerto Rico and other low-wage islands.[27]

Tax-exempt factories and the food stamps are symmetric. The first is a subsidy to some of the nation's largest corporations.[28] The second is a subsidy to America's poorest people. The island economy, from private enterprise to private citizen, survives on grants from the U.S. taxpayer to everyone's long-run detriment. To give *more* of both tax credits and food stamps will accelerate the crisis. The tax credit must be redesigned to keep firms and jobs in Puerto Rico and create linkages *within* the island, the criteria of which can be specified statistically and simply. The food stamp/cash program must be redesigned to earmark a portion of the coupons for the purchase of locally grown foods, as is currently done with some success in the food program of the Northern Marianas. At the same time, the small mountain family farmer, sometime migrant, sometime factory worker, also must be encouraged to produce food with the help of the agricultural program described earlier in this book. The goal need not be food self-sufficiency. Just growing food would create employment and rebuild the linkages.

New gimmicks are substitutes for clear policies. In the past, there has been copper mining, a superport, free enterprise zones, rice growing, vegetables, and food stamps. This year it is the Caribbean Basin Initiative, twin plants, ocean-thermal energy, kenaf (an industrial field crop), newsprint, and nutrition assistance. A new tax arrangement or technological breakthrough will not in itself restore a people's livelihood, but it may help reconstruct parts of the material support system given up in the most recent decades of "successful" development.

What should all this matter to the United States? The present arrangement is costly to the U.S. taxpayer and harmful to both economies. The time has arrived to revise the Puerto Rico model of development.

THE GOVERNOR'S summer mansion in Jájome Alto looks out over the southern coast of Puerto Rico toward the Caribbean Sea. Below in the village of Jájome Bajo, once a stronghold of the nationalist underground, people hold Bible meetings dressed in sackcloth and subsist on food stamp checks. Not far away, on the superhighway that slices its way through the mountains, a white statue of a *jíbaro* family stands alone like a tombstone in the abandoned hills. The grandchildren of the *jíbaro*—the engineer, chemist, fast-order chef, politician, factory hand, migrant worker—displaced and now returning, all bring their skills and optimism to the new economy.

Notes

Chapter 1. Introduction: The Puerto Rico Model of Development

1. See Magruder, *Son of Boot-Strap,* pp. 135–39.

2. Among the world's 130 countries, Puerto Rico ranks 35th in terms of its income per capita, ahead of most of the so-called developing countries. In the Caribbean and South America, only Venezuela and Trinidad and Tobago, oil-exporting countries, show higher per capita income. In 1977, the GNP per capita for the United States was $8,750, compared to $2,450 for Puerto Rico, $1,060 for Jamaica, and $158 for India. See International Bank for Reconstruction and Development, *World Tables,* table 11, pp. 430–33. Puerto Rico is included in the rankings but not in the country tables!

3. The acquisition of formal colonies was specifically to be avoided according to the framers of the U.S. Constitution. Instead, they provided for territories to be incorporated as states. There was no provision for "permanently associated" states, which are "subject to, but not part of" the United States. See G. Lewis, *Puerto Rico,* chap. 18, "The Problem of Political Status," pp. 409–37.

4. Weisskoff, "A Multisector Simulation Model of Employment, Growth and Income Distribution in Puerto Rico," p. 46; published later in Weisskoff, "Income Distribution and Export Promotion in Puerto Rico," p. 215.

Chapter 2. The Economy at a Glance

1. Mill, "Of the Inverse Deductive, or Historical Method," in *On the Logic of the Moral Sciences.*

2. See U.S. Department of Commerce, *National Income and Product Accounts of the United States, 1929–1965;* and Puerto Rico Planning Board, *Income and Product* (San Juan, various years).

3. See Duesenberry et al., eds., *Brookings Quarterly Econometric Model of the United States;* Houthakker and Taylor, *Consumer Demand in the United States, 1929–1970;* and Leontief, Carter, and Petri, *Future of the World Economy.*

4. See Festinger, *A Theory of Cognitive Dissonance;* and Hirschman, "Obstacles to Development."

5. There are, of course, exceptions. See Bruno, *Interdependence, Resource Use and Structural Change in Israel,* chap. 6.

6. See the essays in Easterlin, ed., *Population and Economic Change in Developing Countries.*

7. In other countries, the debate revolves around the loss of savings from the economy and its flight abroad. In Puerto Rico, such discussion is irrelevant.

8. *Gross product* refers to all the goods and services produced within the society and includes

depreciation on the capital used in production. *Personal income* refers to spendable income of the people of the island. From gross product are subtracted depreciation and indirect business taxes, social security contributions, nondisbursed profits, corporate income tax, and withheld personal income taxes. Various transfers are then added to the product: subsidies and interest payments received by business and families; and remittances from abroad. In fiscal year 1983, the gross product in current dollars totalled some $12.9 billion after all the subtractions and additions were made. Personal income amounted to $12.7 billion, exceeding the gross product. Of personal income, $2.9 billion, or 23 percent, was federal transfers. See Puerto Rico Planning Board, *Economic Report to the Governor 1983,* appendix table 9, p. A-9, for detailed accounts.

9. One must be careful here not to imply that in the absence of the subsidies, the society would have been less equal, as measured by the Gini coefficient of .466. We cannot evaluate the absence of the transfers without a complete model.

Chapter 3. Economic Performance and the Model

1. See the essays in Adelman and Thorbecke, eds., *Theory and Design of Economic Development;* and in Blitzer, Clark, and Taylor, eds., *Economy-Wide Models and Development Planning.*

2. The wage levels may be linked, as in Puerto Rico, directly to the U.S. wage levels, through legislation or international collective bargaining agreements regardless of local labor-market conditions. Government wage-setting has always been attacked by neoclassical economists as inhibiting the free labor-market outcome. However, since Puerto Rico is marked by deep social cleavages and has no real army of its own with which to confront protracted class conflict or to enforce labor compliance, a major social problem is resolved by simply pegging wages to outside arbitration. See Reynolds and Gregory, *Wages, Productivity, and Industrialization in Puerto Rico,* chap. 2, for a description of the older system of negotiation. In some mobile occupations a truly international market sets the wage levels even in the remotest parts of the colony: the needs of the tomato harvest in New Jersey affect the wages of tobacco pickers in rural Puerto Rico.

3. Contrast Baran, *Political Economy of Growth,* and Hirschman, *Strategy of Economic Development,* on this issue.

4. Contrast Levitt and Best, *Externally-Propelled Growth and Industrialization in the Caribbean,* and Baldwin, "Patterns of Development in Newly Settled Regions."

5. See Weisskoff, "Income Distribution and Export Promotion in Puerto Rico," pp. 218–21.

6. *Ibid.,* pp. 219, 221.

7. The revisions of the employment series were received as this book was being prepared for final publication. Wherever possible, the revised series, available in the 1983 *Economic Report to the Governor,* have been incorporated into the text and tables. The administration of the decennial United States Population Census in Puerto Rico, with the island's high population density and rural dispersion, has always been a challenging and controversial undertaking. There are thought to be strong incentives for the populace to present information consistent with what the respondent believes to be prospective benefits. Moreover, the response in 1980 to a census carried out through the mail and through the selected follow-up interviews may have been less complete than expected. Nevertheless, the U.S. census remains the major benchmark for the global population of the island. The Puerto Rico Department of Labor and Human Resources administers its own monthly sample survey of some 6,300 households and uses this to estimate monthly the rates and characteristics of employment and unemployment. Nevertheless, the reconciliation of these samples of the work force with the census totals is undertaken only at the benchmark year, namely, at the conclusion of the decade. See Puerto Rico Department of Labor, "The Revision of Data of Employment and Unemployment Based on the Population Census of 1980" (San Juan, n.d.); and "Monumental 'Error' Estadístico Desata," *El Reportero* (San Juan), May 30, 1983.

Chapter 5. Games Economists Play

1. Compare the arguments of Conrad and Meyer, *Economics of Slavery and Other Studies in Econometric History;* Gerschenkron, *Economic Spurt That Failed;* and McCloskey, *Enterprise and Trade in Victorian Britain;* to the story of L'Engle, *Swiftly Tilting Planet.*
2. Economists who vitriolically oppose the use of these fixed networks satisfy themselves with more flexibility and less detail. See chap. 3 in Blitzer, Clark, and Taylor, eds., *Economy-Wide Models and Development Planning.*
3. See Hirschman, "Political Economy of Import Substituting Industrialization in Latin America"; and Weisskoff, "Growth and Decline of Import Substitution in Brazil—Revisited."

Chapter 6. The Economy That Might Have Been

1. This is, in fact the observation of James Ingram, who writes, "When no domestic production exists, it is difficult to distinguish between an 'excise tax' and an import duty. . . . Puerto Rico has imposed a sizable number of excise taxes." See *Regional Payments Mechanisms,* pp. 6–7.
2. For example, David Ricardo concludes, "And therefore it follows, if I am right, that the same cause which may increase the net revenue of the country may at the same time render the population redundant. . . ." See *Principles of Political Economy* (London: Everyman's Library, 1965), chap. 31, "On Machinery," p. 264.
3. I am indebted to the Chilean economist Pedro Vuskovic for the following interpretation.

Chapter 7. The Economics of the Puerto Rican Problem

1. See Clark et al., *Porto Rico and Its Problems,* pp. 468–74. These have been described also as "part subsistence farms." See Luther H. Gulick, Jr., *Rural Occupance in Utuado and Jayuya Municipios, Puerto Rico,* Research Paper 23 (Chicago: Department of Geography, University of Chicago, 1952), pp. 58–59.
2. See Stewart et al., *People of Puerto Rico,* chaps. 8–9.
3. See Reynolds and Gregory, *Wages, Productivity and Industrialization in Puerto Rico,* chap. 7, "Assembling an Industrial Labor Force."
4. Modern economics may not recognize this distinction, although colonial historians and the peasantry certainly do. In economics, even the traders or speculators are said to earn, or make money for their services, their risk, their foresight, and so on. The trader may pay taxes to the state, and the state returns some of the original value to the peasant as a grant for his local school or road. Under the Spanish, the grant is more likely to have been for the San Juan government or for military support to help collect taxes and enforce the penal codes.
5. See Robert Manners, "Tabara: Subcultures of a Tobacco and Mixed Crops Municipality," in Stewart et al., *People of Puerto Rico,* p. 132.
6. As early as 1946, Bartlett, writing for the Planning Board, had suggested "various methods for 'adjusting' population to wealth,"namely, emigration and birth control. See Bartlett and Howell, *Puerto Rico y su problema de población,* p. 13. See also Meek, ed., *Marx and Engels on the Population Bomb,* pp. 37–49; Mass, *Population Target,* pp. 87–108; History Task Force, *Labor Migration under Capitalism,* chap. 5; and Schultz, "A Family Planning Hypothesis."
7. Of an adult population of 2.3 million in 1980, 1.5 million were not working. The labor force here is divided into active and inactive, and the nonworking share of the labor force includes both the inactive and the unemployed portion of the active. Traditional analysis focuses on two of these relationships, labor force participation and unemployment. It is important to look as well at

the share of all nonworking adults and the overall dependency ratio, which includes children and nonworking adults relative to the total population. This index of dependency varied slightly during the 1940–80 period, hovering around 75 percent. The difference, however, between the dependency rate of 77 percent in 1960 and 74 percent in 1980 is that the decline in share of children from 41 percent in 1960 to 28 percent in 1980 had been offset by the rise in share of dependent, or nonworking, adults.

8. Ingenious accounting conventions permit companies to shift profits to Puerto Rico from other branches by underinvoicing the cost of imported raw materials and overinvoicing the price of exported products. This leads to the appearance of high profits in the Puerto Rican branch plant, which are erroneously attributed to the extraordinary high productivity of local labor, or to the machinery, or to the climate. These are, then, profits created elsewhere and maneuvered to Puerto Rico, where they are not taxed and from whence they can, like a faithful dog, return to their owner when he whistles. Hence, the presumption that investment generates, causes, or earns profits is inappropriate.

Chapter 8. The Decade of Economic Cataclysm: Food Stamp Savior
Comes to Puerto Rico

1. Research for this chapter was supported by the Food and Nutrition Service of the U.S. Department of Agriculture and by the Institute for Policy Studies in Washington, D.C. The author acknowledges the perceptive insights of Oscar Lamourt-Valentín of Lares, Puerto Rico.

The Food Stamp Act had been operational in the United States since 1964 but had been limited to the fifty states and the District of Columbia. On January 11, 1971, Public Law 91-671 amended the Food Stamp Act of 1974 by redefining "State" to mean "the fifty States and the District of Columbia, Guam, Puerto Rico, and the Virgin Islands of the United States," clearly allowing "the territories to participate in the program." See House Report 91-402 to the Committee on Agriculture, p. 12. A second amendment allowed Puerto Rico to enter the program with its own "standards of eligibility" and its own schedule of benefits, which could be the same or lower than the food stamp benefits received by poor families in the United States. These criteria would, in accordance with Section 5(b) of Public Law 91-671, "reflect the average per capita income and cost of obtaining a nutritionally adequate diet in Puerto Rico and the respective territories." See U.S. Statutes at Large, 1970–71, vol. 84, pt. 2 (Washington, D.C.: Government Printing Office, 1971).

The amendments extending food stamps to Puerto Rico remained academic for some time, as no program was authorized for the island. Public Law 93-86, passed on August 10, 1973, compelled all counties to make food stamps available to its needy unless "impossible or impractical." However, due to administrative difficulties, the implementation of the program in Puerto Rico was gradual. A court suit brought by the San Juan Legal Services Corporation and the Washington-based Food Research Action Coalition (FRAC) was successful, and the Food and Nutrition Services of the Department of Agriculture was instructed to introduce the program throughout Puerto Rico at an accelerated pace. Hundreds of centers to certify the qualified poor were staffed. More than fifteen thousand stores, merchandisers, and wholesalers were instructed in the detailed regulations, and the commercial banks set up the apparatus to exchange the stamps for money.

As much as 75 percent of Puerto Rico's inhabitants qualified for the program under U.S. standards of poverty. Within six months, the program, administered fifteen hundred miles away from a small office in suburban New Jersey, absorbed 10 to 12 percent of U.S. food stamp resources. By June 1975, the Food and Nutrition Service oversaw the distribution of nearly $50 million a month in bonus stamps to nearly two million people.

2. That food stamps are not used exclusively for food, as specified in the regulations, need not

detract from our analysis. It should not surprise us that, because food stamps represent purchasing power and are so widely held, they substitute for and are treated as currency. Food stamps are exchanged directly for gasoline, rum, and medicine, contrary to the regulations, which must be regarded as an inconvenience, necessitating circumvention in an imaginative and discrete manner. See, for example, Office of Inspector General, Audit: Northeast Region, Audit Report 2713-72-Hy, "The Food and Nutrition Service—Food Stamp Program, Department of Social Services, San Juan, Puerto Rico, As of March 13, 1980," May 29, 1980.

3. A business that has accepted food stamps for articles other than food may also find itself in the embarrassing position in which its food stamp redemptions exceed its total food sales, an accounting indiscretion which automatically triggers an investigation by the Food and Nutrition Service.

4. Such an inflation does not occur when food stamps are distributed within a large, already monetarized society, such as the United States. Here, the food subsidy maintains a slim modicum of survival for the poor, as in the Bedford-Stuyvesant section of Brooklyn or the South Side of Chicago, where food stamps serve as the lifeline to the needed products. But in the small, closed economy, such subsidies undercut the informal network of barter, exchange, and gifts by forcing the creation of a cash market, creating commerce, and throwing business to importing and distributing enterprises.

5. Cash on hand that is not lent out actually represents forgone earnings, especially if that money is essentially free to the bank, like the food stamp float, and requires no interest to the depositors.

6. See *Moody's Bank and Finance Manual,* annually *1975* through *1980,* for the time profiles of assets for Puerto Rican banks, especially the Banco de Ponce, Banco Popular, and Banco Comercial de Mayagüez. The Banco Popular experienced a four-fold increase in its assets and a doubling of its loans from 1975 to 1979.

7. See comments by Jesse Helms, Republican senator from North Carolina, in U.S. Senate, *Proposed Reauthorization of the Food and Agriculture Act of 1977 (Food Stamps),* p. 27.

8. Since July 1982, food coupons have been replaced by cash grants paid by check to each family. The elimination of the coupon merely simplifies the conversion of the grant into cash, which can then be used openly for any transaction. The need for a black-market middle person is bypassed, but our analysis is otherwise unchanged.

Chapter 9. The Decade of Economic Cataclysm: The Economic Record

1. In a normal closed economy, private investment would stimulate dynamic growth. Gross investment in Puerto Rico has been more or less constant at $1.7 to $2.0 billion per year between 1971 and 1979, with the exception of the major decline in 1977 in private and public construction. Gross domestic investment fell in 1982 and 1983 to $1.2–1.4 billion in current terms, the lowest since 1970. Another cycle of economic difficulty begins. See Puerto Rico Planning Board, *Economic Report to the Governor 1983,* table 2.

2. The degree to which import inflation is passed into or is kept out of the local economy has to do with the rigidity of markups of the intermediaries. The full price increase of imports may not be passed on to consumers if retailer margins are declining. This may have occurred as the supermarkets strove to achieve a larger market share and undercut traditional *colmados,* or corner stores.

3. The population series itself has recently been revised in the light of the preliminary count of the 1980 census. The commonwealth's population estimate was 300 thousand higher than the U.S. census count for 1980 and was based on erroneous data for net return migration to Puerto Rico supplied by the Port Authority. The revised series (see table 9.2) is based on a corrected net flow series from the airlines. Earlier data had reported only "revenue departures" and "seats

filled" (rather than "people occupying" the seats). The former concept omits nonpaying passengers (airlines employees and others), and the latter omits infants. Data on arrivals are difficult to verify and data on charter flights are even less well documented. In any case, the net flows are such small residuals compared to the great volume of passengers that the minor miscounts in the total volumes result in major changes in the net migration.

4. Local manufactured food includes imported raw food processed in Puerto Rico for export. Hence, it overestimates local food manufactured for local use.

5. Again, an overestimation, since local agriculture consists of food for local consumption and for export as well.

6. Weisskoff and Wolff, "Linkages and Leakages."

7. See Ricardo Campos and Frank Bonilla, "Bootstraps and Enterprise Zones: The Underside of Late Capitalism in Puerto Rico and the United States," *Review* 5, no. 4 (Spring 1982), pp. 556–90.

8. See, for example, Wanniski, *Way the World Works,* chap. 12, "Experiment in Puerto Rico."

9. See North American Congress on Latin America, "Puerto Rico."

10. In 1981, the U.S. Congress became alarmed at the projected rising costs of the Puerto Rico food stamp program. To reduce spending, the Omnibus Budget Reconciliation Act of 1981 (PL 97-35) replaced food stamps with a block grant to Puerto Rico with a ceiling fixed at $825 million. The new system, known as the Nutrition Assistance Program, distributes monthly checks to needy families, rather than coupons. A 1983 report of the Food and Nutrition Service concludes that under the fixed grant, Puerto Rico has been forced to reduce the value of benefits and the number of participating families in the program. As a result, the report concludes, a slight decline in the nutritional standards of some families is expected. See U.S. Department of Agriculture, Food and Nutrition Service, "Evaluation of the Puerto Rican Nutrition Assistance Program," chap. 8.

Chapter 10. The Other Side of Paradise: Puerto Ricans in the United States

1. See, for example, the introduction to O. Lewis, *La Vida.*

2. See Senior, *Strangers—Then Neighbors;* and Fitzpatrick, *Puerto Rican Americans.*

3. See Senior et al., *Puerto Ricans;* Cordasco, *Puerto Ricans on the United States Mainland;* and Leavitt, *Puerto Ricans.*

4. See, for example, Soto, *Spiks;* and Pietri, *Puerto Rican Obituary,* for stories and poems. See also History Task Force, *Labor Migration under Capitalism;* and Garza, ed., *Puerto Ricans in the U.S.*

5. See O. Lewis, *La Vida.* The academic literature on the economics of migration is vast, ranging from statistical to polemic. For orthodox economic approaches, see Reynolds and Gregory, *Wages, Productivity, and Industrialization in Puerto Rico;* and Friedlander, *Labor Migration and Economic Growth.* For statistical studies, see the following studies published by the Puerto Rico Planning Board, Bureau of Social Planning; *Puerto Rican Migrants: A Socio-Economic Study* (San Juan, 1972); *A Comparative Study of the Labor Market Characteristics of Return Migrants and Nonmigrants in Puerto Rico* (San Juan, July 1973); and Steven Zell, Puerto Rico Planning Board, Bureau of Social Planning, *Two Studies of Puerto Rican Labor Mobility,* vol. 1, *Labor Mobility among Social Security Covered Workers in the Puerto Rican Labor Force* (San Juan, 1974). For sociopolitical approaches, see Maldonado-Denis, *Puerto Rico y Estados Unidos;* Maldonado-Denis, *Puerto Rico: A Socio-Historic Interpretation,* esp. pp. 302–24; and Luis Nieves Falcón, *El emigrante puertorriqueño* (Río Piedras, P.R.: Editorial Edil, 1975).

6. These statistics correspond to a descriptive reality, which depends on the vocabulary and ideology of the analyst. The narrower income distribution may be the result of less social mobility and more prejudice. Higher individual earnings reflect the predominance of urban industrial and

service-sector employment, which is high paying compared to work as a Mexican American farmhand. On the other hand, living costs are notoriously exorbitant in the ghetto.

7. Inferences can be made, with caution, from the U.S. Census sample results for the Puerto Rican population in the United States. How much of the observed changes are cyclical, structural, or due simply to changes in the sample coverage? "Between March, 1972, and March, 1973," the introduction to the 1974 edition reads, "the CPS sample was changed to reflect new information available from the 1970 Census on the geographical distribution of the population of the United States." The results for March 1973 and after "are not directly comparable to the estimates from the CPS of earlier years." See U.S. Census, *Current Population Report* P-20, no. 250, "Persons of Spanish Origin in the United States: March, 1973" (Washington, D.C., 1974), p. 8. The lack of comparability has to do with the classification of children if the wife is of Spanish origin but the husband (head of household) is not; a change in the identification of those of Mexican origin; and a change in the sampling variability due to a change in the sample base from 5 percent of the entire population in the 1970 census to 1/800. While these changes might affect the data on overall population and certain characteristics of the young, it is difficult to dismiss or disregard the trends in other characteristics in the adult Puerto Rican population.

8. See Mass, "Emigration and Sterilization in Puerto Rico," in *Population Target,* pp. 87–108; and Presser, *Sterilization and Fertility Decline in Puerto Rico.* Compare Brown, *Dynamite on Our Doorstep;* and O. Lewis, *La Vida.*

9. Compare the profiles in Berger and Mohr, *Seventh Man,* to the Puerto Rican migration literature cited in note 5. See Dominguez, "From Neighbor to Stranger," for parallels among the migrations from the American, British, Hispanic, and French islands.

10. See Moreno Fraginals, "The Work," *Sugarmill,* pt. 5.

11. Those workers who return to Puerto Rico have labored more months in more jobs in more industries in more locations, and yet face higher unemployment, than those who never left Puerto Rico. A Puerto Rican working man who emigrated to the United States and returned to Puerto Rico is on the average thirty-three years old, compared to thirty-eight years for the average nonemigrant; he has worked eighteen jobs, compared to ten for the nonemigrant; in six rather than three industries and locations; during thirty-six rather than thirty-seven quarters of the year. The migrant population shows a greater initial concentration in agriculture. By 1967, the men who had returned to Puerto Rico were employed to a greater extent in construction and agriculture and less in commerce and government. The women who returned show somewhat greater stability, beginning and ending with a greater share in manufacturing.

12. See, for example, Marqués's classic, *Oxcart;* and Levine, *Benjy Lopez.*

Chapter 11. Puerto Rico as Prototype: The Intellectual Background

1. See Corretjer, *La lucha por la independencia de Puerto Rico;* testimony of the Commander of the U.S. Naval Forces, Caribbean, in the U.S. House of Representatives, *Naval Training Activities on the Island of Vieques, Puerto Rico,* pp. 51–53; and John Enders, *La presencia militar de los Estados Unidos en Puerto Rico* (Río Piedras, P.R.: Proyecto Caribeño de Justicia y Paz, 1981).

2. See Hirschman, ed., *Latin American Issues,* pp. 3–42; Girvan, "Development of Dependency Economics in the Caribbean and Latin America," is the exception.

3. See esp. Reynolds, "Wages and Unemployment in a Labor Surplus Economy"; and Reynolds and Gregory, *Wages, Productivity, and Industrialization in Puerto Rico.* But the literature goes back to Galbraith and Solo, "Puerto Rican Lessons in Economic Development"; Hanson, *Transformation;* Baer, "Puerto Rico"; Jaffe, *People, Jobs, and Economic Development;* Haring, "External Trade as an Engine of Growth"; and Picó, "Economic Development in Puerto Rico."

4. "Puerto Rico," in Szulc, ed., *United States and the Caribbean,* p. 93. Ironically, Frank

McDonald's chapter, "The Commonwealth Caribbean," tells us more about Puerto Rico, while Kalman Silvert's conclusions, "The Caribbean and North America," ignore their fundamental differences.

5. Stephansky, "Puerto Rico," p. 93.

6. See U.S. House of Representatives, *Caribbean Basin Policy.*

7. Stephansky, "Puerto Rico," p. 94.

8. "Industrialization of the British West Indies," p. 30.

9. For the first image, one is reminded of the coat of arms of the Commonwealth of Puerto Rico. On the second image, we are reminded of the Christmas extravaganza in San Juan of flying down a planeload of snow, hardly an enduring phenomenon. Lewis was not keen on allowing just any industry. He outlined eight criteria (wage shares, horsepower, and so on) and then ranked forty-two industries by these criteria.

10. Compare Demas, *Economics of Development in Small Countries with Special Reference to the Caribbean,* chap. 4; "Employment Strategies in the Commonwealth Caribbean," to W. A. Lewis, "Economic Development with Unlimited Supplies of Labour." Demas writes that the "two main intellectual influences underpinning the attempts to create a new economic, social, and political order in the West Indies in the post-1945 world were the Moyne Commision Report, 1938, and the philosophy of industrial development evolved in the early 1950's from the experience of Puerto Rico." See *Political Economy of the English-Speaking Caribbean,* p. 7.

11. See Demas, *Economics of Development in Small Countries,* p. 32, n. 32. The citation of Hoselitz is from "Patterns of Economic Growth," *Canadian Journal* 21 (1955), pp. 420–21.

12. *Essays on Caribbean Integration and Development,* p. 107.

13. See Levitt and Best, *Externally-Propelled Growth and Industrialization in the Caribbean;* and Beckford, *Persistent Poverty,* on plantation economies. See Girvan, *Foreign Capital and Economic Underdevelopment in Jamaica;* Jefferson, *Post-War Economic Development of Jamaica;* C. Thomas, *Monetary and Financial Arrangements in a Dependent Monetary Economy;* St. Pierre, "Political Factor and the Nationalization of the Demarara Bauxite Co., Guyana"; and Armstrong, Daniel, and Francis, "Structural Analysis of the Barbados Economy, 1968." See Brown and Brewster, "Review of the Study of Economies in the English-Speaking Caribbean," for summary hypotheses and some 171 references. See also Eduardo Seda-Bonilla, "Dependence as an Obstacle to Development: Puerto Rico," and Lloyd Best, "Independent Thought and Caribbean Freedom," both in Girvan and Jefferson, eds., *Readings in the Political Economy of the Caribbean.* The literature of the British Caribbean is refreshing and extensive.

14. W. A. Lewis, "Economic Development with Unlimited Supplies of Labour"; and Reynolds, "Wages and Unemployment in a Labor Surplus Economy."

15. Reynolds, "China as a Less Developed Economy."

16. Only in response to the most basic of challenges does the modern neoclassical economist turn away from economic arguments and rely on political factors. See Birnberg and Resnick, *Colonial Development,* for an attempted reconciliation.

17. See Chenery and Taylor, "Development Patterns," p. 397, for charts of the primary and industrial sectors' shares "among countries and over time."

18. *Caribbean,* p. x.

19. *Ibid.,* p. xii, and chap. 7, "Caribbean Nation Building 1804–1970," esp. pp. 159, 162, 169, 175.

20. *Ibid.,* p. 211.

21. *Ibid.,* p. 166. Also see Corretjer, *La patria radical.*

22. See G. Lewis, *Growth of the Modern West Indies,* on the British islands; see Mintz, "Caribbean as a Socio-Cultural Area"; and Maingot, "Diplomacy and Policy Toward West Indian Socialism in the Mare Nostrum," on West Indian politics. Compare Jonnard, *Caribbean Investment Handbook,* to Wachtel, *New Gnomes.* Compare Hagelberg, *Caribbean Sugar Industries,* to Girvan, *Corporate Imperialism,* on Caribbean bauxite.

Chapter 12. Puerto Rico as Caribbean Prototype: The Statistical Background

1. See W. Lewis, "Economic Development with Unlimited Supplies of Labour," and "Unlimited Supplies of Labour: Further Notes"; but see also Reynolds, "Wages and Unemployment in a Labor Surplus Economy," for its application to Puerto Rico. And see Fei and Ranis, *Development of the Labor Surplus Economy,* for further elaboration.

2. See Hymer and Resnick, "Model of an Agrarian Economy with Non-agricultural Activities," for a theoretical treatment of the other activities.

3. See Mintz's introduction to Guerra y Sanchez, *Sugar and Society.*

4. Contrast the early writings of Taylor, "Neo-Malthusianism in Puerto Rico," with Meade, "Mauritius."

5. Presser, *Sterilization and Fertility Decline in Puerto Rico,* estimates that by 1965, "one-third of all Puerto Rican mothers from 20–49 years of age were sterilized" (p. 179), and that the sterilization of one-sixth of the same age group of women by 1953–54 had not resulted in a decline in fertility. She concludes that, in the absence of a large government or private campaign, the "popularity" of sterilization was a "response by Puerto Rican women who were searching for an effective way to limit the size of their families."

Chapter 13. Failings of the Labor-Surplus Model

1. Compare International Bank for Reconstruction and Development, *World Development Report 1978,* with Amnesty International, *Amnesty International Report 1977.*

2. "That is, unless this time we encountered Them, around and around. It is not a cycle without ports we long to reach. Nancy waits for poor Charlie in Puerto Rico. . . . Joined by all the girls in her town, they sang together . . . /oh now we reach it—/now, now!/The whistling hub of the world./It's as if God had spun a whirlpool,/Flung up a new continent./

"And then we would have each other out of sight, our tears lessening with each circuit, for we were set for our first sight of Them, and they, the women, were waiting with us, for on us their release depended, since they were prisoners on that island" (Doris Lessing, *Briefing for a Descent into Hell* [New York: Knopf, 1971], quoted from Vintage edition, 1981, pp. 14–15).

3. See Weisskoff and Wolff, "Development and Trade Dependence."

4. A colonial administration notoriously resolved conflicts with its own legions or with resident or mercenary armies. Colonialism then could hardly be replaced by a harmoniously working economic model. The construction of a national economy, even in the labor-surplus path, invites constant intervention by international and neocolonial armies.

5. See Corretjer, *La lucha por la independencia de Puerto Rico;* and Geertz, *Agricultural Involution.*

6. See Perelman, *Farming for Profit in a Hungry World.*

7. See Weisskoff, "Income Distribution and Economic Growth in Puerto Rico, Argentina, and Mexico," for early documentation on the widening of the income distribution. The literature today is vast: see Chenery et al., *Redistribution with Growth;* and Frank and Webb, eds., *Income Distribution and Growth in Less-Developed Countries,* for different reviews and approaches.

8. Analyses of actual crises usually focus on the precipitating political issues. The point here is to evaluate the failings of the economic structures as they become evident. Thus, the American invasion of Grenada in 1983 may be viewed as a response to the attempt by the smallest of nations to change its economic model. Likewise, the austerity programs of the International Monetary Fund seek to enforce conformity to their economic model in return for packages of loans from the Western community. In reaction, note the riots in the Dominican Republic and Haiti in April and May 1984. See Selwyn Ryan, "Grenada Questions: A Revolutionary Balance Sheet," and Bernard Diederich, "Troubled Island of Hispaniola," *Caribbean Review* (Summer 1984).

9. See speeches of Pedro Albizu Campos in *Obras Escogidas 1923–1935,* vol. 1 (San Juan: Editorial Jelofe, 1975).

10. "The authors . . . find this view unacceptable," Adelman and Robinson (*Income Distribution Policy in Developing Countries*) conclude in their World Bank–sponsored study, in which they apply one of the most comprehensive and mechanical models to South Korea.

First, it took a very long time . . . for the industrial revolution to begin to furnish substantial benefits to the poor. The poor in modern less-developed countries are justifiably more impatient. And second, the vast majority of the poor . . . are very poor indeed, with ubiquitous malnutrition, actually approaching the point of starvation in many areas. . . . The costs of renegotiating the social contract are never low, but they cannot be avoided. . . . The question is not whether there will be change; it is rather in what direction and to what extent. Will there be a relatively peaceful transition to a more equitable economy and society, with some structural change but with the essential aspects of a free market economy preserved? . . . Or will there be a violent revolution with great costs and unpredictable outcome for the future path of the economy and society? Our results indicate that the first course is an economic possibility. Whether it is a political possiblity as well is still an open question (pp. 201–2).

Chapter 14. Consumption as a Subversive Activity

1. See the descriptions of living standards in the studies of field and town life in Stewart et al., *People of Puerto Rico,* pt. 3.

2. See Weisskoff and Figueroa, "Traversing the Social Pyramid."

3. See the descriptions of the standard of living in Raymond L. Scheele, "The Prominent Families of Puerto Rico," in Stewart et al., *People of Puerto Rico;* and G. Lewis's chapters "Class and Community" and the "Debate on 'Americanization,' " in *Puerto Rico.*

4. See Sinha et al., *Poverty, Income Distribution and Employment;* and Adelman and Robinson, *Income Distribution Policy in Developing Countries.* Adelman and Robinson find the radical economic solution attractive in economic terms, much to their surprise and to the surprise of their World Bank sponsors: "It is perhaps surprising that the socialist package comes off as well as it does. In terms of the overall distribution, it is in fact superior to any other strategy. . . . it is only the people in the top three deciles who suffer relative to the basic run. . . . The six lowest deciles are better off" (p. 172).

5. See Weisskoff, "Growth and Decline of Import Substitution in Brazil—Revisited," p. 668.

6. A recent high-level study recommended import substitution policies for Puerto Rico, and cited my earlier work. See Comité Interagencial de la Estratégia de Puerto Rico, *El desarrollo económico de Puerto Rico,* pp. 65–71.

7. See Weisskoff and Wolff, "Linkages and Leakages."

8. "An even more fundamental question is raised by the genuine possibility that the distribution of income is so deeply embedded in the structure . . . that it can only be affected by a major, and presumably violent, upheaval. . . . Such an approach should only be regarded as a solution of last resort. It is, therefore, most important to explore how much can be done to reduce inequality starting from the existing social, political and economic framework and working gradually within an acceptable time period." Adelman and Robinson, *Income Distribution Policy in Developing Countries,* p. 2.

Chapter 15. History and Counterhistory

1. See Amnesty International, *Amnesty International Report 1977;* Chomsky and Herman, *Washington Connection and Third World Fascism;* and U.S. House of Representatives, *Human Rights in Guatemala,* and *U.S. Arms Transfer Policy in Latin America.*

2. On Hong Kong, see Lim, "General Equilibrium Model of an Export Dependent Economy."

On Peru, see Figueroa, "Income Distribution, Employment and Development," or its summary, "Income Distribution, Demand Structure and Employment." On Brazil, see Francisco P. Lopes, "Inequality Planning in the Developing Economy (Ph.D. diss., Harvard University, 1972). On Pakistan, see Soligo, "Factor Intensity of Consumption Patterns, Income Distribution and Employment Growth in Pakistan." On Ecuador, see Tokman, "Income Distribution, Technology and Employment in Developing Countries: An Application to Ecuador." Many of the early studies are reviewed in Morawetz, "Employment Implications of Industrialization in Developing Countries"; and Cline, "Distribution and Development." On Sri Lanka, see Pyatt, Roe, and associates, *Social Accounting for Development Planning with Special Reference to Sri Lanka*. On South Korea, see Adelman and Robinson, *Income Distribution Policy in Developing Countries*. On India, see Radha Sinha et al., *Poverty, Income Distribution and Employment*. All these models are constructed for conservative scenarios, as Adelman and Robinson state clearly: "to this end, we have developed a model . . . a laboratory for investigating the potential impact of standard economic policy . . . intended to improve the relative and absolute incomes of the poor" (p. 2).

3. "Basic needs programs have been initiated through which public amenities are distributed to the rural poor. By thus putting the world's poor on welfare, they constitute the last card of the disarticulated alliance in attempting to reproduce the objective possibility of functional dualism. Today, they are at the core of the programs of international agencies" *The Agrarian Question and Reformism in Latin America* (Baltimore: Johns Hopkins University Press, 1981), p. 254.

4. See Mintz, "Culture History of a Puerto Rican Sugar Cane Plantation, 1876–1949"; Mintz, *Worker in the Cane;* and Sidney W. Mintz, "Reflections on Caribbean Peasantries," *New West Indian Guide* 57, nos. 1 and 2 (1983), pp. 1–15, esp. his comments on agriculture and Caribbean cuisine. On the nineteenth-century sugar industry, see Andrés A. Ramos Mattei, "Los Libros de Cuenta de la Hacienda Mercedita, 1861–1900: Apuntes para el Estudio de la Transición Hacia el Sistema de Centrales en la Industria Azucarera de Puerto Rico," CEREP Cuaderno no. 4 (San Juan, 1975).

5. On the system of *libreta,* or forced wage labor, in the coffee sector, see Fernando Picó, *Libertad y servidumbre en el Puerto Rico del siglo XIX: los jornaleros utuadeños en vísperas del auge del café* (Río Piedras, P.R.: Ediciones Huracán, 1979). For publication of 856 registered *libretas,* work histories, and personal descriptions, see Fernando Picó, *Registro general de jornaleros, Utuado, Puerto Rico (1849–50)* (Río Piedras, P.R.: Ediciones Huracán, 1976).

6. The transition of economic control and the creation of the new production system is analyzed in José A. Herrero, "La Mitología del Azúcar, un Ensayo de Historia Económica de Puerto Rico: 1900–70," CEREP Cuaderno no. 5 (San Juan, 1975); and A. G. Quintero, "Puerto Rico 1870–1940, from Mercantilist to Imperialist Colonial Domination," CEREP Cuaderno (San Juan, n.d.). A close reading of the primary materials written during the early years of American occupation testifies to the hardship imposed on workers, merchants, and landowners by the substitution of U.S. currency at a rate arbitrarily fixed by the military administration. See Davis, *Report on Civil Affairs of Puerto Rico 1899*, pp. 29–33. Also see the text of General Order no. 30 for the command fixing the exchange rate, pp. 104–5. Davis notes: "The only way to force American money into circulation . . . is to withdraw the pesos, thereby creating such a deficiency as will result in the American money leaving the vaults. . . . As long as an exchange value for the peso is arbitrarily fixed at 60, this provincial money will remain in the island. . . . Local businessmen and native officials . . . have argued that it would be but just and equitable to establish a new official rate of exchange of . . . 75 cents American money. . . ." (pp. 30–32).

One journalist reported:

Under such circumstances, any policy which tends to still further decrease the purchasing power of their silver . . . must do a serious injustice to the natives of this island. . . . It also means the crushing out of commercial activity among the indigenous population, and the aggrandizement of every monied American who may desire to invest his capital in this rich and fertile region. As financier, are we willing to further oppress a people who have suffered much already at the hands of rapacious rulers? . . . What argument can be advanced to defend our government against the severest criticism for having, through military power, set an arbitrary rate of exchange, whereby every peso collected at fifty cents by our Treasury may be reminted, after the addition of five cents' worth of silver into one of our own silver dollars?

See William Dinwiddie, *Puerto Rico: Its Conditions and Possibilities* (New York: Harper, 1899), pp. 223–24. See also Juan Manuel Delgado, *Grandes acontecimientos en la historia de Ciales* (Ciales, P.R.: Sociedad Ciales Histórico, 1979). New data are now becoming available for a rewriting of the entire transition period from Spanish to American rule in Puerto Rico.

7. See Gayer, *Sugar Economy of Puerto Rico;* and History Task Force, *Labor Migration under Capitalism.* See also Angel Quintero Rivera, "Socialista y Tabaquero: la Proletarización de los Artesanos," *Sin Nombre* 8, no. 4 (Jan.–March, 1978), pp. 101–37, and the series by A. Quintero Rivera, "La Clase Obrera y el Proceso Político en Puerto Rico," *Revista Ciencias Sociales* 18, nos. 3–4 (Sept.–Dec. 1974), pp. 61–110; vol. 19, no. 1 (March 1975), pp. 47–100; and vol. 19, no. 3 (Sept. 1975), pp. 261–300.

8. See the speeches of Albizu Campos, especially in his dealings between the police and the National Sugarworkers Union, in *La conciencia nacional puertorriqueña* (México, D.F.: Siglo 21, 1972) and in *Obras escogidas 1923–1935* (San Juan: Editorial Jelofe, 1975). See also Brown, *Dynamite on Our Doorstep,* for a somewhat dramatized account of social discontent. See also the sources quoted in Angel Quintero Rivera, *Workers' Struggle in Puerto Rico: A Documentary History,* translated by Cedric Belfrage (New York: Monthly Review, 1976), pp. 113–21.

9. G. Lewis, *Puerto Rico,* chap. 7, describes and analyzes the 1932–40 period of the early New Deal, when a series of federal relief agencies were sent to Puerto Rico. "It is easy to see, in retrospect, what went wrong," wrote Lewis. "The New Deal had grown up as a movement of response to American problems. It transferred to Puerto Rico without much recognition of the truth that those methods which succeed in a national democracy may not necessarily succeed in a dependent colony. What was 'liberalism' for American became, at best, 'enlightened imperalism' for Puerto Ricans. This was better than unenlightened imperialism; but it was imperialism, nonetheless. . . . The imperialism of neglect had merely been exchanged for the imperialism of liberal paternalism" (p. 140). See also Mathews, *Puerto Rican Politics and the New Deal;* and Tugwell, *Stricken Land,* which G. Lewis calls "the epitaph of enlightened colonialism" (*Puerto Rico,* p. 140).

10. The Land Authority, Planning Board, a budget bureau, a statistical service, Minimum Wage Board, Transportation Authority, Communications Authority, Water Resource Authority, Housing Authority, Development Company, Development Bank, reorganization of the University of Puerto Rico, the School of Public Administration, all important institutions to this day.

11. Credit for the successful challenge to the large landholdings should also be given, of course, to Tugwell and the 1941 land law, "which gave the new Land Authority the legal power of eminent domain against the sugar corporations and the power to buy lands condemned through legal proceedings." See Lewis, *Puerto Rico,* p. 153.

12. Perloff, *Puerto Rico's Economic Future;* and Koenig, *Comprehensive Agricultural Program for Puerto Rico.* Compare to Alain de Janvry, *The Agrarian Question and Reformism in Latin America* (Baltimore: Johns Hopkins University Press, 1981), chap. 7.

13. See Alexander, "Luis Muñoz Marín and the Puerto Rico Miracle," in *Prophets of the Revolution: Profiles of Latin American Leaders,* pp. 74–197; also Charles D. Ameringer, "The Tradition of Democracy in the Caribbean; Betancourt, Figueres, Muñoz and the Democratic Left," *Caribbean Review* 11, no. 2 (Spring 1982), p. 28ff.

14. See Tugwell, *Stricken Land,* p. 64; and W. A. Lewis, *Labour in the West Indies.* Paul Blanshard calls the unrest in the Caribbean, "the modern labor rebellion," and he links the events and conditions in the British and American West Indies. See *Democracy and Empire in the Caribbean* (New York: Macmillan, 1947), pp. 21–28. See also Annette Baker Fox, *Freedom and Welfare in the Caribbean* (New York: Harcourt, Brace, 1949), pp. 29–33, for a similar analysis. John Gunther relates his impressions of Puerto Rico, of Muñoz-Marín, and of the wartime

defense preparations. He called Puerto Rico, "the Gibraltar to the Canal . . . the key to our Caribbean defense system." See *Inside Latin America* (New York: Harper, 1941), pp. 432–35.

15. See Bergad, *Coffee and the Growth of Agrarian Capitalism in Nineteenth-Century Puerto Rico,* pp. 134–44.

16. The history of the use of force in internal politics in Puerto Rico is documented in the civil liberties reports reviewed in G. Lewis, *Puerto Rico.* The point here is merely to note that it is an ongoing factor in Puerto Rican affairs. See also Corretjer, *La lucha por la independencia de Puerto Rico.* For a revisionist history of this period, see Emilio González Díaz, "Ideología Popularista y Estrategias de Desarrollo en Puerto Rico, 1940–50," CEREP Cuaderno no. 3 (San Juan, n.d.), and A. G. Quintero Rivera, "La Base Social de la Transformación Ideológica del Partido Popular Democrático en la Década de 1940–1950," paper presented at the Conference for Planning National Social Development (San Juan, May 4, 1975).

17. See, for example, the U.S. Justice Department investigation surrounding the alleged police entrapment at Cerro Maravilla in 1978 (*Miami Herald,* Dec. 11, 1983). Tugwell himself wrote retrospectively about the commonwealth: "Muñoz . . . showed his people the neatest trick of all—how they could have their cake and eat it. They could rid themselves of 'foreigners' and yet have all the assistance, on which they had become dependent, as a right. . . . How could the *independentistas*—who would have thrown away all these gifts—or the statehood party . . . compete with the status represented by Muñoz." See Rexford G. Tugwell, *The Art of Politics as Practiced by Three Great Americans: Franklin Delano Roosevelt, Luis Muñoz Marín, and Fiorello H. La Guardia* (Garden City, N.Y.: Doubleday, 1958), p. 50.

18. See P. Sraffa, *Production of Commodities by Means of Commodities, Prelude to a Critique of Economic Theory* (Cambridge: Cambridge University Press, 1972); and North American Congress on Latin America, "Puerto Rico."

19. An alternative system of political economy holds axiomatically that all value comes from human work. Profit is simply unpaid wages. The economic game is then to get labor away from those who have a monopoly on it—the work force—by having them compete with each other, driving down their own wage. This leaves those who have a monopoly on capital—the corporations and banks—to appropriate as surplus value the difference between the value that labor produces and the wage that the laborer receives. It was an astute and innovative Henry Ford who discovered that if he raised the wage of his workers and selected only the best applicants for each job, he could receive a value from these workers greater than the increased wage he paid them. And more value forthcoming from the work force meant more surplus value. See E. Wolff, "The Rate of Surplus Value in Puerto Rico," *Journal of Political Economy* 83, no. 5 (1975), pp. 935–49.

Chapter 16. Crops versus Coupons: Puerto Rican Agriculture, Record of the Descent

1. Puerto Rico Planning Board, *Economic Report to the Governor,* for the years 1960–70 contain many comparisons with European industrial countries, especially with respect to their industrial share and population densities.

2. Calculated from U.S. Census Bureau, *1980 Census of Population and Housing,* PHC80-P-53, "Puerto Rico," Preliminary reports (Washington, D.C.: U.S. Department of Commerce, February 1981).

3. Many observations in this section are made on the basis of my tenure as a rural resident and agricultural worker in Lares during 1980.

4. On the cane culture, see Mintz, *Worker in the Cane.*

5. Average plot sizes are from the *U.S. Census of Agriculture, 1964,* table 6, p. 9; and *1978,* table 16, p. 6.

6. At the turn of the century, the *Encyclopedia Britannica* (1904) described the dominance of local agriculture before the coming of the U.S. sugar plantation: "The rice, which is the principal food of the labourer, is a mountain variety grown without flooding. On the lowland pastures, . . . great herds of excellent cattle are reared to supply butcher-meat for St. Thomas and the French Islands. In general, Porto Rico may be described as extremely fertile, and its exports more than double in value those of Jamaica" (p. 547). In 1883, the major exports were sugar and molasses, coffee, honey, and tobacco.

7. See Koenig, *Comprehensive Agricultural Program for Puerto Rico;* also Koenig, *Role of Cooperatives in the Production and Marketing of Fruits and Vegetables in Puerto Rico,* Pts. 1 and 2 (Washington, D.C., 1970).

8. See Nathan Koenig and Checchi and Co., "The Sugar Industry in Puerto Rico: An Integrated Program for the Future" (Washington, D.C., December 1971); and Staff of the Interagency Strategy Committee for the Finance Council, "The Agricultural Economy of Puerto Rico: Evaluation and Policy Suggestions" (San Juan, October 1975).

9. See Perelman, *Farming for Profit in a Hungry World.*

10. See Alain de Janvry, *The Agrarian Question and Reformism in Latin America* (Baltimore: Johns Hopkins University Press, 1981), for a comprehensive theory and classification of responses.

11. The parallels de Janvry describes for the Latin American peasantry, indeed of the whole process of proletarianization, is strikingly similar to the Puerto Rican experience. He writes of the Russian process, "Thus the rural proletariat very often has the appearance of a peasant, owing to his control over a small plot of land, even though the social relations that characterize it are more those of a worker. It is the existence of this allotment-holding rural laborer which accounts in part for the Narodniks' insistence on the permanence of the peasantry, even under capitalism" (*Ibid.,* p. 99).

Chapter 17. Conclusion: Toward a New Political Economy

1. Weisskoff and Wolff, "Linkages and Leakages."

2. See Joseph Schumpeter, "Money, Credit, and Cycles," in *A History of Economic Analysis* (New York: Oxford University Press, 1954), pp. 1117–34. Business cycles are little understood and are understudied in modern economics. After all, the dominant paradigm, that of Keynesian thought, teaches us that depressions can be avoided through the correct management of final demand.

3. See the recommendations of the Tobin Commission: Staff of the Interagency Strategy Committee, *The Economic Development of Puerto Rico: A Strategy for the Next Decade* (November 1975).

4. See San Juan *Star,* October 30, 1983.

5. See Weisskoff, "Food Stamps and the Puerto Rican Economy."

6. Koenig, *Comprehensive Agricultural Program for Puerto Rico,* pp. i–v. The population of 3 million projected by Koenig turned out to be the actual population in 1980.

7. Public Law 97-35 of the U.S. Congress (The Omnibus Budget Reconciliation Act of 1981) replaced Puerto Rico's food stamp program by a block grant fixed at an annual level of $825 million for food assistance. Since July 1, 1982, the government of Puerto Rico has distributed this bonus as cash grants rather than as food coupons. The final charade of food aid was dropped; the grants are simply cash subsidies through the people to U.S. imports. (See U.S. Department of Agriculture, Food and Nutrition Service, Office of Analysis and Evaluation, "Evaluation of the Puerto Rico Nutrition Assistance Program.") Of the $825 million, $25 million has been earmarked for special agricultural projects, which include a loan fund for farmers, a crop-protection spraying program, and a tick eradication program. The irony is that responsibility for these programs has been placed in the hands of the Puerto Rico Department of Social Services and

overseen by the Middle-Atlantic Region of the Federal Food Stamp Office in Robbinsville, New Jersey. Neither agency has much experience in food production.

8. See N. Koenig, *The Role of Cooperatives in the Production and Marketing of Fruits and Vegetables in Puerto Rico* (Washington, D.C.: Checchi and Co., 1970). See also Nathan Koenig and Checchi and Co., "The Sugar Industry in Puerto Rico: An Integrated Program for the Future, A Proposal for Diagnosing Puerto Rico's Sugar Industry," submitted to the Puerto Rico Department of Agriculture December 1971 and February 1973. A general revision of the global agricultural setting had been made by José Vicente Chandler, *Conceptos, Plan y Programa para una Agricultura Moderna en Puerto Rico* (San Juan, January 1978). Chandler projected food consumption to 1988 and then examined the water and land available for each crop, their yields, costs, and inputs. He concluded that agriculture could be modernized at a cost of $27.5 million a year for the twelve-year period. His program, however, emphasizes sugarcane, rice, and vegetables. "If necessary," Chandler writes, "Puerto Rico could produce all the food required by its population provided some changes are made in food preferences. . . . In the plans and programs described in this document, total self-sufficiency is not contemplated but a combination of economic agricultural enterprises producing the great majority of the island's food requirements and some items for export, such as vegetables for the U.S. winter market and fresh pineapples and other tropical fruits" (p. 499).

9. See Tahal Consulting Engineers, Ltd., with the Commonwealth of Puerto Rico Department of Agriculture and The State of Israel Ministry of Agriculture, "Programa Estratégico para el Desarrollo Integrado del Sector Agropecuario en el Próximo Decenio," 4 vols. (San Juan, February 1984).

10. See "Puerto Rico Tax Revisions: Benefits Are Curbed for Some," *New York Times,* September 15, 1982. See also, "USA Repudiates the 936 (Tax Exemption)," *El Nuevo Día,* December 4, 1984.

11. See "Why Latin America's Debt Crisis Won't Go Away," *Business Week,* April 16, 1984.

12. This neglect is most clearly seen in the numerous studies on the Puerto Rican economy. Of the 600 pages in the Tobin Commission report, only 24 pages are devoted to agriculture. See Staff of the Interagency Strategy Committee, "The Agricultural Economy of Puerto Rico: Evaluation and Policy Suggestions" (San Juan October 1975); and "A New Agriculture," in Interagency Strategy Committee, *The Economic Development of Puerto Rico: A Strategy for the Next Decade* (November 1975). Reprinted as *El desarrollo económico de Puerto Rico: una estratégia para la próxima década* (Río Piedras, P. R.: Editorial Universidad de Puerto Rico, 1976). Four years later, the U.S. Department of Commerce coordinated an Interagency Task Force whose *Economic Study of Puerto Rico* devoted 15 of its 1,079 pages to a superficial analysis of agriculture.

13. See A. Berg, *The Nutrition Factor: Its Role in National Development* (Washington, D.C.: Brookings, 1973), on similar transitions to temperate-climate diets. See Cabanillas, Ginorio, and Quiros de Mercado, *Cocine a Gusto;* and Lillian Colon de Reguero and Sylvia M. Rodriguez de Santiago, *Tabla de Composición de Alimentos de Uso Corriente en Puerto Rico* (Río Piedras, P. R.: Editorial Universidad de Puerto Rico, 1978), on the advantages and uses of local foods. See also Laurence Simon, "Misdevelopment in Puerto Rico," *Food Monitor* (May/June 1980), pp. 4–8. A cruel irony is the appearance of these "inferior" West Indian fruits, roots, nuts, and vegetables in North American health stores at premium prices! How closely the average Puerto Rican diet has come to the average U.S. diet is measured by data from the U.S. Department of Agriculture, Human Nutrition Information Service, *Food Consumption and Dietary Levels of Households in Puerto Rico, Summer and Fall 1977,* 1982 Analysis of Nationwide Food Consumption Survey, cited in U.S. Department of Agriculture, Food and Nutrition Service, "Evaluation of the Puerto Rican Nutrition Assistance Program," pp. viii–7.

14. According to the 1980 census, the population is still rather dispersed, and there are several ways of viewing the dispersion within the island. In 1980, 52 percent of the population resided in the four standard metropolitan statistical areas (SMSAs), compared to the 44 percent in 1970. However, the SMSAs are rather broadly defined, and only 24 percent of all Puerto Ricans live in the urban zones within the SMSAs. The population in the urban portion of the townships, or

municipios, totals 57 percent, leaving 43 percent of the people living in the rural zones. See U.S. Census Bureau, *1980 Census of Population and Housing,* Preliminary report, PHC80-P-53 Puerto Rico (February 1981).

15. This would entail a national commitment to the small-sized unit as well as the large, more easily monitored farms of the credit agencies. See Yujiro Hayami and Vernon W. Ruttan, *Agricultural Development: An International Perspective* (Baltimore: Johns Hopkins University Press, 1971), esp. chaps. 8 and 9, on comparing the transfer of technologies.

16. See Shlomo Reutlinger and Marcelo Selowsky, *Malnutrition and Poverty: Magnitude and Policy Options,* Occasional Paper 23 (Baltimore: Johns Hopkins University Press for the World Bank, 1976), pp. 46–52, for an analysis of the utility-maximizing consumer facing a variety of food programs. See also Marcelo Selowsky, "Target Group Oriented Food Programs: Cost Effective Comparisons, *American Journal of Agricultural Economics* 61, no. 5 (December 1979), pp. 988–94, for a comparison of food subsidies, food stamps, and direct-feeding programs.See Carlos Umpierre and Ernesto Ruíz Ortiz, *A mis amigos de la locura* (San Juan: Litografia Metropolitana, 1970); and Luis Rafael Sánchez, *La guaracha del macho Camacho* (Buenos Aires: Ediciones de la Flor, 1976).

17. See *Reportero* (San Juan), February 28, 1984, for a summary of the report of the Committee for Puerto Rico's Economic Development (COPRED) and the response by the Center for the Study of Puerto Rican Reality (CEREP). Also see Elías Gutierrez, "The Transfer Economy of Puerto Rico: Towards an Urban Ghetto," and José Joaquín Villamil, "Puerto Rico 1948–1979: The Limits of Dependent Growth," both in *Time for Decision: The United States and Puerto Rico,* edited by Jorge Heine (Lanham, Md.: North-South, 1983).

18. A prelude to any change in the economic paradigm may be political independence, but a change in status hardly guarantees major economic alteration. Independence could be negotiated with the United States and the same economic policies be continued. The rental fee for the U.S. naval base at Roosevelt Roads could be taken as "payment" in lieu of food stamps. Outmigration could continue. Or, should the world price of copper rise sufficiently to justify its exploitation, the cities could become even more congested as people free the lands in the western municipalities for strip mining. See Logic, Inc., *Cobre,* vol. 2, "Impacto de la Minería en el Sector Agropecuario de Puerto Rico" (San Juan, n.d.).

19. Nathan Koenig, interview March 16, 1981, quoted in Weisskoff, "Food Stamps and the Puerto Rican Economy."

20. See Committee to Study Puerto Rico's Finances (Tobin Commission), *Report to the Governor* (December 1975).

21. See "New Wave from Puerto Rico," *New York,* May 17, 1982.

22. Puerto Rico Planning Board, *Economic Report to the Governor 1984* (San Juan, 1985), table 23.

23. See Mathematica Policy Research, "Evaluation of the Nutrition Assistance Program in Puerto Rico," Prepared for the Food and Nutrition Service, vol. 2 (Washington, D.C.: June 1985), p. vi.

24. U.S. Census Bureau, *Census of Agriculture 1982,* vol. 1, pt. 52, Puerto Rico (Washington, D.C.: GPO, 1984), tables 18 and 38–59.

25. From the worksheets of the U.S. Census Bureau, State Estimates Division, and from the Puerto Rico Planning Board.

26. See U.S. Census Bureau, Current Population Reports, series P–20, no. 396, *Persons of Spanish Origin in the United States March 1982* (Washington, D.C.: GPO, 1985), tables 7 and 14.

27. See Puerto Rico Economic Development Administration, "Analysis of the President's Tax Credit in Section 936 of the U.S. Internal Revenue Code" (San Juan, n.d.); and "Puerto Rico and the Caribbean Basin Initiative" (San Juan, May 1985).

28. See Economic Development Administration, "Leading Companies Manufacturing in Puerto Rico" (San Juan, n.d.), for Fortune 500 firms.

Bibliography

Adelman, Irma, and Sherman Robinson. *Income Distribution Policy in Developing Countries: A Case Study of Korea.* Oxford: Oxford University Press for the World Bank, 1978.

Adelman, I., and E. Thorbecke, eds. *The Theory and Design of Economic Development.* Baltimore: Johns Hopkins Press, 1966.

Albizu Campos, Pedro. *La conciencia nacional puertorriqueña.* Compiled by Manuel Maldonado-Denis. Mexico, D.F.: Siglo Veintiuno, 1972.

Albizu Campos, Pedro. *Obras Escogidas.* Vol. 1, *1923–1935.* Compiled by J. Benjamin Torres. San Juan: Editorial Jelofe, 1975.

Alexander, Robert J. *Prophets of the Revolution: Profiles of Latin American Leaders.* New York: Macmillan, 1969.

Amnesty International. *Amnesty International Report 1977.* London: Amnesty International Publications, 1977.

Armstrong, W. E., S. Daniel, and A. A. Francis. "A Structural Analysis of the Barbados Economy, 1968." *Social and Economic Studies* 23, no. 4 (December 1974): 493–520.

Baer, Werner. "Puerto Rico: An Evaluation of a Successful Development Program." *Quarterly Journal of Economics* 73 (November 1959): 645–72.

Baer, Werner. *The Puerto Rican Economy and United States Economic Fluctuations.* Río Piedras, P.R.: Social Science Research Center, 1962.

Baerrensen, Donald W. *The Border Industrialization Program of Mexico.* Lexington, Mass.: D. C. Heath, 1971.

Baldwin, Robert E. "Patterns of Development in Newly Settled Regions." *The Manchester School of Economics and Social Studies* 24 (May 1956): 161–79.

Baran, Paul A. *The Political Economy of Growth.* New York: Monthly Review Press, 1957.

Bartlett, Frederick P., and Brandon Howell. *Puerto Rico y su problema de población.* Informe Técnico 2. Santurce, P.R.: Junta de Planificación, Urbanización y Zonificación, 1946.

Beckford, George L. *Persistent Poverty.* New York: Oxford University Press, 1972.

Bergad, Laird W. *Coffee and the Growth of Agrarian Capitalism in Nineteenth-Century Puerto Rico.* Princeton, N.J.: Princeton University Press, 1983.

Berger, John, and Jean Mohr. *A Seventh Man: Migrant Workers in Europe.* New York: Viking Press, A Richard Seaver Book, 1975.

Bienstock, Herbert. *Labor Force Experience of the Puerto Rican Worker.* New York: Center for Study of the Unemployed, Graduate School of Social Work, New York University, 1968.

Birnberg, Thomas B., and Stephen A. Resnick. *Colonial Development: An Econometric Study.* New Haven: Yale University Press, 1975.

Blitzer, Charles R., Peter B. Clark, and Lance Taylor, eds. *Economy-Wide Models and Development Planning.* Oxford: Oxford University Press for the World Bank, 1975.

Brewster, Havelock, and Clive Y. Thomas. *The Dynamics of West Indian Economic Integration.* Mona, Jamaica: Institute of Social and Economic Research, University of the West Indies, 1967.

Brown, Adlith, and Havelock Brewster. "A Review of the Study of Economies in the English-Speaking Caribbean." *Social and Economic Studies* 23, no. 1 (March 1974): 48–68.

Brown, Wenzell. *Dynamite on Our Doorstep: Puerto Rican Paradox.* New York: Greenberg, 1945.

Bruno, Michael. *Interdependence, Resource Use and Structural Change in Israel.* Jerusalem: Bank of Israel, 1965.

Cabanillas, Berta, Carmen Ginorio, and Carmen Quiros de Mercado. *Cocine a Gusto.* Río Piedras, P.R.: University of Puerto Rico Press, 1950.

Carter, Anne P. *Structural Change in the American Economy.* Cambridge, Mass.: Harvard University Press, 1970.

Caves, Richard E. "Export-led Growth and the New Economic History." In *Trade, Balance of Payments and Growth.* Edited by Jagdish Bhagwhati, et al. New York: American Elsevier, 1971.

Caves, Richard E. " 'Vent for Surplus' Models of Trade and Growth." In *Trade, Growth, and the Balance of Payments.* Edited by R. E. Baldwin. Chicago: Rand McNally, 1965.

Chenery, Hollis, et al. *Redistribution with Growth.* London: Oxford University Press, 1974.

Chenery, Hollis B., et al., eds. *Studies in Development Planning.* Cambridge, Mass.: Harvard University Press, 1971.

Chenery, H. S., and L. Taylor. "Development Patterns: Among Countries and Over Time." *Review of Economics and Statistics* 50, pt. 4 (November 1968): 391–416.

Chomsky, Noam, and Edward S. Herman. *The Washington Connection and Third World Fascism.* Vol. 1, *The Political Economy of Human Rights.* Boston: South End Press, 1979.

Clark, Victor S., et al. *Porto Rico and Its Problems.* Washington, D.C.: Brookings, 1930.

Cline, William R. "Distribution and Development: A survey of literature." *Journal of Development Economics* 1 (1975): 359–400.

Cline, William R. *The Potential Effect of Income Redistribution on Economic Growth in Six Latin American Countries.* New York: Praeger, 1972.

Comité Interagencial de la Estrategia de Puerto Rico. *El desarrollo económico de Puerto Rico: Una estrategia para la próxima década (Informe Echenique).* Informe preparado para el Consejo Financiero del Gobernador, November 1975. Río Piedras, P.R.: University of Puerto Rico Press, 1976.

Committee to Study Puerto Rico's Finance. *Report to the Governor.* San Juan: December 11, 1975. Published in Spanish as *Informe al Gobernador del Comité Para el Estudio de las Finanzas de Puerto Rico (Informe Tobin).* Río Piedras, P.R.: University of Puerto Rico Press, 1976. (Spanish edition includes text of the hearings.)

Conrad, Alfred H. "Redistribution through Government Budgets in the United States,

1950." *Income Redistribution and Social Policy.* Edited by Alan T. Peacock. London: Jonathan Cape, 1954.

Conrad, Alfred H., and John R. Meyer. *The Economics of Slavery and Other Studies in Econometric History.* Chicago: Aldine, 1964.

Cordasco, Francesco, with E. Bucchioni and D. Castellanos. *Puerto Ricans on the United States Mainland: A Bibliography.* Totawa, N.J.: Rowman & Littlefield, 1972.

Corretjer, Juan Antonio. *La lucha por la independencia de Puerto Rico.* 5th ed. Guaynabo, P.R.: Cooperativa de Artes Gráficas, "Romualdo Real": 1977.

Corretjer, Juan A. *La patria radical.* Santurce, P.R.: Liga Socialista Puertorriqueña, 1978.

Davis, George W. *Report on Civil Affairs of Puerto Rico 1899.* Washington, D.C.: Government Printing Office, 1900.

Demas, William G. *The Economics of Development in Small Countries with Special Reference to the Caribbean.* Montreal: McGill University Press, 1965.

Demas, William G. *Essays on Caribbean Integration and Development.* Mona, Jamaica: Institute of Social and Economic Research, University of the West Indies, 1976.

Demas, William G. *The Political Economy of the English-Speaking Caribbean.* Study Paper 4. Caribbean Ecumenical Consultation for Development, 1971.

Dominguez, Virginia R. *From Neighbor to Stranger: The Dilemma of Caribbean Peoples in the United States.* Occasional Paper 5. New Haven: Antilles Research Program, Yale University, 1975.

Duesenberry, James S., et al., eds. *The Brookings Quarterly Econometric Model of the United States.* Chicago: Rand McNally, 1965.

Dutta, M., and P. L. Sharma. "Alternative Estimators and Predictive Power of Alternative Estimators: An Econometric Model of Puerto Rico." *Review of Economics & Statistics* 55, no. 3 (August 1973): 381–85.

Dutta, M., and V. Su. "An Econometric Model of Puerto Rico." *Review of Economic Studies* 36, no. 3 (July 1969): 319–33.

Easterlin, Richard A., ed. *Population and Economic Change in Developing Countries.* Chicago: University of Chicago Press, 1980.

Economic Commission for Latin America. "The Growth and Decline of Import Substitution in Brazil." *Economic Bulletin for Latin America* 9, no. 1 (March 1964): 1–59.

Euripides. *The Bacchae and Other Plays.* Translated by Philip Vellacott. Harmondsworth: Penguin Books, 1954.

Evans, W. Duane, and Marvin Hoffenberg. "The Interindustry Relations Study." *Review of Economics and Statistics* 34, no. 2 (May 1952): 97–142.

Fei, John C. H., and Gustav Ranis. *Development of the Labor Surplus Economy: Theory and Policy.* Homewood, Ill.: Richard D. Irwin, 1964.

Fernández-García, ed. *El Libro de Puerto Rico* [*The Book of Puerto Rico*]. San Juan: El Libro Azul, 1923.

Festinger, Leon. *A Theory of Cognitive Dissonance.* Stanford: Stanford University Press, 1957.

Figueroa, Adolfo. "Income Distribution, Demand Structure and Employment: The Case of Peru." *Journal of Development Studies* 11, no. 2 (January 1975): 20–31.

Figueroa, Adolfo. "Income Distribution, Employment and Development: The Case of Peru." Ph.D. diss., Vanderbilt University, 1972.

Fitzpatrick, Joseph P. *Puerto Rican Americans: The Meaning of Migration to the Mainland.* Englewood Cliffs, N.J.: Prentice-Hall, 1971.

Fleischer, B. M. "Puerto Rican Migration to the United States." *Review of Economics and Statistics* 45 (1963): 245–48.

Food and Agriculture Organization. *Production Yearbook.* Rome: FAO, various years.

Frank, Charles R., Jr., and Richard C. Webb, eds. *Income Distribution and Growth in Less-Developed Countries.* Washington, D.C.: Brookings, 1977.

Friedlander, Stanley L. *Labor Migration and Economic Growth: A Case Study of Puerto Rico.* Cambridge, Mass.: MIT Press, 1965.

Galbraith, John K., and Richard H. Holton. *Marketing Efficiency in Puerto Rico.* Cambridge, Mass.: Harvard University Press, 1955.

Galbraith, J. K., and C. S. Solo. "Puerto Rican Lessons in Economic Development." *The Annals of the American Academy of Political and Social Science* 285 (January 1953): 55–59.

Garza, Catarino, ed. *Puerto Ricans in the U.S.: The Struggle for Freedom.* New York: Pathfinder Press, 1977.

Gautier-Mayoral, Carmen, and María del Pilar Argüelles. *Puerto Rico y la ONU.* Río Piedras, P.R.: Editorial Edil, 1978.

Gayer, Arthur D. *The Sugar Economy of Puerto Rico.* New York: Columbia University Press, 1938.

Geertz, Clifford. *Agricultural Involution.* Berkeley: University of California Press, 1963.

Gerschenkron, Alexander. *An Economic Spurt that Failed: Four Lectures in Austrian History.* Princeton, N.J.: Princeton University Press, 1977.

Girvan, Norman. *Corporate Imperialism: Conflict and Expropriation.* White Plains, N.Y.: M.E. Sharpe, 1976.

Girvan, Norman. "The Development of Dependency Economics in the Caribbean and Latin America: Review and Comparison." Mona, Jamaica: Department of Economics, University of the West Indies, 1972.

Girvan, Norman. *Foreign Capital and Economic Underdevelopment in Jamaica.* Mona, Jamaica: Institute of Social and Economic Research, University of the West Indies, 1971.

Girvan, Norman, and O. Jefferson, eds. *Readings in the Political Economy of the Caribbean.* Kingston, Jamaica: New World Group, 1971.

Goodsell, Charles T. *Administration of Revolution: Executive Reform in Puerto Rico under Governor Tugwell, 1941–1946.* Cambridge, Mass.: Harvard University Press, 1965.

Guerra y Sánchez, Ramiro. *Sugar and Society in the Caribbean: An Economic History of Cuban Agriculture.* New Haven: Yale University Press, 1964.

Hagelberg, G. B. *The Caribbean Sugar Industries: Constraints and Opportunities.* Occasional Paper 3. New Haven: Antilles Research Program, Yale University, 1974.

Hanson, Earl Parker. *Transformation: The Story of Modern Puerto Rico.* New York: Simon & Schuster, 1955.

Haring, J. E. "External Trade as an Engine of Growth." *Economia Internazionale* 14 (February 1961): 97–118.

Heine, Jorge, ed. *Time for Decision: The United States and Puerto Rico.* Lanham, Md.: North-South, 1983.

Hirschman, Albert O. *A Bias for Hope: Essays on Development and Latin America.* New Haven: Yale University Press, 1971.

Hirschman, Albert O., ed. *Latin American Issues: Essays and Comments.* New York: Twentieth Century Fund, 1961.

Hirschman, Albert O. "Obstacles to Development: A Classification and a Quasi-Vanishing Act." *Economic Development and Cultural Change* 13 (July 1965): 385–93.

Hirschman, Albert O. "The Political Economy of Import Substituting Industrialization in Latin America." *Quarterly Journal of Economics* 82, no. 1 (February 1968): 1–32.

Hirschman, Albert O. *The Strategy of Economic Development.* New Haven: Yale University Press, 1958.

History Task Force, Centro de Estudios Puertorriqueños. *Labor Migration under Capitalism: The Puerto Rican Experience.* New York: Monthly Review Press, 1979.

Houthakker, H. S., and Lester D. Taylor. *Consumer Demand in the United States, 1929–1970: Analyses and Projections.* Cambridge, Mass.: Harvard University Press, 1966.

Hymer, Stephen A., and Stephen Resnick. "A Model of an Agrarian Economy with Nonagricultural Activities." *American Economic Review* 59, pt. 4 (September 1969): 493–506.

Ingram, James C. *Regional Payments Mechanisms: The Case of Puerto Rico.* Chapel Hill: University of North Carolina Press, 1962.

Interagency Task Force coordinated by the U.S. Department of Commerce. *Economic Study of Puerto Rico: Report to the President.* Vols. 1, 2. Washington, D.C.: U.S. Department of Commerce, December 1979.

International Bank for Reconstruction and Development. *World Development Report 1978.* New York: Oxford University Press, 1978.

International Bank for Reconstruction and Development. *World Tables.* 2d ed. Baltimore: Johns Hopkins University Press, 1980.

Jaffe, Abram, J. *People, Jobs, and Economic Development: A Case History of Puerto Rico.* Glencoe, Ill.: Free Press, 1959.

Jefferson, Owen. *The Post-War Economic Development of Jamaica.* Mona, Jamaica: Institute of Social and Economic Research, University of the West Indies, 1972.

Jonnard, Claude M. *Caribbean Investment Handbook.* Park Ridge, N.J.: Noyes Data, 1974.

Kitto, H.D.F. *Greek Tragedy: A Literary Study.* Garden City, N.Y.: Doubleday-Anchor, n.d.

Knight, Franklin W. *The Caribbean: The Genesis of a Fragmented Nationalism.* New York: Oxford University Press, 1978.

Koenig, Nathan. *A Comprehensive Agricultural Program for Puerto Rico.* U.S. Department of Agriculture in Cooperation with the Commonwealth of Puerto Rico. Washington, D.C.: Government Printing Office, 1953.

Kuznets, Simon. *Modern Economic Growth: Rate, Structure, and Spread.* New Haven: Yale University Press, 1966.

Leavitt, Ruby Rohrlich. *The Puerto Ricans: Cultural Change and Language Deviance.* Tucson: University of Arizona Press, 1974.

L'Engle, Madeleine. *A Swiftly Tilting Planet.* New York: Dell, 1978.

Leontief, Wassily. *Input-Output Economics.* New York: Oxford University Press, 1966.

Leontief, Wassily, Anne P. Carter, and Peter A. Petri. *The Future of the World Economy: A United Nations Study.* New York: Oxford University Press, 1977.

Levine, Barry B. *Benjy Lopez: A Picaresque Tale of Emigration and Return.* New York: Basic Books, 1980.

Levitt, Kari, and Lloyd Best. *Externally-Propelled Growth and Industrialization in the Caribbean.* 4 vols. Montreal: McGill University, 1969.

Lewis, Gordon K. *The Growth of the Modern West Indies*. New York: Monthly Review Press, 1968.

Lewis, Gordon K. *Notes on the Puerto Rican Revolution*. New York: Monthly Review Press, 1974.

Lewis, Gordon K. *Puerto Rico: Freedom and Power in the Caribbean*. New York: Monthly Review Press, 1963.

Lewis, Oscar. *La Vida: A Puerto Rican Family in the Culture of Poverty—San Juan and New York*. New York: Random House, Vintage Books, 1965.

Lewis, W. Arthur. "Economic Development with Unlimited Supplies of Labour." *Manchester School* (May 1954): 139–91.

Lewis, W. Arthur. "Evolution of the Peasantry in the British West Indies." Pamphlet 656. London: Colonial Office, 1936.

Lewis, W. Arthur. "Industrial Development in Puerto Rico." Report of the Caribbean Commission, 1951.

Lewis, W. Arthur. "Industrialization of the British West Indies." Report of the Caribbean Commission, 1951.

Lewis, W. Arthur. *Labour in the West Indies: The Birth of a Workers' Movement*. 1938. Reprint. London: New Beacon Books, 1977.

Lewis, W. Arthur. "Unlimited Supplies of Labour: Further Notes." *Manchester School* 26 (January 1958): 1–32.

Lim, Edwin R. "A General Equilibrium Model of an Export Dependent Economy." Ph.D. diss., Harvard University, December 1969.

Lloyd, Peter J. *International Trade Problems of Small Nations*. Durham, N.C.: Duke University Press, 1968.

Magruder, Martha Dreyer. *Son of Boot-Strap*. Santurce, P.R.: Permanent Press, 1976.

Maingot, Anthony P. "Diplomacy and Policy Toward West Indian Socialism in the Mare Nostrum." Conference Paper. Washington, D.C.: Wilson Center, March 1978.

Maldonado-Denis, Manuel. *Puerto Rico: A Socio-Historic Interpretation*. Translated by Elena Vialo. New York: Vintage Books, 1972.

Maldonado-Denis, Manuel. *Puerto Rico y Estados Unidos: emigración y colonialismo. Un análisis sociohistórico de la emigración puertorriqueña*. México, D.F.: Siglo Veintiuno, 1976.

Mann, Arthur J. "Economic Development, Income Distribution, and Real Income Levels: Puerto Rico, 1953–1977." Paper presented to the American Economics Association, December 1982.

Marqués, René. *The Oxcart [La Carreta]*. Translated by Charles Pelditch. New York: Scribners Sons, 1969.

Mass, Bonnie. *Population Target: The Political Economy of Population Control in Latin America*. Toronto: Latin American Working Group and the Women's Press, 1977.

Mathews, Thomas. *Puerto Rican Politics and the New Deal*. Gainesville: University of Florida Press, 1960.

McCloskey, Donald N. *Enterprise and Trade in Victorian Britain*. London: Allen & Unwin, 1981.

Meade, J. E. "Mauritius: A Case Study in Malthusian Economics." *Economic Journal* 71, no. 283 (September 1971): 521–34.

Meek, Ronald L., ed. *Marx and Engels on the Population Bomb*. Berkeley: Ramparts Press, 1971.

Mill, John Stuart. *On the Logic of the Moral Sciences*. Book 6, *A System of Logic*. Edited by Henry M. Magid. Indianapolis: Library of Liberal Arts, Bobbs-Merrill, 1965.

Mingo, John J. "Capital Importation and Sectoral Development: A Model Applied to Postwar Puerto Rico." *American Economic Review* 59, no. 3 (June 1974): 273–90.

Mintz, Sidney W. "The Caribbean as a Socio-Cultural Area." In *Peoples and Cultures of the Caribbean*. Edited by Michael M. Morawitz. Garden City, N.Y.: Natural History Press, 1971.

Mintz, Sidney W. "The Culture History of a Puerto Rican Sugar Cane Plantation, 1876–1949." *Hispanic American Historical Review* 33, no. 2 (May 1953): 224–51.

Mintz, Sidney W. *Worker in the Cane*. New Haven: Yale University Press, 1960.

Morawetz, David. "Employment Implications of Industrialization in Developing Countries: A Survey." *Economic Journal* 84 (September 1974): 481–542.

Moreno Fraginals, Manuel. *The Sugarmill: The Socioeconomic Complex of Sugar in Cuba 1760–1860*. Translated by Cedric Belfrage. New York: Monthly Review Press, 1976.

North American Congress on Latin America. "Puerto Rico: The End of Autonomy." *Report on the Americas* 15 (March–April 1981): 2–36.

Okun, Arthur M. "Desarrollo Económico de P.R. en la Década del '50: Proyecciones y Realidad." *Revista de Ciencias Sociales* 5, no. 2 (June 1961): 223–54.

Ortiz, Fernando. *Cuban Counterpoint: Tobacco and Sugar*. New York: Vintage Books, 1970.

Peacock, Alan T. *Income Redistribution and Social Policy*. London: Jonathan Cape, 1954.

Perelman, Michael. *Farming for Profit in a Hungry World: Capital and the Crisis in Agriculture*. New York: Allanheld, 1976.

Perloff, Harvey S. *Puerto Rico's Economic Future: A Study in Planned Development*. Chicago: University of Chicago Press, 1950.

Picó, Rafael. "Economic Development in Puerto Rico." In *International Cooperation and Problems of Transfer and Adaptation*. Washington, D.C.: Government Printing Office, 1963.

Picó, Rafael, *The Geographic Regions of Puerto Rico*. Río Piedras, P.R.: University of Puerto Rico Press, 1950.

Pietri, Pedro. *Puerto Rican Obituary*. New York: Monthly Review Press, 1973.

Pomfret, R. "Some Interrelationships between Import Substitution and Export Promotion in a Small Economy." *Weltwirtschaftliches Archiv* 3, no. 4 (1975): 714–27.

Presser, Harriet B. *Sterilization and Fertility Decline in Puerto Rico*. Population Monograph 13. Berkeley: Institute of International Studies, 1973.

Puerto Rico Planning Board. *Economic Report to the Governnor*. San Juan: various years.

Pyatt, Graham, Alan R. Roe, & Associates. *Social Accounting for Development Planning with Special Reference to Sri Lanka*. Cambridge: Cambridge University Press, 1977.

Quesada, Carlos. "La Inversión Extranjera: Un país, Puerto Rico, un Caso, la Consolidated Cigar Corporation." *Revista de Ciencias Sociales* 14, no. 4 (December 1970): 471–510.

Reynolds, Lloyd G. "China as a Less Developed Economy." *American Economic Review* 65, no. 3 (June 1975): 418–28.

Reynolds, Lloyd G. "Wages and Unemployment in a Labor Surplus Economy." *American Economic Review* 55 (March 1965).

Reynolds, Lloyd G., and Peter Gregory. *Wages, Productivity, and Industrialization in Puerto Rico*. Homewood, Ill.: Richard D. Irwin, 1965.

Ridker, R. G. "Discontent and Economic Growth." *Economic Development and Cultural Change* 9, no. 1 (October 1962): 1–15.

Robinson, E.A.G., ed. *Economic Consequences of the Size of Nations.* New York: St. Martin's Press, 1960.

Ross, David F. *The Long Uphill Path: A Historical Study of Puerto Rico's Program of Economic Development.* San Juan: Talleres Gráficos Interamericanos, 1966.

St. Pierre, Maurice. "The Political Factor and the Nationalization of the Demarara Bauxite Co., Guyana." *Social and Economic Studies* 24, no. 4 (December 1956): 481–502.

Schultz, T. Paul. "A Family Planning Hypothesis: Some Empirical Evidence from Puerto Rico." Memorandum RM 5405-RC/AID. Santa Monica: Rand, December 1967.

Senior, Clarence. *Puerto Rican Emigration.* Rio Piedras, P.R.: Social Science Research Center, University of Puerto Rico, 1947.

Senior, Clarence. *Strangers—Then Neighbors: From Pilgrims to Puerto Ricans.* New York: Freedom Books, 1961.

Senior, Clarence, et al. *The Puerto Ricans: Migration and General Bibliography.* New York: Arno Press, 1975.

Sinha, Radha, et al. *Poverty, Income Distribution and Employment: A Case Study of India.* London: Krom and Helm, 1979.

Soligo, Ronald. "Factor Intensity of Consumption Patterns: Income Distribution and Employment Growth in Pakistan," Paper 44. Houston: Program of Development Studies, Rice University, 1973.

Soto, Pedro Juan. *Spiks.* Translated by Victoria Ortiz. New York: Monthly Review Press, 1973.

Stead, William H. *Fomento: The Economic Development of Puerto Rico.* Planning Pamphlet 103, Washington, D.C.: National Planning Association, March 1958.

Steiner, Stan. *The Islands: The Worlds of the Puerto Ricans.* New York: Harper & Row, 1974.

Stewart, Julian H., et al. *The People of Puerto Rico: A Study in Social Anthropology.* Urbana: University of Illinois Press, 1956.

Szulc, Tad, ed. *The United States and the Caribbean.* Englewood Cliffs, N.J.: Prentice-Hall, 1971.

Taylor, Milton C. "Neo-Malthusianism in Puerto Rico." *Review of Social Economy* 10, no. 1 (March 1952): 42–54.

Thomas, Clive Yolande. *Monetary and Financial Arrangements in a Dependent Monetary Economy: A Study of British Guiana, 1945–1962.* Mona, Jamaica: Institute of Social and Economic Research, University of the West Indies, 1965.

Thomas, Piri. *Down These Mean Streets.* New York: Knopf, 1967.

Thurow, Lester C. "Puerto Rican Industrialization Incentives for the 1970's and 1980's." Report prepared for the Puerto Rican Planning Board. December 1970.

Tokman, Victor E. "Income Distribution, Technology and Employment in Developing Countries: An Application to Ecuador." *Journal of Development Economics* 2, no. 1 (March 1975): 49–80.

Tugwell, Rexford Guy. *The Stricken Land: The Story of Puerto Rico.* Garden City, N.Y.: Doubleday, 1947.

Tumin, Melvin, with Arnold S. Feldman. *Social Class and Social Change in Puerto Rico.* Princeton, N.J.: Princeton University Press, 1961.

United Nations Department of Economic and Social Affairs. *A System of National Accounts and Supporting Tables.* Studies in Methods, series F, no. 2, rev. 2. New York: U.N., 1964.

United Nations Department of Economic and Social Affairs. *Yearbook of National Accounts Statistics.* New York: U.N., various years.

U.S. Department of Agriculture, Food and Nutrition Service, Office of Analysis and Evaluation. "Evaluation of the Puerto Rico Nutrition Assistance Program." Report Submitted to the Committees on Agriculture, U.S. Congress. Washington, D.C., March 9, 1983.

U.S. Department of Commerce. *National Income and Product Accounts of the United States, 1929–1965.* Washington, D.C.: Government Printing Office, 1969.

U.S. House of Representatives. *The Caribbean Basin Policy.* Hearings before the Subcommittee on Inter-American Affairs of the Committee on Foreign Affairs. Washington, D.C.: Government Printing Office, 1981.

U.S. House of Representatives. *General Farm Bill of 1981 (Food Stamp Program).* Hearings before the Subcommittee on Domestic Marketing, Consumer Relations, and Nutrition, of the Committee on Agriculture. Serial no. 97-G, pt. 2. Washington, D.C.: Government Printing Office, 1981.

U.S. House of Representatives. *Human Rights in Guatemala.* Hearings before the Subcommittees on Human Rights and International Organizations and on Inter-American Affairs of the Committee on Foreign Affairs. Washington, D.C.: Government Printing Office, 1981.

U.S. House of Representatives. *Naval Training Activities on the Island of Vieques, Puerto Rico.* Hearings before the Panel to Review the Status of Navy Training Activities on the Island of Vieques of the Committee on Armed Services. Washington, D.C.: Government Printing Office, 1980.

U.S. House of Representatives. *U.S. Arms Transfer Policy in Latin America.* Hearings before the Subcommittees on International Security and Scientific Affairs and on Inter-American Affairs of the Committee on Foreign Affairs. Washington, D.C.: Government Printing Office, 1981.

U.S. Senate. *Hearings before the United States-Puerto Rico Commission on the Status of Puerto Rico.* Vol. 3, *Economic Factors in Relations to the Status of Puerto Rico.* Washington, D.C.: Government Printing Office, 1966.

U.S. War Department, Porto Rico Census Office. *Report on the Census of Porto Rico, 1899.* Washington, D.C.: Government Printing Office, 1900.

Wachtel, Howard M. *The New Gnomes: Multinational Banks in the Third World.* Washington, D.C.: Transnational Institute, 1977.

Wagenheim, Kal. *A Survey of Puerto Ricans on the U.S. Mainland in the 1970's.* New York: Praeger, 1975.

Wanniski, Jude. *The Way the World Works.* New York: Simon & Schuster, Touchstone Books, 1978.

Weisskoff, Richard. "Crops vs. Coupons: Agricultural Development and Food Stamps in Puerto Rico." *Time for Decision: The United States and Puerto Rico.* Edited by Jorge Heine. Lanham, Md.: North-South, 1983.

Weisskoff, Richard. "Demand Elasticities for a Developing Economy: An International Comparison of Consumption Patterns." In *Studies in Development Planning.* Edited by H. B. Chenery, et al. Cambridge, Mass.: Harvard University Press, 1971.

Weisskoff, Richard. "Economic Models of the Caribbean." In *Caribbean Basin Policy.*

Hearings before the Subcommittee on Inter-American Affairs of the Committee on Foreign Affairs, U.S. House of Representatives. Washington, D.C.: Government Printing Office, 1981.

Weisskoff, Richard. "Food Stamps and the Puerto Rican Economy." In *Proposed Re-Authorization of the Food and Agricultural Act of 1977—Food Stamps,* pt. 2. Hearings before the Committee on Agriculture, Nutrition, and Forestry, U.S. Senate. Washington, D.C.: Government Printing Office, 1981.

Weisskoff, Richard. "The Growth and Decline of Import Substitution in Brazil—Revisited." *World Development* 8 (September 1980): 647–75.

Weisskoff, Richard. "Income Distribution and Economic Growth in Puerto Rico, Argentina and Mexico." *Review of Income and Wealth* 16, no. 4 (December 1970): 303–32.

Weisskoff, Richard. "Income Distribution and Export Promotion in Puerto Rico." In *Advances in Input-Output.* Edited by K. Polenske and J. Skolka. Cambridge, Mass.: Ballinger, 1976.

Weisskoff, Richard. "Patrones de gastos de consumo en Puerto Rico." *Revista de Ciencias Sociales* 21 (September-December 1979): 363–410.

Weisskoff, Richard, and Adolfo Figueroa. "Traversing the Social Pyramid: A Comparative Review of Income Distribution in Latin America." *Latin American Research Review* 9, no. 2 (Summer 1976): 71–112.

Weisskoff, Richard, et al. "A Multisector Simulation Model of Employment, Growth and Income Distribution in Puerto Rico: A Re-evaluation of 'Successful' Development Strategy." U.S. Department of Labor Research Report, July 1971.

Weisskoff, Richard, and Edward Wolff. "Development and Trade Dependence: The Case of Puerto Rico, 1948–1963." *Review of Economics and Statistics* 57, no. 4 (November 1975): 470–77.

Weisskoff, Richard, and Edward Wolff. "Linkages and Leakages: Industrial Tracking in an Enclave Economy." *Economic Development and Cultural Change* 25 (July 1977): 607–28.

Weisskoff, Richard, and Edward Wolff. "The Structure of Income Inequality in Puerto Rico." *Journal of Development Economics* 9 (1981): 205–28.

Index

The Johns Hopkins University Press

FACTORIES AND FOOD STAMPS

This book was composed in Linotron Times Roman
by the Composing Room of Michigan from a design
by Susan Bishop.
It was printed on 50-lb. Sebago paper and bound
in Holliston Roxite cloth by the Maple Press
Company.